324585

KU-200-723

Matt Lichtenberg

To my long-time girlfriend Kate, whose love and support I treasure.

Jim Travis

To Joanne who taught me the meaning of love, and Billy,
who taught me the meaning of life.

CREATING
DYNAMIC PRESENTATIONS
with STREAMING MEDIA

WITHDRAWN

THE LEARNING CENTRE
HAMMERSMITH AND WEST
LONDON COLLEGE
GLIDDON ROAD
LONDON W14 9BL

0181 741 1688

PLEASE CHECK
FOR CD-ROM
ON RETURN

Create professional-quality online training, sales presentations, company briefings, and more with Microsoft® Producer for PowerPoint® 2002

Hammersmith and West London College

324585

Matt Lichtenberg and Jim Travis

PUBLISHED BY
Microsoft Press
A Division of Microsoft Corporation
One Microsoft Way
Redmond, Washington 98052-6399

Copyright © 2002 by Microsoft Corporation

HAMMERSMITH AND WEST
LONDON COLLEGE
LEARNING CENTRE

1 4 JAN 2002

DAW. L362599. £22.58
324585
658.452
Business Studies

All rights reserved. No part of the contents of this book may be reproduced or transmitted in any form or by any means without the written permission of the publisher.

Library of Congress Cataloging-in-Publication Data
Lichtenberg, Matt, 1974-
     Creating Dynamic Presentations with Streaming Media / Matt Lichtenberg, Jim Travis.
         p. cm.
     Includes index.
     ISBN 0-7356-1436-9
     1. Computer graphics. 2. Microsoft Producer. 3. Business presentations--Graphic methods--Computer programs. I. Travis, Jim, 1963- II. Title.

     T385 .L57   2001
     658.4'52'028566869--dc21   2001052177

Printed and bound in the United States of America.

1 2 3 4 5 6 7 8 9   QWT   7 6 5 4 3 2

Distributed in Canada by Penguin Books Canada Limited.

A CIP catalogue record for this book is available from the British Library.

Microsoft Press books are available through booksellers and distributors worldwide. For further information about international editions, contact your local Microsoft Corporation office or contact Microsoft Press International directly at fax (425) 936-7329. Visit our Web site at www.microsoft.com/mspress. Send comments to *mspinput@microsoft.com*.

JScript, Microsoft, Microsoft Press, PowerPoint, Windows, and Windows Media are either registered trademarks or trademarks of Microsoft Corporation in the United States and/or other countries. Other product and company names mentioned herein may be the trademarks of their respective owners.

The example companies, organizations, products, domain names, e-mail addresses, logos, people, places, and events depicted herein are fictitious. No association with any real company, organization, product, domain name, e-mail address, logo, person, place, or event is intended or should be inferred.

Acquisitions Editor: Alex Blanton
Project Editor: Aileen Wrothwell

Body Part No. X08-24249

Contents

Introduction xi

Part I   Introducing Microsoft Producer 1

Chapter 1   What is Microsoft Producer? 3
What Can I Do with Microsoft Producer? 3
Working with Microsoft Producer 4
    Getting Content into Microsoft Producer 4
    Editing in Microsoft Producer 5
    Synchronizing Your Presentation 6
    Previewing Your Presentation 6
    Publishing Your Presentation 7
What Other Software Works with Microsoft Producer? 7
What Hardware Can I Use with Microsoft Producer? 7
    Video Capture Devices 8
    Audio Capture Devices 8
Your Presentation: the Final Product 8
Understanding Windows Media Technologies 9
    Streaming Media 9
    Windows Media Tools 9
How Is Microsoft Producer Different from PowerPoint? 11
Usage Scenarios for Microsoft Producer 11
    Creating Business-to-business Communications 12
    Creating Internal Corporate Communications 13
    Creating Training Events 14
    Creating Sales and Marketing Presentations 16

Chapter 2   The Microsoft Producer User Interface 17
Using the Menus 17
    File Menu 18
    Edit Menu 20
    View Menu 21

Tools Menu 23

Clip Menu 25

Play Menu 26

Help Menu 28

Using the Toolbar 28

Using the Tabs 29

The Media Tab 29

The Table of Contents Tab 32

The Preview Presentation Tab 33

Using the Timeline 34

The Timeline Tools 35

The Timeline Display 36

The Timeline Tracks 36

Part II   Preparing to Create Presentations **39**

Chapter 3   Creating an Engaging Presentation **41**

Planning Your Presentation 41

Considering Your Audience 42

Determining the Purpose of Your Presentation 42

Considering Time Constraints 42

Considering Budgetary Constraints 43

Scheduling Your Presenter 43

What Makes an Engaging and Effective Presentation? 44

Guidelines for the Speaker 44

Using Digital Media in Your Presentation 48

Tips for Video Screen Captures 51

Chapter 4   Setting up Hardware and Software **55**

Video Formats 55

Video Sources 57

Video Cameras 57

Web Cameras 58

Analog or DV VCRs 58

Satellite or Cable TV 58

Broadcasting Standards 59

Understanding Capture Devices 60

Video Interfaces 60

Video Capture Devices 64

Audio Sources 66
Configuring Capture Devices 66
Device Driver Software 67
Connecting Video Capture Devices 67

Chapter 5   Preparing to Record Digital Media **73**
Planning the Video in Your Presentation 73
Choosing a Recording Site 75
Choosing Recording Accessories 77
Preparing an Office for Recording 80
Lighting 80
Improving Sound 82
Choosing a Background 83
Creating a Presentation Plan 85
Creating a Basic Script 85
Using Storyboards 85
Rehearsing the Presentation 86

Chapter 6   Recording High-quality Audio and Video **89**
Video and Computers 89
How Codecs Work 90
Bandwidth Considerations 91
Recording Video 92
Basic Recording Steps 92
Common Video Camera Features 93
Advanced Features and Effects 94
Some Basic Shots 96
Setting up Shots 97
Recording Video to Edit 100
Recording High-quality Audio 101

Part III   Creating Presentations Using Microsoft Producer **103**

Chapter 7   Starting a New Presentation **105**
Using the New Presentation Wizard 105
Choosing a Presentation Scheme 108
Entering Information About Your Presentation 111
Using PowerPoint Slides or Still Images 113
Synchronizing Slides—Now or Later 116
Completing the Wizard 116

Synchronizing Slides and Still Images 117
Starting a New, Empty Project 119
Importing Digital Media Files 120
Saving Your Project 124
Saving Project Archives—Pack and Go 124

Chapter 8 Capturing Video, Audio, and Still Images **129**
Before You Begin Capturing Content 129
Starting the Capture Wizard 131
Starting the Capture Wizard through the New Presentation Wizard 131
Starting the Capture Wizard through the Tools Menu 132
Using the Capture Wizard 133
Narrating Slides with Video and Audio 135
Capturing Video and Audio 141
Capturing Still Images from Video 145
Capturing Images from Your Computer Screen 146
Capturing Video from Your Computer Screen 148
Understanding Capture Settings 151
Considerations for Choosing Capture Settings 153
Choosing Video and Audio Devices 154

Chapter 9 Editing on the Timeline **161**
Working with the Media Tab 162
Adding Files to the Timeline 163
Creating Clips from Video Files 163
Determining Where Files Are Added on the Timeline 164
Setting Default Durations for Digital Media Files 166
Adding Web Links 167
Adding Templates to the Timeline 168
Removing Files from the Timeline 168
Editing Video and Audio 169
Trimming Video and Audio 169
Splitting Files and Clips 170
Combining Clips 171
Adding Video Transitions 171
Adding Video Effects 173
Moving and Copying Files on the Timeline 174
Working with Audio 175
Using Audio Effects 175

Normalizing Audio on the Timeline 175
Adjusting Audio Levels 176
Editing the Table of Contents 176
Creating or Editing the Introduction Page 178
Previewing Presentations 179
Setting Security Zones for Previewing 179
Editing a Project 182

Chapter 10 Microsoft PowerPoint Presentations in Producer **193**
Using Slides in Your Presentations 193
Using PowerPoint to Edit Slides in Producer 194
When to Edit Slides 195
Inserting Images in Slides 195
Editing Imported Slides in PowerPoint 196
Using the Microsoft Producer PowerPoint Add-in 199
Working with Slide Timings 200
Understanding Add-in Security Issues 201
Using Slide Animations and Transitions 203
Using Time-based Animations 204
Using On-click Animations 204
Viewing Slide Animations in Producer 206
Video and Audio in PowerPoint Slides 207

Chapter 11 Publishing Your Presentation **209**
Understanding the Publishing Process 209
Files Published by Microsoft Producer 210
Understanding Servers 210
Selecting a Publishing Profile 214
Publishing with E-services 216
Using the Publish Wizard 218
Publishing to My Computer 218
Publishing to a CD 224
Publishing to My Network Places 229
Publishing to a Web Server 233
Understanding Presentation Playback 240
Specifying a Profile for Presentation Playback 241
Using Other Playback Parameters 242

Part IV   Advanced Producer Topics **245**

Chapter 12   Customizing Producer Templates **247**

Template Basics 247

    CSS Selectors and Properties 247

    Template Naming and Styles 249

    Choosing a Presentation Template 250

Getting Started 251

    Naming a Presentation Template 253

Customizing a Presentation Template 254

    Customizing Background Images 255

    Customizing the Media Player 261

    Working with Slides 266

    Customizing HTML Display 269

    Customizing the Table of Contents 271

Chapter 13   Customizing Your Presentations **275**

Opening Web Content in a New Window 275

Customizing CD AutoPlay 276

    Creating a New Scan.hta File 277

    Editing an Existing Scan.hta File 278

Getting a Jump Start on a Presentation 282

Creating a Microsoft PowerPoint Template 283

Annotating Slides for Your Presentation 285

Switching Published Video Files 287

Copying a Published Presentation 288

Chapter 14   Creating Custom Publishing Solutions **291**

Customizing Registry Keys 292

Custom Publishing with E-services 299

Displaying a Custom Publish Wizard 303

Building a Simple E-service 305

Making Your E-service Public 312

Taking the Next Step 316

Glossary **319**

Index **325**

About the Authors **331**

Introduction

This book will show you how to create dynamic and compelling presentations using Microsoft Producer for PowerPoint 2002. Producer lets you take Microsoft PowerPoint-based presentations to a more persuasive level by synchronizing your PowerPoint slides with video and audio to create dynamic rich-media presentations. The video and audio you use can be recorded from a video tape or captured live in Producer. You can also import and use existing digital media files.

In addition to using video, audio, and PowerPoint slides, you can also use other digital media files such as still images, HTML pages, or even Web content from a live Web site. You can use the different presentation templates available in Producer or custom templates you create to change the appearance of your presentation.

You can then easily publish your presentation to a variety of locations, depending on how you want to distribute it. Presentations can be published to your own computer, a corporate intranet site, a Web site, a shared network location, or a recordable CD. This flexibility ensures that your message reaches your audience no matter where they are.

Microsoft Producer makes extensive use of Windows Media Technologies. The audio and video in your presentation is in Windows Media Format, a streaming media format that lets you incorporate high-quality audio and video in your presentations. The video and audio are highly compressed because they use Windows Media audio and video codecs to make them smaller, and therefore easier to distribute over the Web, on a corporate intranet site, or over a traditional local area network (LAN). Finally, you can use other Windows Media Technologies to stream your presentations over a corporate LAN, corporate intranet site, or over the Internet so others can watch the presentations you create online.

Who Is This Book For?

This book is for people who want to create compelling, rich-media presentations. This book is designed, much like the software, for people who may be new to using digital media. The goal of this book to walk you through the process of creating rich-media presentations, from the basics of recording video and audio to the publishing of the edited project as a presentation, while covering all the tasks you can do in between to create a great final product. The primary audiences for this book are business users and educators.

Business Users

This book is for business users who want to create rich-media presentations for their corporations or organizations. The types of presentations you might want to create range from internal corporate communications to online training to business-to-business communications. The information or message conveyed in the presentation is up to you. However, this book will help you turn your information into a compelling presentation.

Educators

This book is also for educators who want to deliver online training. The training presentations created using Microsoft Producer can be used for distance learning courses in a college or university, as well as for online training courses for corporations. The topics covered in the presentations do not have to be computer-related. The topic or message again depends on the educator's needs and the message he or she wants to convey. However, this book will help those who want to create and distribute online training.

How Is This Book Organized?

This book is organized to take you through the steps needed to create a dynamic, rich-media presentation. The Help for Microsoft Producer provides useful information about performing Producer's basic tasks, but this book leads you through the entire process from beginning to end to show you how to create professional-looking, compelling presentations in Microsoft Producer.

To help you quickly find the information you are looking for, this book is organized in four parts:

- **Introducing Microsoft Producer**. Contains basic information about Microsoft Producer and the types of presentations you can create.

- **Preparing to Create Presentations**. Explains different concepts you should consider when planning your presentation, including basic information about recording the video and audio you will use.

- **Creating Presentations Using Microsoft Producer**. Shows you how to get the most out of Microsoft Producer—how to create a new presentation, import digital media files, capture video and audio, synchronize slides with video and audio, edit your project, and publish your final presentation.

- **Advanced Producer Topics**. Provides advanced information for getting more out of Microsoft Producer. This section contains detailed tips about how to customize your presentations, and handy tricks to help you get the most out of Microsoft Producer.

Part I: Introducing Microsoft Producer

Chapter 1 introduces you to Microsoft Producer. You will learn about the basic features of Producer, and you'll learn what other software and hardware can be used to help you create dynamic, rich-media presentations. This chapter also provides information about other Windows Media tools and technologies. You'll see scenarios that illustrate the types of presentations you might want to create in Microsoft Producer.

Chapter 2 describes the basic elements of Producer, including an overview of the user interface and complete coverage of all the commands you will be using.

Part II: Preparing to Create Presentations

Chapter 3 provides information about what makes an engaging presentation. In doing so, this chapter provides guidelines for choosing what to include in your presentation and how to successfully incorporate different digital media files. This chapter also includes tips and guidelines for presenters who appear in the presentation's video and audio.

In chapter 4, you will start learning about the different capture devices you can use to record video and audio on your computer. This chapter explains how to configure and connect common capture devices to your computer to prepare for capturing content within Microsoft Producer.

Chapter 5 introduces you to the recording process and provides information about what you can do when preparing to record video and audio for your presentation. It explains what considerations you should make when choosing a recording location, and provides detailed information about how you can set up a common office working environment so that you can record high-quality video and audio for your presentation.

In chapter 6, you will learn basic recording techniques. This includes using features of your video camera to record high-quality video and audio.

Part III: Creating Presentations Using Microsoft Producer

Chapter 7 gets you on your way to creating presentations. This chapter contains information about creating a new presentation using the **New Presentation Wizard** or by starting with a new, blank project. Included in this chapter is information about importing existing digital media files and synchronizing your slides and still images with video and audio. In addition, you will learn how you can use the **Pack and Go** feature to create a project archive so you can move the project from one computer to another, and how to unpack a project archive.

Chapter 8 teaches you how to narrate and capture video and audio, audio only, or still images using the **Capture Wizard**. This chapter explains how you can capture live or recorded video and audio from tape. It also explains how you can successfully capture video or still images from your computer screen. Included in this chapter is specific information about choosing the appropriate settings when capturing video and audio on your computer.

Chapter 9 explains the basics of editing a project on the timeline. You will learn how you can add files to the timeline, how to edit content on the timeline to create your presentation, and then how to preview it. The basic editing procedures that are explained in this chapter include moving and copying files on the timeline, rearranging digital media files on the timeline, trimming files, splitting video and audio files, and combining video and audio clips. You will also see how you can add Web links, presentation templates, and video and audio effects to your project.

Chapter 10 explains how you can use Microsoft PowerPoint presentations in the presentations you create in Producer. This chapter explains how you can edit slides in PowerPoint through Microsoft Producer. This chapter also discusses the Microsoft Producer for PowerPoint 2002 add-in program that lets you record slide timings during a live presentation, so you can easily incorporate synchronized video and audio with the slides. Finally, this chapter discusses how slide animations and slide transitions work when added to a PowerPoint presentation and then used in a Producer presentation.

After editing your Microsoft Producer project, it's time to publish it as a presentation. Chapter 11 discusses how you can publish your presentation on a Windows Media server, on a Web server, to a shared network location, to your own computer, or to recordable CD. You will learn how to publish your presentation so others can watch it on a corporate intranet site, on a Web site, on a shared network location, or from a recordable CD. Included in this chapter is information about how you can determine which profiles should be used when publishing the presentation.

Part IV: Advanced Producer Topics

Chapter 12 discusses how you can edit an existing presentation template so you can customize the presentations you create for your organization. Even though Microsoft Producer has many different presentation templates installed by default for you to use in your presentations, you can also create your own customized presentation templates.

Chapter 13 provides a variety of tips for using Microsoft Producer. This chapter also discusses how to create your own PowerPoint design templates, which you can then apply to the slides that are part of your Producer presentation.

Finally, chapter 14 discusses creating a basic e-service. The topics discussed are intended to help you get started and to provide information about how you can create a basic e-service to customize the publishing process.

What's on the Companion CD?

A companion CD-ROM is included with this book to provide you with the following tools and information that will help you create presentations with Microsoft Producer.

Microsoft Software

The following Microsoft software has been included on the companion CD for your convenience:

- **Microsoft Producer for PowerPoint 2002**. Install Microsoft Producer for PowerPoint 2002 so you can create your own rich-media presentations.

- **Microsoft Windows Media Player 7.1**. Discover, organize, and play all of your favorite digital media files. Windows Media Player 7.1 delivers the best digital media experience for Microsoft Windows and the Web. Windows Media Player allows you to play back your Microsoft Producer presentations in a Web browser.

  Note that you do not need this version of Windows Media Player if your computer is running Microsoft Windows XP, which includes a newer version of the Player.

- **Microsoft Windows Media Encoder 7.1**. Use Windows Media Encoder to convert both live and prerecorded audio, video, and computer screen images to Windows Media Format for live and on-demand delivery.

- **Advanced Script Indexer**. Insert markers, URLs, and script commands into a Windows Media Audio (WMA) or Windows Media Video (WMV) file, and changes the title, author, and other text information that is embedded in a Windows Media file.

Content

The companion CD contains the following content files, which you can use as you are learning about Producer:

- **Sample digital media files**. The CD contains sample digital media files, so you can experiment with sample digital media content if you choose.

- **Sample presentations**. The CD also contains sample presentations, so you can see examples of presentations that were created by using Microsoft Producer.

- **Tips and tricks**. Several additional tips and tricks are included to help you get more out of Microsoft Producer.

Acknowledgements

Written by: Matt Lichtenberg and Jim Travis

Reviewed and revised by: Bill Birney and Mark Galioto

Project managed by: Terrence Dorsey, Seth McEvoy, and Tom Woolums

Edited by: Terrence Dorsey and Kari Rosenthal Annand

Illustrations and production by: Greg Lovitt

Indexed by: Terrence Dorsey and Cathy McDonald

Companion CD produced by: C. Keith Gabbert and Kari Rosenthal Annand

Sample CD content provided by: Gary Schare and Ellen Wechsler

Technical content reviewed by: Matthew Clapham, Eric Juteau, May Lau, Mike Matsel, J.P. McKinney, Ian Mercer, R. Cutts Peaslee, James Peters, Jen Rowe, Ellen Wechsler, and Kristen Whalen.

Legal review by: Debbie Donaty

Marketing information provided by: Marcus Matthias

Additional editorial assistance provided by: Bill Birney, Karl Erickson, Gregory Finch, John Shaw, and Tom Woolums.

Companion CD additional contributors: Henry Bale and Robert L. Porter

Special thanks to Microsoft Press editors: Alex Blanton and Aileen Wrothwell

System Requirements

Use the following information to make sure your computer is compatible with Microsoft Producer and the content provided on the companion CD.

Microsoft Producer for PowerPoint 2002

Microsoft Producer requires the following minimum system requirements:

- Microsoft Windows 2000 with Service Pack 1 or Microsoft Windows XP operating system.

- 400 megahertz (MHz) processor. A processor speed of 600 MHz or higher is recommended when capturing from a digital video device.

- 128 megabytes (MB) of RAM.

- 2 gigabytes (GB) of free hard disk space.

- An audio capture device to capture audio.

- A video (DV or analog) capture device to capture video.

- Microsoft PowerPoint 2002.

- Microsoft Windows Media Player 6.4 or later. Windows Media Player 7.0 or later is recommended.

- Microsoft Internet Explorer 5.0 or later.

- An Internet or network connection to publish a presentation to a Web site, intranet site, e-service provider, or shared network location.

Companion CD

To use the content on the companion CD, you must have Microsoft Internet Explorer 5.0 or later installed on your computer.

Microsoft Press Support Information

Every effort has been made to ensure the accuracy of the book and the contents of this companion CD. Microsoft Press provides corrections for books through the World Wide Web at:

http://www.microsoft.com/mspress/support/

To connect directly to the Microsoft Press Knowledge Base and enter a query regarding a question or issue that you may have, go to:

http://www.microsoft.com/mspress/support/search.asp

If you have comments, questions, or ideas regarding the book or this CD-ROM, or questions that are not answered by querying the Knowledge Base, please send them to Microsoft Press via e-mail to:

mspinput@microsoft.com

or via postal mail to:

> Microsoft Press
> Attn: Creating Dynamic Presentations with Streaming Media Editor
> One Microsoft Way
> Redmond, WA 98052-6399

Please note that product support is not offered through the above addresses.

Part I
Introducing Microsoft Producer

Chapter 1: What is Microsoft Producer?
Chapter 2: The Microsoft Producer User Interface

What is Microsoft Producer?

This chapter is intended to give you a broad overview of Microsoft Producer and what you can accomplish using it. Our goal is to explain how the features in Microsoft Producer help you to create dynamic, rich-media presentations—ones that let you go beyond using simple text and images.

Microsoft Producer lets you share your message with others through the Web, through a corporate intranet or extranet, or through a third-party e-service provider. You can easily incorporate audio, video, HTML files, and still images with your Microsoft PowerPoint presentations to create dynamic, distributable, rich-media presentations.

What Can I Do with Microsoft Producer?

You can install and run Microsoft Producer on a computer that is running the Microsoft Windows 2000 or Windows XP operating system and Microsoft PowerPoint 2002. Microsoft Producer is a standalone application that lets you take your Microsoft PowerPoint slides and synchronize them with audio and video. This can be audio and video that you have already recorded on your computer or new audio and video content that you record in Microsoft Producer. Furthermore, you can add still images and HTML files to your presentations.

The final product is a rich-media presentation that you can distribute on a company intranet site, on an e-service provider's site, on a CD, or to the Web so clients, colleagues, or anyone with Microsoft Internet Explorer can watch.

Working with Microsoft Producer, you can create a variety of presentations based on your specific needs. Later in this chapter, you will see a list of different scenarios in which you might use Microsoft Producer.

Figure 1.1 shows a presentation that is being edited in Microsoft Producer.

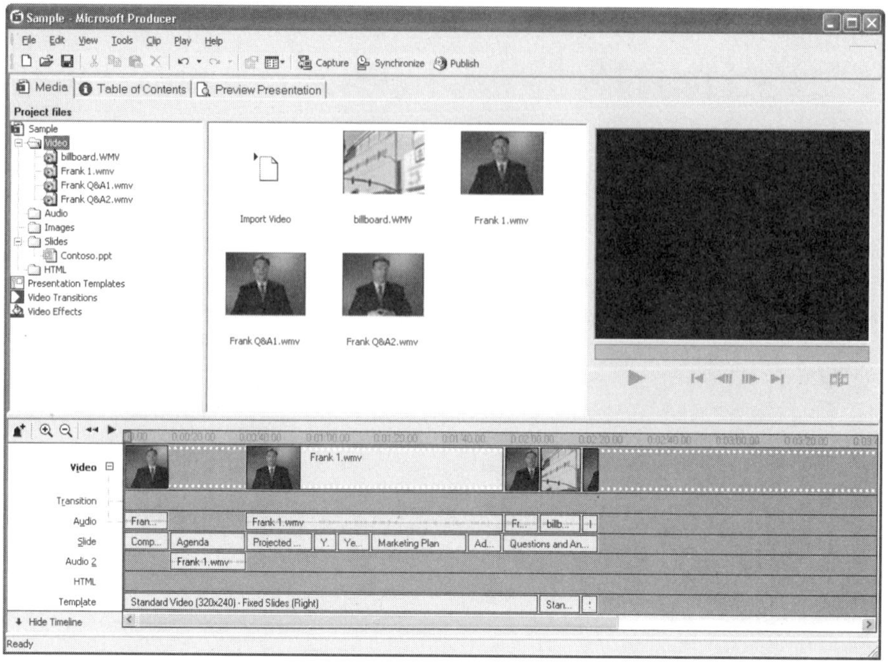

Figure 1.1 — Editing a presentation in Microsoft Producer.

Working with Microsoft Producer

Before you start working with Microsoft Producer and this book, it's helpful to know what features are included in Microsoft Producer and where they are discussed in this book. The following section is designed to do just that.

Getting Content into Microsoft Producer

The first task is to bring digital media files into your Microsoft Producer project. The files that you can use in your projects can include audio, video, Microsoft PowerPoint slides, still images, and HTML files.

Because you can import a wide variety of digital media file formats, you will be able to use many of your existing still images, HTML files, audio files, video files, or Microsoft PowerPoint slides. Techniques for importing existing digital media files and a listing of supported file types are discussed in greater detail in chapter 7.

You can capture audio and video in Microsoft Producer if you have an appropriate capture device connected to or installed in your computer. You can record from a wide variety of video capture devices, such as Web cameras, analog video cameras, digital video

(DV) cameras, and analog or DV VCRs. These features enable you to capture full-motion video—either live or from tape—or to simply capture individual still images from video.

You can also use a standalone audio capture device such as a microphone to capture audio. If you plan to capture audio and video using an analog or DV camera or VCR, you need to have a video capture card connected and properly installed on your computer. Detailed information about capture devices, including instructions for connecting capture devices to your computer, is discussed in chapter 4.

If a capture device is properly installed and detected on your computer, you can then record video and audio in Microsoft Producer. The video and audio you record play an important role in the presentations you create; they're one of the key elements that helps turn your standard, old-fashioned slide shows into dynamic, rich-media presentations.

Other capturing options include recording video and audio (or audio only) alongside your PowerPoint slides or recording video or still images of your computer screen.

Regardless of the recording you want to make for your presentation, the **Capture Wizard** walks you step-by-step through the capturing process and lets you choose what type of recording you want to make. The type of content you capture is up to you. Chapter 8 discusses capturing in greater detail and provides step-by-step instructions for the different capturing options that are available in Microsoft Producer.

Editing in Microsoft Producer

After you have imported digital media files or recorded the video and audio you want to use in your presentation, you can then begin arranging them in your project. You start by adding them to the *timeline*. The timeline is the Microsoft Producer workspace in which you arrange the various elements that will appear in your presentation. The timeline enables you to edit the entire project or elements of the project, such as individual audio and video files.

When working with video and audio, you will often need to edit or hide some unwanted material. For example, a video file might contain the frantic preparation and last-minute changes that took place during recording. You probably won't want to show this part in your presentation. However, you might not want to delete those last-minute changes because they could be used for a separate training video.

You can use Microsoft Producer to trim unwanted video and audio out of your presentation. This lets you hide the unwanted footage from your audience without deleting those scenes from the source video file. Trimming and other video editing tasks you can accomplish in Microsoft Producer are discussed in chapter 9.

To aid in synchronizing slides with audio and video, Microsoft Producer provides a timeline workspace. Once you have the files for your presentation laid out on the timeline, you may want to rearrange the digital media files. You can quickly do this by dragging the files from one part of the timeline to another or by using the menu commands to cut, copy, and paste files. And if you later decide that you have a file on the timeline that you do not need anymore, you can easily remove that file from the timeline so it does not appear in your final presentation. Moving, copying, and removing files is discussed in chapter 9.

In addition to editing video footage, you can enhance your presentations by adding video *transitions* and *effects*. Microsoft Producer provides many different video transitions and effects that you can add to your presentation. A video transition plays between two video clips, slides, or still images, while a video effect applies a new style or appearance to your still images or video content. Chapter 9 discusses adding and using video transitions and effects in your Microsoft Producer presentations.

To help your audience understand the topics discussed in your presentation, you can create a *table of contents*. The table of contents in your presentation is much like the table of contents you see in a book; it provides a way for your audience to see the topics or subjects that will be discussed. Just like a table of contents in a book lists page numbers for chapters or topics, the table of contents for your presentation contains links to a specific topic or part of your presentation. This way, viewers can simply click a link to go to that part of the presentation. When they click a table of contents link, they will go to the corresponding video, text, images, or PowerPoint slides that are contained in that topic. Chapter 9 discusses the table of contents in detail and provides step-by-step instructions for creating and editing a table of contents.

Synchronizing Your Presentation

You can choose to synchronize existing video and audio files with your Microsoft PowerPoint slides. This is an important feature of Microsoft Producer because it lets you take different digital media files, such as audio, video, still images, and slides, and then quickly synchronize them to create a rich-media presentation. Synchronizing is done through the synchronize slides feature. Synchronizing your slides to existing audio and video files is discussed in chapter 7.

In addition to synchronizing existing audio and video files with your slides, you can also choose to capture new video and audio while synchronizing it with your PowerPoint slides. You can do this by narrating your slides to video with audio or audio only in the **Capture Wizard**. This is discussed in chapter 8.

Previewing Your Presentation

As you work on your project in Microsoft Producer, you can preview it to see how the presentation will appear after you publish it. By previewing, you can get a "sneak peek" of your project before publishing it to a local computer, Web server, Windows Media server, or e-service provider.

Microsoft Producer lets you preview in two different tabs: the **Media** tab and the **Preview Presentation** tab. Each tab gives you a different view of your presentation. Chapter

9 of the book describes previewing your projects, including differences between previewing your project in the **Media** tab and the **Preview Presentation** tab.

Publishing Your Presentation

When you have finished editing your project, you are then ready to publish the presentation. When you publish the project as a presentation, all of the digital media in your project, including any video, audio, HTML files, PowerPoint slides, and templates, is compiled into one final presentation. You can then take the final presentation and the files contained in it and publish it to a local computer, Web server, Windows Media server, e-service provider, or even to a CD that you can then distribute.

Chapter 11 describes publishing in detail, and provides examples of each publishing scenario (for example, publishing to a local computer, Web server, Windows Media server, e-service provider, or a CD). These scenarios include step-by-step procedures along with information about each publishing option.

What Other Software Works with Microsoft Producer?

You can use many different types of digital media in your presentations. The presentations you create can use still images, HTML files, PowerPoint slides, video, and audio. The software you use to create these original files is completely up to you, as long as you can save the source files in file formats that can be imported into Microsoft Producer.

For example, you can create your HTML files by using a WYSIWIG (What You See Is What You Get) HTML editor, such as Microsoft FrontPage, or you can use a simple text editor, such as Notepad. As long as the software you choose lets you save in a supported file format, you can use the applications you are most comfortable with to create the original still images, video, audio, and HTML files you want to use in your Microsoft Producer presentations.

You can use slides that were created by any version of PowerPoint, but to run Microsoft Producer and import PowerPoint slides to your Microsoft Producer presentations, you must have Microsoft PowerPoint 2002 installed on your computer.

To watch your published Microsoft Producer presentation, both you and your audience must have Windows Media Player 6.4 or higher installed—Windows Media Player 7.0 or higher is recommended. In addition to having Windows Media Player installed, Microsoft Internet Explorer 5.0 or higher is needed to view your published presentation.

What Hardware Can I Use with Microsoft Producer?

Recording video and audio for your Microsoft Producer presentations requires you to have specific hardware properly installed and connected to your computer. To record audio and video for your presentations, you need to have video and audio capture devices installed on your computer.

Video Capture Devices

To record video in Microsoft Producer, you must have an appropriate capture device connected to and recognized by your computer. A capture device is a piece of hardware, such as a Web camera, a VCR, or an analog or digital video (DV) camera that lets you record video to your computer.

To record video and audio to your computer using a DV or analog camera or VCR, you must use a video capture device, such as a video capture card, that is installed on your computer. If you plan to use an analog video camera, you will need to use an analog capture device. However, if you have a DV camera, you can use an analog or digital capture card. An IEEE 1394 DV capture card, sometimes called a FireWire card, can be used to transfer digital video from your camera, whether live or from tape, to your computer.

Today, some new computers already include a video capture device, such as FireWire card, to connect your DV camera or VCR. However, a majority of computers require that a separate video capture card or device be installed on your computer.

Chapter 4 of this book discusses capture devices, including the types of video capture devices and connecting these devices to your computer.

Audio Capture Devices

Just like you need a video capture device to record video to your computer, you also need to have an audio capture device, such as an audio card, connected and properly detected by your computer to record audio. Many sound cards let you connect an external audio capture device such as a microphone to your computer, so you can record audio on your computer.

In Microsoft Producer, you can record audio, such as a narration of a slide show. Connecting and using capture devices is discussed in chapter 4 of this book.

Your Presentation: the Final Product

The final product of your project is the published presentation. This contains all of the different digital media files and effects you added to your Microsoft Producer project, and is the presentation that your audience can watch in their Web browsers. The final presentation is created by publishing the project.

The presentation can be published to a variety of locations including a Web site, corporate intranet site, a shared network location, your local computer, or to a recordable or rewriteable CD. The process of publishing a presentation is discussed in chapter 11.

Understanding Windows Media Technologies

When you record video and audio in Microsoft Producer, it is encoded into Windows Media Format. Audio and video files in Windows Media Format can be streamed from a Windows Media server, which means that the audio and video can be seen or listened to while the file is being delivered to the viewer's computer. These files also can contain links from the audio or video to slides or other files. This is how the slides or other files stay synchronized with the video or audio.

Typical multimedia files like AVI or WAV files cannot be synchronized with other files easily, which is why Windows Media Format is used. Any audio and video in your final published presentation is saved in Windows Media Format.

Windows Media lets you easily distribute high-quality audio and video over a network, such as a corporate intranet or Web site. This is because high-quality Windows Media files are much smaller than original audio or video files in most other formats.

Streaming Media

Traditionally, audio and video needed to be downloaded to your computer before it could be played. However, Windows Media changes this by enabling *streaming* audio and video. Instead of having to wait a long time for a file to be completely downloaded, video and audio in Windows Media Format can be played as the file is delivered, or streamed, to the local machine. This eliminates the "download and wait" issues that used to be associated with retrieving audio and video from the Internet.

In addition, a streamed file does not remain on the user's computer. The audio or video data is transferred to the user's computer and played, but never saved to a file; users have to access the original source of the streaming audio or video every time they want to access it. This functionality gives content creators more control over how and when their content is used.

The various possible methods for delivering your presentation are discussed later in this book. Chapter 11 will discuss different publishing options, the publishing profiles available in Microsoft Producer, along with step-by-step instructions about how to publish your project as a presentation.

Windows Media Tools

The following sections describe some of the Windows Media software that you are likely to encounter when working with Microsoft Producer. These tools are not required to create successful presentations, but you might want to know about them anyway.

Windows Media Player

Windows Media Player is the software that lets you play Windows Media files on your computer. The audio and video files you play in Windows Media Player can be stored locally on your computer, or you can play Windows Media files that are streamed from a media server or downloaded from a Web server. Additionally, you can play other popular audio file types such as MP3, and other video file types such as AVI or MPEG. You can also use Windows Media Player to listen to Internet radio stations from around the world.

In addition to playing music, Windows Media Player acts as an entertainment center for your computer. You can use Windows Media Player to organize all the video and audio you have on your computer. You can copy CDs to your computer to save new music in Windows Media Format, and you can create (*burn*) CDs from lists of songs stored in Windows Media Player.

Windows Media Services

Windows Media Services lets you stream and distribute digital media files over the Internet or over a local network. A computer running Windows Media Services is known as a Windows Media server. This server is much like a Web server, but it can be used to distribute streaming digital media content over the Internet or a local network.

A Windows Media server is designed to distribute Windows Media files by *streaming* them across a network. Streaming eliminates the traditional "download and wait" experience that occurs when a Windows Media Format file is stored on and distributed from a Web server.

If you have Windows Media Services installed on a computer running Windows 2000 Server, you can set up this service to distribute Windows Media files over your corporate network or over the Internet. This server hosts Windows Media-based files that are stored on the computer, and you can also broadcast live events.

Windows Media Encoder

Windows Media Encoder lets you encode video and audio content from a Web camera, DV camera, analog video camera, or a DV or analog VCR connected to a capture device on your computer. The video you encode using Windows Media Encoder can be taken from a source such as a video camera or from tape, and it is encoded into Windows Media Format. In addition to recording from a camera or VCR, you can also record video screen captures—video of the actions that occur on your computer screen—into Windows Media files.

When you encode content using Windows Media Encoder, you can choose to record both audio and video, or audio only. You can encode to a file, to a live broadcast stream, or to both at the same time.

In addition to encoding content live or from tape, you can also use Windows Media Encoder to encode (and broadcast, if necessary) existing audio and video files into Windows Media Format.

Windows Media Encoder also lets you deliver a live stream. This lets users watch or listen to the content you are encoding and streaming using Windows Media Player. If your audience consists of 50 people or less and you want to stream live content, you can use Windows Media Encoder as an alternative to using Windows Media Services to stream and distribute the content.

A software development kit (SDK) is available for Windows Media Encoder. This SDK enables software developers to use Microsoft Visual Basic or C++ to build customized applications that incorporate Windows Media encoding technologies.

You can use any existing content you may have already encoded using Windows Media Encoder and then import it directly into Microsoft Producer. This lets you use existing audio and video files that you have already encoded in your Microsoft Producer presentations.

How Is Microsoft Producer Different from PowerPoint?

A question that you might be asking is "How is Microsoft Producer different from Microsoft PowerPoint?" Well, that question is pretty easy to answer. You use Microsoft PowerPoint to create slides (and HTML files) that can serve as the basic building blocks for your final presentation in Microsoft Producer. PowerPoint lets you create versatile slideshows and presentations that can be used on their own or incorporated into a presentation using Microsoft Producer.

You then import what you have added in PowerPoint into Microsoft Producer and combine your PowerPoint creation with other types of digital media to create rich-media presentations.

In Microsoft Producer, you can take the PowerPoint presentation and enhance it by adding video, audio, HTML files, effects, or transitions, and then synchronize these with your original PowerPoint slides. The final result is a seamless, rich-media presentation that you can deliver over a corporate network, intranet, extranet, CD, or Web site to effectively communicate your message.

Usage Scenarios for Microsoft Producer

Microsoft Producer lets you create the presentations that *you* want to create. You probably have a good idea of what you want to say and what you want to accomplish—you have a purpose for creating the presentation.

This chapter describes some scenarios in which you might use Microsoft Producer. It is intended to give you an idea of what Microsoft Producer can be used for. The scenarios described in this chapter are by no means exhaustive—they are merely a few of the situations in which you could use Microsoft Producer to create a presentation, whatever your purpose or goal. Later in this book, specifically within part III, instructions are provided to show you *how* to create presentations within the context of the categories of scenarios described in this chapter.

The following scenarios are broken down into several different categories. These categories include:

- Creating business-to-business communications
- Creating internal corporate communications
- Creating training events
- Creating sales and marketing presentations

Creating Business-to-business Communications

Nearly every business today works with other businesses on a daily basis. An important part of these business relationships, which at times become close partnerships, is keeping your business partners informed about changes or new services within your company. After all, one of the best ways to sustain a lasting business relationship is to effectively communicate with your business partners.

Microsoft Producer is a tool that provides another way for you to communicate with other companies and organizations. This section describes some examples of this business-to-business communication.

Introducing a New Product

For business-to-business communication, many companies have online catalogs for their business partners to see new and existing products they offer. Often, these catalogs consist of basic images and text describing the featured product. However, sometimes the text and simple graphics limit a company's ability to adequately inform customers about the product being featured.

Using Microsoft Producer, you could change all this by creating a rich-media presentation that shows your new product line and gives detailed information about the products, as well as the new advantages they offer.

For example, let's say your company designs large industrial machines and you want to demonstrate the advantages of the new machine over the older model. You could create a presentation that includes slides comparing the specifications of the older model and newer model. You could also have video that features someone demonstrating the new features and their benefits compared to the older model. This lets you tell other companies about your new model, as well as show them how the new features work through audio and video.

Throughout the presentation, you could also display an HTML page that links to the page in your online catalog that lets customers order this new product. You don't have to change the way your buying and processing system works, and you can link to it directly from your sales presentation.

Introducing a New Service

Selling a service is much like selling a product. You may want to show the results of the new service that you have delivered to other clients. For example, a consulting company might be expanding from its core computer training service, adding Web site design services for their corporate clients.

In this situation, you could use Microsoft Producer to create a presentation that has an individual discussing the company's new services. In addition to that, the presentation could feature video screen captures and still images—both of which you can record in Microsoft Producer—to show Web sites you have designed for other clients. By using Microsoft Producer, you could post these presentations to a corporate extranet, to an e-service provider site, or to the Web itself.

Introducing a New Web Site

Part of today's business world is its ever-changing appearance. Today, especially with the Web, corporate extranets and intranets are constantly changing; in many cases, new features and information are being added daily. Sometimes, it's difficult for employees or customers to keep track of and learn about changes. In situations like this, you could use Microsoft Producer to create a presentation that introduces a new site and its features.

For example, if your company does electronic business with other companies, where purchasing is handled online, you might update the site, add new features, or institute new procedures for online purchasing, all of which affect your external corporate customers.

You could use Microsoft Producer to create a presentation that has screen shots and video screen captures of the new online purchasing procedures, and then include video that demonstrates these new procedures and how they affect your customers. Furthermore, you could include HTML pages that provide links to information about how to contact support personnel at your company for any additional questions customers might have about these changes.

Creating Internal Corporate Communications

Aside from communicating with other businesses, organizations need to communicate with their own employees. After all, employees play a crucial role in the success of a company. However, with the expanding size and geographic reach of companies today, company-wide meetings can be both expensive and impractical. It's difficult, if not impossible, to gather every employee of a large company into one central location.

It can also be a matter of time and convenience. With Microsoft Producer, you can choose to post presentations to a corporate network location or intranet site. While this enables wide distribution, it also provides another benefit as well: it lets employees view the presentation on-demand, when their schedule allows for it.

The following are some examples of situations in which Microsoft Producer can be used to create presentations for internal corporate communications.

Online Company-wide Meetings

An online company meeting lets your company deliver important information to all of its employees online. Given the large size of companies today, and the ever changing landscape of business, it's often difficult for companies to inform their employees about important changes or news that affects the company and how it does business. Microsoft Producer lets you quickly create an online presentation that communicates this important information.

For example, news might come out that concerns employees, whether it's a change in management, a new corporate structure, or just information that could affect employee morale. A presentation created in Microsoft Producer could feature key management representatives discussing the changes. If the meeting is to discuss changes in management structure, you could incorporate Microsoft PowerPoint slides that contain an organizational chart showing the new management structure. While the slides display in the presentation, you could include video that shows managers explaining these changes.

After you record the presentation, you could publish it to your corporate intranet. This lets employees, shareholders, or journalists see the meeting when they have the time.

Creating Training Events

Computers have changed the way training is accomplished within companies. Over the past few years, computer-based training has become extremely popular. However, some existing computer-based titles can be expensive, and at times ineffective if they do not meet your company's specific needs.

This is where Microsoft Producer can be beneficial for your company. Producer lets you quickly create online training classes, and then redistribute these classes over the company's network, intranet, over the Web, or by using a third-party e-service provider.

With Microsoft Producer, you can design online training classes for a wide variety of topics. Presentations can be designed to teach about both computer and non-computer topics as well.

Creating Online Software Training

Software training has traditionally been provided in a classroom environment. However, making sure employees get the training they need can be difficult in a modern corporate setting due to the time and distance issues related to coordinating a computer trainer's time with company employees. Perhaps more importantly, companies have to invest a lot of time and resources for computer training. By using Microsoft Producer, the time and resources it takes to make an online training class can be significantly reduced.

In Microsoft Producer, the training presentation could feature a variety of digital media that help staff and employees learn about a software application. The video for your presentation can be recorded during an actual training class, and then repurposed for distribution on a company-wide basis. For example, the video portion of the presentation could combine video of the computer trainer describing procedures and video screen captures of the steps being accomplished. The presentation can also contain slides that list, in step-by-step procedures, the commands or features demonstrated in the video.

After this presentation has been created, you could then post it to a corporate intranet site. By putting the presentation online, users can view the presentation at any time—whether for new-employee training or to refresh their knowledge of the tasks shown in the presentation.

If necessary, the presentation (or a group of presentations) could be copied to a CD so other employees can play these presentations on their own computers when they are not connected to the corporate network or Internet. Chapter 11 discusses how to copy a presentation to a recordable or rewritable CD.

Creating Non-computer Training

Typically, people associate online training with computers classes, but your corporation could easily use Microsoft Producer for other training needs. For example, you could create presentations to train sales and marketing staff on non-technical issues, such as key points about new products in a company's product line. In presentations such as this, videos and still images could be shown while slides appear presenting technical issues or specifications for the product they are selling, regardless of what type of product the staff is going to be selling.

Distance Learning and Online Classes

Many of the scenarios up to this point have concentrated on business needs and corporate audiences. However, distance learning classes have become popular at a growing number of universities. Producer can be used to create presentations for this kind of instruction.

Professors or instructors can record their class lectures and synchronize the video or audio with Microsoft PowerPoint slides, and then post the entire presentation on a Web site that is only accessible to students in this class. By providing lectures or other class presentations online, students can have access to previous class sessions and materials. Furthermore, within the presentation, links could be placed so that students can download any additional class handouts.

Creating Sales and Marketing Presentations

The previous scenarios have concentrated on corporate customers or students as the audience. However, Microsoft Producer can also be used for everyday consumers. By creating presentations in Microsoft Producer, people marketing products and services on the Web can target consumers.

For example, a realtor could create a presentation that shows a property he or she is offering. The presentation itself could include slides that describe the different attributes of the property, such as the size of the house, the number of bedrooms, the number of baths, and the land it's on, while showing synchronized video that shows the corresponding view of the property. The presentation could also include an HTML page that links to the listing of the house or comparable properties on the realtor's Web site.

By adding video and audio, synchronized HTML, PowerPoint slides, or other images, a realtor can not only improve the online listing, he or she can begin selling the house without ever having met the potential buyers!

CHAPTER 2

The Microsoft Producer User Interface

The Microsoft Producer user interface is designed to help you immediately start making presentations. The basic elements of the user interface include menus, a toolbar, tabs, and a timeline. This chapter will give you a quick introduction to the Microsoft Producer interface. More extensive information is provided by the Microsoft Producer Help.

Using the Menus

You can perform common tasks in Microsoft Producer by selecting commands from the menus. For example, Figure 2.1 shows the **New Presentation Wizard** command being selected from the **File** menu.

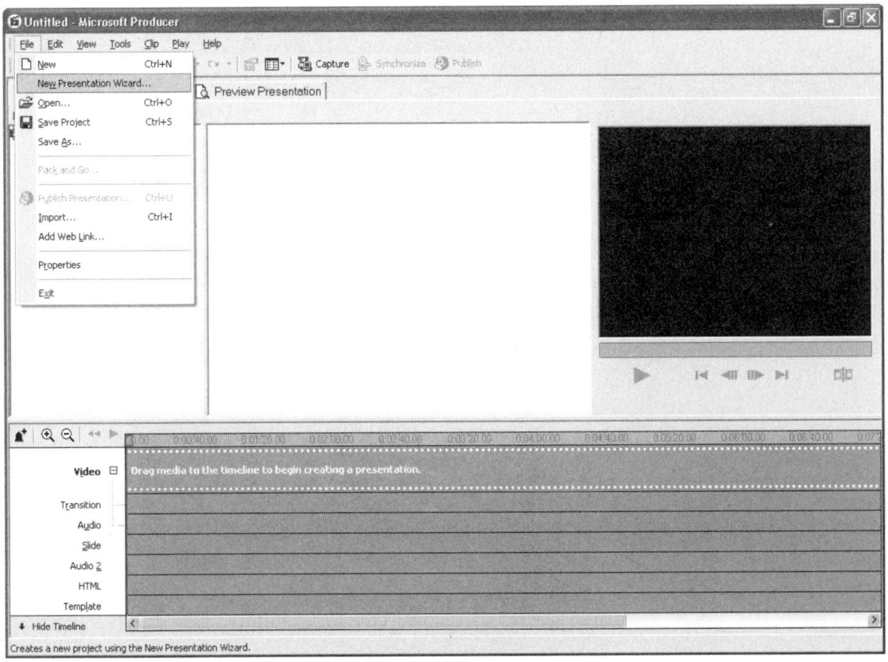

Figure 2.1 — Selecting the **New Presentation Wizard** command.

The following sections provide brief descriptions of the menu commands. When applicable, the shortcut keys for the specific command appear in parentheses.

File Menu

The **File** menu provides commands that help you create new projects or work with existing projects you have created in Microsoft Producer.

New (Ctrl+N)

Use this command to start a new project. When you use this command to create a new project, the timeline is empty. You can then import existing digital media files, or capture new audio and video files, and add them to the timeline.

New Presentation Wizard

Use this command to start the **New Presentation Wizard** that walks you through the process of creating and adding digital media to a new project. The **New Presentation Wizard,** shown in Figure 2.2, lets you choose a template for your presentation and import existing digital media files or record new audio and video. The wizard automatically adds the imported or recorded content to the timeline for your current project, which you can then edit and rearrange.

New Presentation Wizard

Welcome to the New Presentation Wizard

This wizard helps you create a new presentation by walking you through the following steps:

- Selecting a presentation template
- Importing files into your project
- Capturing new video, audio, or still images
- Synchronizing slides to video and audio
- Previewing the presentation

To continue, click Next.

Press F1 for Help at any time in this wizard.

| < Back | Next > | Finish | Cancel |

Figure 2.2 — The introduction page of the **New Presentation Wizard**.

Open (Ctrl+O)

Use this command to open an existing Microsoft Producer project. Project files in Microsoft Producer have a .MSProducer file name extension. After you open the project, all of the associated digital media files appear in the **Media** tab, and any files that have been added to the timeline are displayed there.

Save Project (Ctrl+S)

Use this command to save the changes you made to the current project. By saving the project, you will record any changes you have made to the project, including any files you placed on the timeline and all the imported or recorded digital media. When you open the project later, you can continue working from where you last saved the project file.

Save As

Use this command to save an existing project with a new name or to a different location. This lets you start working on the existing project later without having to import, capture, add, or arrange existing digital media files in the project again.

Pack and Go

Use **Pack and Go** to archive your projects for migration to another computer for additional work or for storage. The project archive contains copies of all files used in the project and all timeline settings. You can then unpack the project archive on another computer and continue editing the project.

Publish Presentation (Ctrl+U)

Use this command to start the **Publish Wizard**. The **Publish Wizard** lets you publish the current project to a corporate intranet site, extranet site, Web site, CD, or third-party e-service provider. After you publish your presentation, others can then watch it in their Web browsers on the site to which you have published the presentation.

Import (Ctrl+I)

Use this command to import existing digital media files, such as still images, Microsoft PowerPoint slides, HTML files, audio, or video files, into your current project. Whether you created your project through the **New Presentation Wizard** or you opened an existing project file, you can import additional digital media to use in the current project.

Add Web Link

Use this command to insert a live Web page or a link to a live Web page in your presentation. A Web link lets you incorporate live Web content into your presentation.

Properties

Use this command to view information about the current project, including when the project was created and modified, as well as display presentation information such as the title, presenter name, and description of the presentation. In the **Properties** dialog box, you can also preview the estimated amount of disk space required to store your presentation based on different audience connection speeds, and see estimates of the amount of time your audience would have to wait to watch your presentation based on their connection speed.

Recent projects

At the bottom of the **File** menu is a list of projects you have worked on recently. You can click one of these to open a specific project in Microsoft Producer—as an alternative to using the **Open** command on the **File** menu.

Edit Menu

The **Edit** menu lets you make changes to your existing project and to digital media files in Microsoft Producer. The following commands are on the **Edit** menu.

Undo (Ctrl+Z)

Use this command to undo the most recent task or action in Microsoft Producer.

Redo (Ctrl+Y)

Use this command to redo the last undone action. For example, if you imported a file and then used the **Undo** command to un-import the file, and you then changed your mind that you do want to import that file, you could click **Redo** to re-import the file.

Cut (Ctrl+X)

Use this command to move a file from one part of the timeline to another. When you use the **Cut** command, the file will be removed from the timeline. You can then use the **Paste** command to insert the file on a new part of the timeline.

Copy (Ctrl+C)

Use this command to copy a file from the contents pane to the timeline or from one part of the timeline to another. When you use the **Copy** command, the file is copied to the Clipboard. You can then use the **Paste** command to insert a copy of the file on the timeline.

Paste (Ctrl+V)

Use this command to paste a file you have copied or cut in Producer to the timeline.

Delete (Del)

Use this command to delete the current selection. The current selection may include one file, many files, or selected text.

Clear Timeline (Ctrl+Del)

Use this command to remove all files from the timeline. This is useful if you decide you want to start over without having to create a new project and import or capture digital media files again.

Select All (Ctrl+A)

Use this command to select all the files in a specified area. For example, if you last clicked on the **Video** track of the timeline and used the **Select All** command, all of the files on the **Video** track would be selected.

Rename (F2)

Use this command to rename a selected item in the contents pane of the **Media** tab. For example, you can rename clips that are created from video files.

Edit Slide

Use this command to edit Microsoft PowerPoint slides that have been imported into Microsoft Producer. When you choose this command, Microsoft PowerPoint starts so you can edit your PowerPoint presentation. You can edit a PowerPoint presentation with a .ppt file name extension or a presentation that was saved in PowerPoint as a Web page with an .htm file name extension.

Replace Web Link

Use this command to replace a live Web page or a link to a live Web page that is selected in your presentation. This command lets you change the Web address or the link that is displayed.

Presentation Scheme

Use this command to open the **Presentation Scheme** dialog box. You can then specify the font, font size, and colors that are displayed in the presentation.

View Menu

The **View** menu provides commands that enable you to switch between the different tabs, show or hide the toolbar, status bar, or timeline, and specify how icons are displayed in the **Media** tab. The following commands are on the **View** menu in Microsoft Producer.

Media Tab (Ctrl+1)

Use this command to display the **Media** tab, which shows all the digital media files available in your current project. This includes any imported or recorded audio and video, as well as any imported still images, HTML files, and Microsoft PowerPoint presentations. For all projects, standard folders that contain presentation templates, video transitions, and video effects are also displayed. The **Media** tab is discussed later in this chapter.

Table of Contents Tab (Ctrl+2)

Use this command to display the **Table of Contents** tab, which allows you to see and edit table of contents entries and information that displays on the introduction page of your presentation. The **Table of Contents** tab is discussed later in this chapter.

Preview Presentation Tab (Ctrl+3)

Use this command to display the **Preview Presentation** tab, which lets you preview your project as it will appear after it has been published. The **Preview Presentation** tab is discussed in more detail later in this chapter.

Timeline (Ctrl+T)

Use this command to show or hide the timeline, which is shown in Figure 2.3.

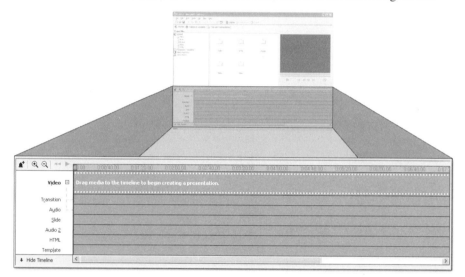

Figure 2.3 — The timeline in Microsoft Producer.

Toolbar

Use this command to show or hide the Microsoft Producer toolbar. The toolbar is displayed below the menus.

Status Bar

Use this command to show or hide the status bar. The status bar is displayed under the timeline, and it provides a description of a menu command when you point to or select one.

Thumbnails

Use this command to display small bitmap images, called thumbnails, of the digital media files in the **Media** tab.

Large Icons

Use this command to display large icons that indicate the file type for files in the **Media** tab.

Details

Use this command to see detailed information about imported digital media files in the **Media** tab.

Arrange Icons by

Use this command to display files in the **Media** tab according to various file properties. The properties you can sort by depend on the selected folder in Microsoft Producer. For example, if you select the **Video** folder, you can arrange files based on information such as the name, source size, duration, type, date, dimensions, frame rate, or the source location of the files.

Refresh (F5)

Use this command to refresh the view of the current project.

Zoom Timeline In (Alt++)

Use this command to decrease the time interval shown on the timeline. This lets you see more precise timing information about the arrangement of the files added to the timeline.

Zoom Timeline Out (Alt+-)

Use this command to increase the time interval shown on the timeline. This lets you see more general information about the arrangement of the files added to the timeline.

Zoom To Fit

Use this command to have Microsoft Producer automatically adjust the zoom level of the timeline so all of the timeline contents display on the timeline on your computer screen. This prevents you from needing to scroll across the screen using the horizontal scroll bar to see all the contents on the timeline.

Tools Menu

The **Tools** menu provides commands for you to use when creating and editing your projects in Microsoft Producer. The following commands are on the **Tools** menu.

Capture (Ctrl+R)

Use this command to start the **Capture Wizard**, which you can use to capture new audio, video, and still images in Microsoft Producer. Chapter 8 provides detailed information about using the **Capture Wizard**.

Synchronize

Use this command to synchronize slides on the timeline with video and audio on the timeline. Chapter 7 discusses synchronizing slides with video and audio.

Rearrange Items On, Slide Track

Use this command to arrange the order items appear on the **Slide** track by moving items up or down in the resulting dialog box.

Rearrange Items On, HTML Track

Use this command to arrange the order items appear on the **HTML** track by moving items up or down in the resulting dialog box.

Rearrange Items On, Template Track

Use this command to arrange the order items appear on the **Template** track by moving items up or down in the resulting dialog box.

Presentation Templates

Use this command to see the available templates that you can use in your project. Templates are stored in the **Presentation Templates** folder in the **Media** tab.

Video Transitions

Use this command to see the available video transitions that you can add between any combination of video and still images on the **Video** track of the timeline. Transitions are stored in the **Video Transitions** folder in the **Media** tab. Chapter 9 discusses working with video transitions in your projects.

Video Effects

Use this command to see the available video effects that you can add to video and still images on the **Video** track of the timeline. All available video effects are stored in the **Video Effects** folder in the **Media** tab. Chapter 9 discusses working with video effects in your projects.

Add Table of Contents Entry (Ctrl+K)

Use this command to add a table of contents entry at the current position of the playback indicator on the timeline. You can then type a name and choose what item the entry is associated with. Chapter 9 provides detailed information about adding and editing entries in the table of contents.

Timeline Snaps

Use this command to change the location of a marker—called a *timeline snap*—on the timeline.

Add Timeline Snap (Ctrl+Shift+P)

Use this menu command to add timeline snaps, which help you synchronize digital media on the timeline. Chapter 9 discusses using timeline snaps to synchronize digital media elements in your projects.

Create Clips

Use this command to separate a selected video file into smaller clips through clip detection. Chapter 9 provides information about clip detection.

Normalize Timeline Audio

Use this command to have audio on the timeline adjusted automatically so it plays back at a uniform level in your presentation.

Audio Levels

Use this command to display the **Audio Levels** dialog box, which enables you to balance sound levels between audio on the **Audio 2** track and the video sound track on the **Audio** track.

Options

Use this command to display the **Options** dialog box, which provides controls for configuring Microsoft Producer.

Clip Menu

The **Clip** menu provides commands that let you work with video and audio files in your project. Most of the commands on this menu are used when you are editing your project. The following commands are on the **Clip** menu.

Add To Timeline (Ctrl+D)

Use this command to add the file selected in the **Media** tab to the timeline. As an alternative to using this command, you can also drag files displayed in the **Media** tab to the timeline.

Audio, Mute

Use this command to specify that the selected audio file is not heard when the file or presentation is played.

Audio, Fade In

Use this command to specify that the selected audio file starts to play quietly, and then increases to the final playback level over a short amount of time when the audio is played in your presentation.

Audio, Fade Out

Use this command to specify that the selected audio starts to play at the regular playback level, and then decreases in volume as the audio ends playback until the audio cannot be heard.

Video, Effects

Use this command to add or remove video effects to selected video or image files on the **Video** track of the timeline.

Video, Fade In

Use this command to specify that the selected video fades in from black.

Video, Fade Out

Use this command to specify that the selected video plays back regularly, and then fades to black as the video ends playback.

Set Start Trim Point (Ctrl+Shift+I)

Use this command to set the starting point, or the *trim in* point, of a video or audio file on the timeline.

Set End Trim Point (Ctrl+Shift+O)

Use this command to set the end point, or *trim out* point, of a video or audio file on the timeline.

Clear Trim Points (Ctrl+Shift+Del)

Use this command to remove any trim points you have added to audio or video files on the timeline.

Duration

Use this command to change the amount of time a slide, still image, HTML file, Web link, or presentation template displays in your presentation. You can change the duration of files that are added to the **Slide**, **HTML**, or **Template** tracks on the timeline.

Split (Ctrl+L)

Use this command to split a selected audio or video file on the timeline into two smaller clips.

Combine (Ctrl+M)

Use this command to combine a previously split audio or video file or to combine two contiguous clips that were created through clip detection. Clip detection is described in chapter 9.

Properties

Use this command to view information about a selected item. You can view properties for items in the **Media** tab or on the timeline.

Play Menu

The **Play** menu lets you control playback of individual video or audio files or your entire project. Chapter 9 discusses previewing your files and projects in Microsoft Producer. The following commands are on the **Play** menu.

Play (Ctrl+P)

Use this command to play the current selection in the monitor on the **Media** tab. What plays depends on the current selection. For example, if one video file is selected in the **Media** tab, that video and its associated audio will play in the monitor, as shown in Figure 2.4.

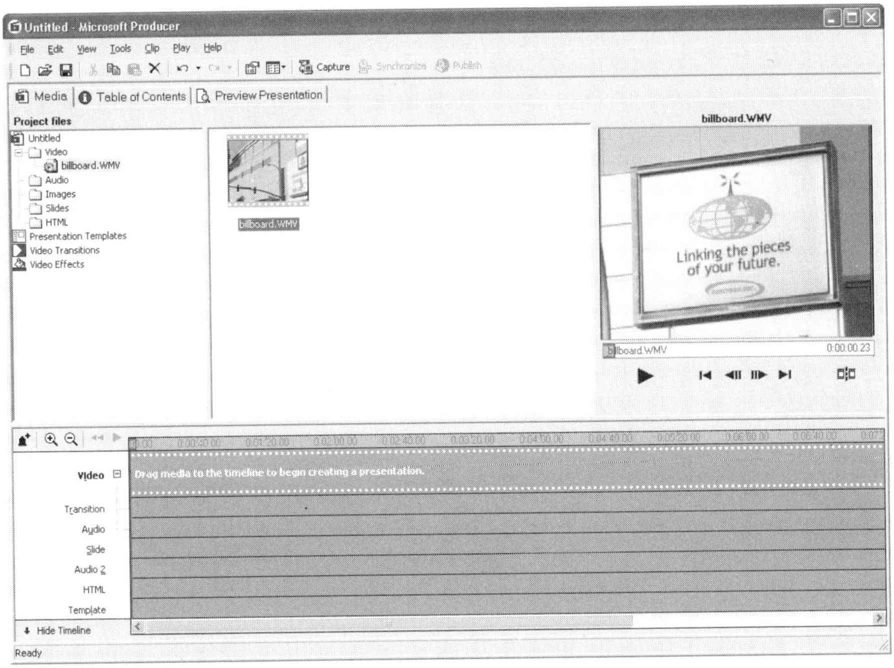

Figure 2.4 — Playing a digital media file in the **Media** tab's monitor.

Play Timeline (Ctrl+W)

Use this command to play the contents of the timeline. Chapter 9 discusses playing files on the timeline.

Rewind (Ctrl+Q)

Use this command to rewind the timeline to the beginning. The next time the timeline is played, it will start from the beginning.

Back (Ctrl+Shift+B)

Use this command to move back one file or clip on the timeline.

Previous Frame (Ctrl+B)

Use this command to move to the frame immediately before the one currently shown in the monitor.

Next Frame (Ctrl+F)

Use this command to move to the frame that is immediately after the frame currently shown in the monitor.

Forward (Ctrl+Shift+F)

Use this command to move forward one file or clip on the timeline.

Help Menu

The **Help** menu gives you access to the Microsoft Producer Help and additional information about Microsoft Producer. The following commands appear on the **Help** menu.

Help Topics (F1)

Use this command to open the Help provided with Microsoft Producer. The Help covers all the features in Microsoft Producer.

Producer on the Web

Use this command to see the additional information about Microsoft Producer that appears on the Web.

About Microsoft Producer

Use this command to display the name, copyright, version number, and product identification for Microsoft Producer.

Using the Toolbar

The toolbar provides an alternate way for you to do many common tasks. Using the toolbar rather than the corresponding menu commands may help you work more quickly and efficiently. To see what each button does, you can point to a button and a ToolTip appears that describes the button's function.

Figure 2.5 shows the toolbar in Microsoft Producer.

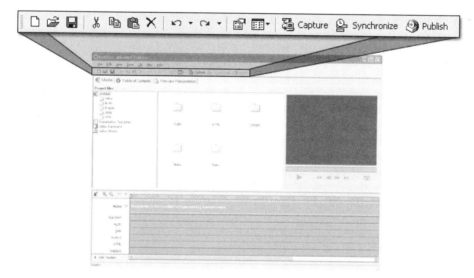

Figure 2.5 — The toolbar.

Table 2.1 shows the buttons on the toolbar and their menu equivalents.

Table 2.1 – Toolbar buttons.

Button	Button name	Corresponding menu command
	New	On the **File** menu, click **New**.
	Open	On the **File** menu, click **Open**.
	Save	On the **File** menu, click **Save Project**.
	Cut	On the **Edit** menu, click **Cut**.
	Copy	On the **Edit** menu, click **Copy**.
	Paste	On the **Edit** menu, click **Paste**.
	Delete	On the **Edit** menu, click **Delete**.
	Undo	On the **Edit** menu, click **Undo**.
	Redo	On the **Edit** menu, click **Redo**.
	Properties	On the **Clip** menu, click **Properties**.
	Views	On the **View** menu, click one of the available options.
	Capture	On the **Tools** menu, click **Capture**.
	Synchronize	On the **Tools** menu, click **Synchronize**.
	Publish	On the **File** menu, click **Publish Presentation**.

Using the Tabs

Each of the Microsoft Producer tabs—the **Media** tab, the **Table of Contents** tab, and the **Preview Presentation** tab—let you see your project differently. The tabs provide you with three different ways for working with your project.

The Media Tab

The **Media** tab is the default view when you first start Microsoft Producer. The **Media** tab lets you see all the imported or recorded files that you can work with for your current project. This is where you work in when beginning a new project and editing it. Chapters 7 and 9 discuss working in the **Media** tab to create and edit a project in Producer.

The **Media** tab is divided into three different panes: the tree pane, contents pane, and monitor. Figure 2.6 shows the different parts of the **Media** tab.

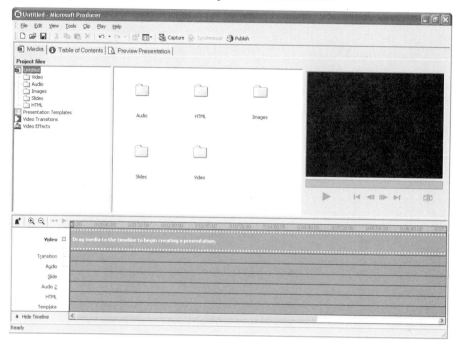

Figure 2.6 — The **Media** tab.

The Tree Pane

The tree pane displays the different types of digital media files you can work with in Microsoft Producer. When you import or record new content, the file for the recorded content is automatically stored in the appropriate folder according to its file type.

In the tree pane, the top five folders are specific to the current project. They only contain files that have been imported or recorded for the current project. Each of these folders can contain the file types described in Table 2.2.

Table 2.2 — Project-specific tree pane folders.

Folder	Description
Video	Contains video files with .asf, .avi, .m1v, .mp2, .mp2v, .mpe, .mpeg, .mpg, .mpv2, .wm, or .wmv file name extensions.
Audio	Contains audio files with .aif, .aifc, .aiff, .asf, .au, .mp2, .mp3, .mpa, .snd, .wav, or .wma file name extensions.
Images	Contains still image files with .bmp, .dib, .emf, .gif, .jfif, .jpe, .jpeg, .jpg, .png, .tif, .tiff, or .wmf file name extensions.
Slides	Contains Microsoft PowerPoint presentations with .ppt or .pps file name extensions. This folder also contains Microsoft PowerPoint slides that were saved as a Web page with an .htm file name extension in PowerPoint and then imported into Producer.
HTML	Contains HTML files with .htm or .html file name extensions.

The folders below the top five folders are default folders that always have the same contents, regardless of project. These folders, described in Table 2.3, appear by default in all Microsoft Producer projects.

Table 2.3 — Default tree pane folders.

Folder	Description
Presentation Templates	This folder contains templates for use in your project. The templates define the layout and view for the duration they appear in the timeline and in your presentation. Chapter 7 discusses working with presentation templates.
Video Transitions	This folder contains video transitions that you can add between two video clips or still images on the timeline. Chapter 9 discusses working with video transition, including information about adding, editing, changing, and adjusting the duration of the transition.
Video Effects	This folder contains different video effects that you can add to a video or still image in the timeline. Chapter 9 discusses working with video effects in Microsoft Producer.

The Contents Pane

The contents pane shows the contents of the folder that is currently selected in the tree pane. When a folder is selected, all the files that are stored in that tree pane folder appear in this area of the **Media** tab. The main purpose of the contents pane is to let you see all the available files you can use for your project. Because the folders are divided by the types of data they contain, you can quickly find the particular file, video transition, or video effect that you want to use in your project.

Chapter 9 discusses working with the contents pane to start a project by adding individual digital media files.

The Monitor

The monitor lets you play individual video files, audio files, and transitions from the contents pane, and it also displays individual still images, slides, HTML files, video effects, and presentation templates. It provides a way for you to see or hear an individual file.

In the monitor, you can also preview parts of your project. Chapter 9 discusses previewing individual files or an entire project.

Below the monitor is a series of monitor buttons. These buttons function just like the buttons on a VCR. They let you navigate through individual files on the timeline or in the contents pane, or you can navigate through all of the files on the timeline for your current project.

To preview individual files or all of the timeline contents, you can use the monitor buttons as an alternative to the menu commands. Both accomplish the same task. However, using the monitor buttons is often quicker than using the menu commands. Table 2.4 describes the monitor buttons and their corresponding menu commands.

Table 2.4 — Monitor buttons and their menu command equivalents.

Button	Button name	Corresponding menu command
▶	**Play**	On the **Play** menu, click **Play**.
◀	**Back**	On the **Play** menu, click **Back**.
◀‖	**Previous Frame**	On the **Play** menu, click **Previous Frame**.
‖▶	**Next Frame**	On the **Play** menu, click **Next Frame**.
▶‖	**Forward**	On the **Play** menu, click **Forward**.
▣▮▣	**Split**	On the **Clip** menu, click **Split**.

The Table of Contents Tab

While working on your project, you might need to edit the table of contents for the final published presentation, as well as the introduction page for your presentation. Use the **Table of Contents** tab to add, edit, delete, or adjust entries in your table of contents. By changing these entries, you can specify how you want your table of contents to appear in your presentation. Figure 2.7 shows the **Table of Contents** tab.

In addition to editing your table of contents, you can also make changes to the introduction page of your final published presentation. This is the page that is displayed before your audience begins to play your presentation.

Chapter 9 discusses editing the table of contents and introduction page for your final presentation.

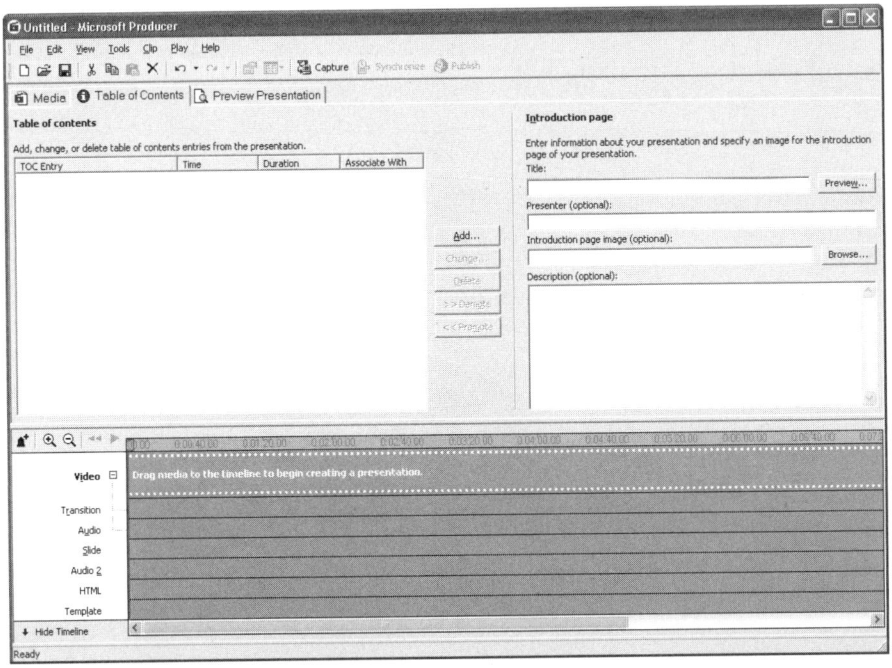

Figure 2.7 — The **Table of Contents** tab.

The Preview Presentation Tab

While working with your project, it is easy to get a sneak preview of what your final presentation will look like by using the **Preview Presentation** tab. This tab lets you see your final presentation as it would appear if you published it. Figure 2.8 shows the **Preview Presentation** tab.

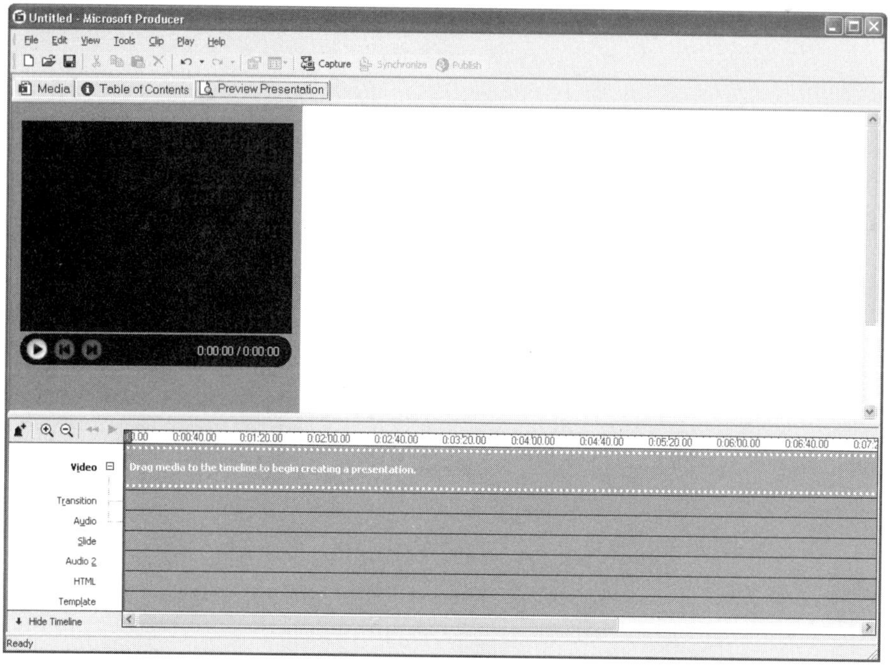

Figure 2.8 — The **Preview Presentation** tab.

Unlike previewing your project in the **Media** tab, previewing your presentation in the **Preview Presentation** tab lets you see all of the elements in your presentation. Because you can see all of the digital media files you have added to the timeline, you get a complete idea of how all the different files within your project would play in the final, published presentation.

Chapter 9 discusses using the **Preview Presentation** tab, including how it differs from previewing in the **Media** tab.

Using the Timeline

The timeline provides the main space for you to work on your projects. It's the canvas for creating your presentation. You can see a chronological listing of all the digital media files that have been added to the timeline and how they all work together to form the complete presentation.

The timeline is divided into multiple parts: the timeline toolbar, the timeline display, and the timeline tracks. Each part plays a valuable role when working on your project in Microsoft Producer.

Figure 2.9 shows the different elements of the timeline.

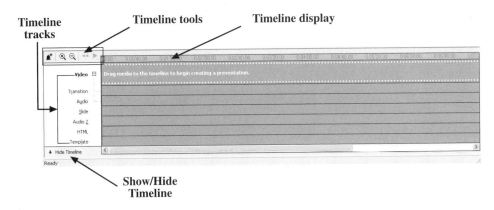

Figure 2.9 — The different elements of the timeline.

The Timeline Tools

Much like the toolbar in Microsoft Producer, the timeline tools provide an alternative to using the menu commands. Using the tools lets you add timeline snaps, zoom in on the timeline, zoom out on the timeline, or rewind and play the timeline. Figure 2.10 shows the timeline tools in Microsoft Producer.

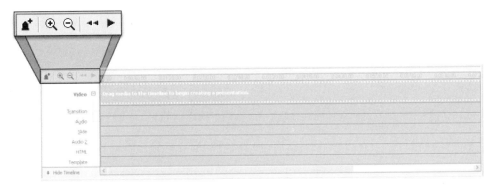

Figure 2.10 — The timeline tools.

Table 2.5 describes the menu equivalent of each tool on the timeline.

Table 2.5 — Timeline tools and corresponding menu commands.

	Tool	Corresponding menu command
⬛⁺	Add timeline snaps	On the **Tools** menu, click **Add Timeline Snap**.
⊕	Zoom timeline in	On the **View** menu, click **Zoom Timeline In**.
⊖	Zoom timeline out	On the **View** menu, click **Zoom Timeline Out**.
◄◄	Rewind the timeline	On the **Play** menu, click **Rewind**.
▶	Play the timeline	On the **Play** menu, click **Play Timeline**.

The Timeline Display

The timeline display is the key to timing the digital media files that appear on the timeline. On the timeline, time is displayed in the form hours:minutes:seconds (H:MM:SS) by default. By using the timeline display, you can determine how long a file on the timeline will play, or how long your entire presentation will play when published.

If you want to increase the time intervals displayed on the timeline, you can click **Zoom Timeline Out** to see a more general overview of your project. However, if you want to see the timeline in more precise time, you can click **Zoom Timeline In**.

The Timeline Tracks

While working on a project in Microsoft Producer, you will most likely be working with a variety of different digital media files. To help keep the files separate from one another, the different types of digital media files, video transitions, video effects, and presentation templates are displayed on different tracks in the timeline.

By keeping these elements on the different tracks, you can quickly see what has been added to the timeline to see how it fits into the timing and appearance of your overall project. The names of the added files appear on the timeline in the individual tracks to help you manage what files appear in your project.

In Microsoft Producer, the following tracks appear in the timeline.

Video Track

Any video files or still images that you add to the timeline are displayed on the **Video** track of the timeline. If you decide to add video effects to one or many different files on this track, a small icon of a paint bucket appears on the track to indicate that a video effect has been added to that file in the timeline. Chapter 9 discusses working with video effects in greater detail.

In Microsoft Producer, you can expand the **Video** track by double-clicking the small plus sign or by pressing Ctrl+Shift+V. When you expand the **Video** track, you can then see the **Transition** and **Audio** tracks.

Transition Track

If you expand the **Video** track, you can see the **Transition** track (and the **Audio** track, discussed next). The **Transition** track lets you see any video transitions that have been added between two video or image files on the timeline. When you add a video transition, you can see how long the transition will play in your final presentation by looking at the shaded region of the **Transition** track. Chapter 9 discusses working with video transitions in greater detail.

Audio Track

Like the **Transition** track, the **Audio** track can only be seen after the **Video** track has been expanded. This track displays the corresponding audio for any video that appears on the **Video** track.

Slide Track

If you have imported any Microsoft PowerPoint slides into your presentation and added them to the timeline, they will appear on the **Slide** track. Adding slides and still images to the timeline is discussed in chapter 9.

Audio 2 Track

Within your presentations, chances are you will be working with different audio files that can contain music or dialog, such as a narration of your presentation. Any added audio files are displayed on the **Audio 2** track of the timeline. Working with audio in Microsoft Producer is discussed in chapter 9.

HTML Track

Another way of effectively conveying your message in your presentation is by adding HTML files that contain pertinent information about the topic to your presentation. When you add any HTML files to the timeline, the files are displayed on the **HTML** track.

Template Track

The **Template** track displays any presentation templates that you have added to the timeline. The templates determine the layout of your presentation—how different elements of the presentation display in a viewer's Web browser. Chapter 9 discusses templates and how they can enhance your overall presentation.

Part II
Preparing to Create Presentations

Chapter 3: Creating an Engaging Presentation

Chapter 4: Setting up Hardware and Software

Chapter 5: Preparing to Record Digital Media

Chapter 6: Recording High-quality Audio and Video

Creating an Engaging Presentation

The most important part of your presentation is your message. Sometimes there can be a tendency to use a technology just for its own sake, rather than using the technology to enhance the message you want to convey to your audience. Of course, that does not mean you should not fully explore the technology. It simply means that you should use different digital media elements in Microsoft Producer to convey and enhance your message. In other words, make sure that the audio, video, slides, HTML content, transitions, and so on serve a purpose in your overall presentation.

Making a presentation engaging and compelling to your audience should be one of your key goals when you are working in Microsoft Producer. To help you meet this goal, this chapter provides tips and guidelines you can follow to make sure that your presentations achieve their specific objectives.

Planning Your Presentation

When creating a presentation, one of the biggest temptations is to start making the presentation right away with little or no advanced planning. At times, planning seems like an extra step because there is a tendency to think that planning is not part of the final presentation. However, the simple considerations you make before creating your presentation can help you save time when working in Microsoft Producer. This section of the book provides you with simple suggestions and considerations to think about in the planning and beginning stages of your presentation.

If you consider some of the issues in this section before you begin work on your project, it can help give direction to your presentation so that it delivers your message clearly and concisely. Planning can also influence the kinds of digital media you use and how you will use Microsoft Producer to create the final presentation.

This chapter concentrates on planning the overall presentation. However, in Microsoft Producer, there are certainly other considerations, especially in regard to recording the video and audio that appears in your presentation. For this reason, this chapter concentrates on the overall presentation. Chapter 5 discusses planning for and recording video and audio for your presentation.

Considering Your Audience

It is important to consider your audience when planning your presentation. By considering your audience, you can determine what they might want to see in your presentation.

If, for example, your organization has a new line of software and your audience is product marketers, you might want to focus your presentation on the new software features that the marketers could then pass on to prospective customers. In this case, you might also want to discuss how this product could help people work more efficiently and show the advantages the new software has over the previous version.

However, if your audience includes employees who are going to be using the new software, you might want the presentation to show how to use the new software. This could include video screen captures, screen shots, and technical instruction about how to accomplish certain tasks using the new software.

In the previous example, the subject matter is the same—the introduction of a new software application. However, by considering the audience for your presentation and their interests, the two presentations probably end up looking very different. This is because the two audiences have different goals. The product marketers want to learn about the software application so they can sell it, whereas the employees want to learn about the new application so they can use it in their daily work. Though at times the audience's goals may overlap, as they easily could in this scenario, consider the main audience and the general purpose of the presentation, and then create the presentation with these issues in mind.

Determining the Purpose of Your Presentation

Closely tied to the idea of considering your audience is determining your purpose. If you aren't sure what the presentation's purpose is, ask yourself, "What do I hope to accomplish through this presentation?" In many communications, whether it is a simple e-mail message or a memo to a group of people, purpose plays an instrumental role in planning and delivering your message.

Continuing with the two example audiences I discussed in the previous section (product marketers and company employees), the two presentations would each have a different purpose. For the product marketers, your purpose is to inform them about the new features and to show them how to sell the product based on these new features. However, if your audience consists of employees who are going to use the software in their everyday work, your purpose is to teach them how to apply the new features to the work they do.

Considering Time Constraints

As with many things you do at work and at home, you will probably have time constraints for creating presentations in Microsoft Producer. For example, your presentation might have a time limit—you might have to limit your presentation to 10 minutes. If this is the case, you must determine which information is absolutely essential and which information can be omitted if time becomes an issue.

Time constraints play a role from the beginning. For example, if you are creating Microsoft PowerPoint slides and then importing them into your Microsoft Producer presentations, you may want to limit the number of slides. Consider the amount of time necessary for setting up the information in the slide, or the time that it will take to go through the points on the slide. Generally speaking, more slides will result in a longer presentation, especially if you plan on narrating the slides and then adding additional video to your presentation.

You will also want to plan for the time available to create your presentation, and then spend the necessary amount of time putting the presentation contents together. You don't want to spend half of the allotted development time creating one slide, and then have the quality of the rest of the slides suffer because there wasn't enough time to do an equally good job.

Considering Budgetary Constraints

Unfortunately, there are very few times when budgetary constraints will not exist in some form or another. Depending on the resources available, you might have to tailor your presentation based on the amount of money set aside for creating online presentations.

Budgetary constraints can exist in many forms. For example, if you have access to a professional studio, you might only have a limited amount of studio time available to you. If you do not have access to a professional studio, you might only have a limited amount of money to spend on recording equipment, such as cameras and accessories, including lighting, tripods, monopods, and so forth.

When these limits exist, you will have to make certain decisions in order to work within your budget. This might mean purchasing a camera with lesser capabilities or going without certain camera accessories. Chapter 4 discusses the difference in cameras and in their performance. This can help you decide which camera is right for your presentations, considering your recording needs and budget.

Scheduling Your Presenter

Gathering the necessary people to record your presentation can be a difficult and time-consuming task. However, by scheduling the participants in advance, you can help guarantee that the recording will go smoothly.

While you are scheduling your presenter and any other participants, it is a good idea to send them a script or plan for recording. This lets the presenters see in advance what they will need to say and can help minimize recording time. Additionally, if your presenters are going to narrate slides in Microsoft Producer, it is a good idea to send them the slides so they can rehearse the narration.

By scheduling your work and sending materials in advance, you can help reduce the time (and possibly the number of takes) needed for recording the video and audio portions of your presentation. Chapter 5 discusses creating a basic script and preparing a location for recording.

What Makes an Engaging and Effective Presentation?

In the past, you may have watched a presentation and noticed that it did not immediately grab and hold your attention. Presentations that are unable to hold the audience's attention are likely to be ineffective. A good practice is to think about past presentations you have watched and think about what you liked or disliked about them.

Regardless of whether you have seen online presentations similar to the ones you can create in Microsoft Producer, this section will provide you with tips and guidelines to follow in order to create effective and dynamic presentations. By following the guidelines and tips discussed in this section, you can create presentations that will grab and hold your audience's attention.

Your content alone does not determine the effectiveness of the presentation. A majority of the effectiveness is determined by how the content is organized and, ultimately, delivered in the presentation. Two key parts of your presentation are the delivery of the message by the speaker and the digital media files contained within the presentation itself.

The following sections do not assume that the creator of the presentation is the presenter, but this may often be the case.

Guidelines for the Speaker

The speaker or presenter plays the key role in the presentation. The presenter can be thought of as the "tour guide" of the presentation because he or she narrates, discusses, or describes what is shown in the presentation. Because of this, the presenter controls the tone and pace of the presentation.

The presenter may not be a professional actor or public speaker. However, not having a professional presenter is not a bad thing. One of the most important attributes for presenters is their ability to show and convey their interest, knowledge, and enthusiasm for the topic discussed in the presentation.

The following sections contain tips and guidelines for the presenter to follow when speaking during the presentation. This information is far from exhaustive. The presenter can do so much more, since professionalism, preparation, and experience can play an important role in the success of a presentation. Following these guidelines can help to increase the effectiveness of the speaker in your presentation.

Speaking Clearly

Speaking clearly is one of the most important tasks for the presenter. After all, the presenter's words provide important information to the presentation's audience. As a presenter, it is sometimes difficult to keep this in mind because so many things are going on simultaneously while recording. However, speaking at an even pace and constantly remembering to enunciate is crucial to the presenter's effectiveness in communicating.

However, the presenter should realize that his or her recorded words and performance can be edited in Microsoft Producer. This can help reassure the presenter that timing does not have to be perfect. If the presenter's timing is off, the recording can be easily synchronized in the presentation using Microsoft Producer. Because of this, it is often easier to videotape the speaker's words (using a digital or analog video camera), record the video into Microsoft Producer, and later edit the video in Microsoft Producer. If you are using a Web camera, you can easily use Microsoft Producer to make a live recording using Microsoft Producer, and then edit and synchronize the recorded video with slides in Microsoft Producer as well.

Synchronizing your presentation and editing video are discussed in part III of this book.

Being Dynamic when Speaking

By displaying enthusiasm in his or her voice to create emphasis on important points, the presenter can convey interest in the subject to the audience. Think about times when you have seen speakers talking monotonously with no visible passion or interest in what they are speaking about. If you saw this on television, did you immediately change the channel? If not, did you find it harder to understand which points were important? You should not expect your audience to take an active interest in a presentation if the presenters themselves seem rather uninterested in what they are speaking about.

Displaying enthusiasm does not mean over-exaggerating, because an audience will quickly pick up on this artificial emotion and may mistake it for sarcasm. When choosing a speaker for your presentations, ask yourself, "Does this presenter have an active interest in the subject, and does he or she convey that interest to the audience watching the presentation?"

In many presentations, regardless of the manner in which it is delivered, there generally needs to be some emotional appeal that is made to the audience—that is, the audience should feel that the speaker cares and wants the audience to care too. For example, if a CEO is delivering a new product announcement or vision for the company, it is important for the company employees to believe the CEO's conviction in the new vision or product. In this type of appeal, the presenter's excitement or commitment to the new vision can help others feel that same sense of excitement and eagerness to work for the goals introduced in the presentation.

The previous example is an instance in which the presenter's passion and interest in the subject play an invaluable role in contributing to the success of the presentation, and more importantly, to the success of the company.

Making Eye Contact with the Camera

When the presenter maintains continued eye contact with the camera, he or she can help to increase the effectiveness of the presentation. Again, thinking back to events you have seen on television, consider how many speakers look directly into the camera—reporters, politicians, news anchors, and so on. This can help to increase the believability and sincerity of the message delivered in the presentation.

Maintaining eye contact with the camera is like looking into the audience's eyes—as if you were speaking to each person in the audience individually, face-to-face. Typically in conversation, it is considered good practice to look into people's eyes when speaking to them. Using this common practice in your Microsoft Producer presentations can help to keep your audience's attention.

Avoiding Space Fillers

Like many of the issues discussed in this section, using "space fillers" when speaking is something that is quite common in everyday conversation. Consequently, these space fillers are often used when a presenter is speaking.

In English, space fillers are words or sounds that serve as a crutch when we are not comfortable with a silent pause. Common space fillers are: "Ummm," "Erhh," "Like," "Usually," "Actually," and so forth. Some speakers may use a nervous laugh to fill uncomfortable pauses. At times, the speaker may seem uncomfortable with moments of silence because he or she might feel like there needs to be some kind of narration throughout the presentation.

Space fillers do not add anything to the presentation, and in the end, can also be distracting when repeated throughout a presentation. As the presenter practices the presentation, he or she should be aware of these space fillers. The speaker should identify them and try to become comfortable with pausing as he or she switches topics or thoughts. If you videotape the speaker giving the presentation, you can always edit out pauses that are too long, but editing out vocalized space fillers can be tough.

Sticking to a Clear Agenda

One of the most detrimental problems that can arise in a presentation is when the speaker seems to be wandering from topic to topic, with no clear direction or sense of purpose. When this occurs, the presentation becomes less effective. By presenting the ideas in a clear and concise manner, your audience will be more likely to believe in what the speaker is discussing in the presentation.

For example, if an organization is presenting a new corporate plan or vision, and the presenter seems to move from one goal to another without clearly explaining each part of the plan, the audience watching the presentation might question the practicality of or commitment to the new vision.

Part of having a clear agenda can mean creating a script or speaking notes. Having brief notes or cue cards about each topic, goal, or slide can help the presenter stay on course—plus, it's a good practice to get into for public speaking.

Avoiding Distractions

When speaking, a presenter should try to keep his or her hands free of distracting items. Many times, a speaker may hold an item and subconsciously fidget with it. For example, the presenter might be holding a pen and clicking the pen nervously while speaking. Keeping hands free of unnecessary objects also lets the speaker use his or her hands when speaking.

During a presentation, it may be necessary to hold an object. For example, if the presentation is a demonstration of a new product, the presenter might hold the new product to show it to the audience. In this case, the object is an instrumental part of the presentation. However, as a general rule, only hold objects that are instrumental to the presentation or play a key role in what the presenter is discussing.

Though cue cards may be helpful to stay on topic, repeated shuffling or playing with cue cards may attract attention to the cards and away from the speaker's points. A presenter might use his or her hands and make gestures with them while talking. Doing this is quite natural and common, and can help emphasize a point. By keeping his or her hands free of objects, the presenter can feel free to use them as he or she might while speaking in a one-on-one conversation.

Discussing Slides, Not Just Reading Them

As discussed in chapter 1, you can use Microsoft Producer to import Microsoft PowerPoint slides for use in your presentations. Many times, your speaker may be narrating these slides through video and audio. When creating this common type of presentation, make sure that the speaker avoids simply reading slides word-for-word during the presentation. When the presenter just reads the slides instead of explaining them, the video and audio do not add value to the existing PowerPoint slides. Remember, the goal is to use audio and video to enhance your presentations.

A common concern a presenter might have is what he or she should say for each slide within the PowerPoint slideshow. To alleviate this concern, consider adding speaker's notes to your slides when you create them in Microsoft PowerPoint. These notes are a great way to keep track of additional content for each slide, and these notes can be viewed on a computer screen or printed out for the presenter when he or she is recording the slide narration. At times, simply glancing at the notes can help a presenter stick to the agenda and add accurate information to the existing slide as it plays in the final Microsoft Producer presentation.

Using Digital Media in Your Presentation

The audio, video, and other digital media you use serve as the individual pieces that, when combined and organized, create your presentation. On their own, the individual digital media files may have little value to your audience. However, when you combine and organize these different files they form one complete, dynamic presentation. Figure 3.1 shows an example of a presentation.

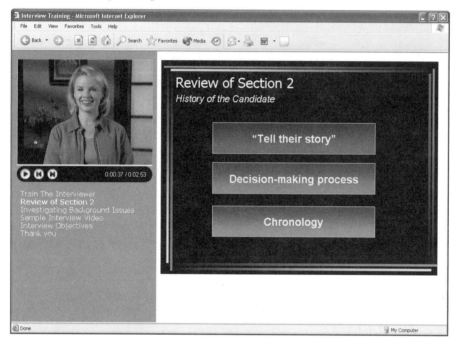

Figure 3.1 — A presentation that includes slides synchronized with video and audio.

Using Different Digital Media Files for Effect

Microsoft Producer lets you use a wide variety of existing digital media files in your presentations. One of the biggest challenges in creating a presentation, however, is to use those various types of digital media without creating a distraction for the viewer. There needs to be a tradeoff between a presentation that is dynamic and one that is gaudy. When you have a specific purpose in using different types of digital media, you can create a tasteful, yet dynamic, presentation that coherently conveys your message.

One example of using different digital media types is combining your Microsoft PowerPoint slides with audio and video. For example, you might want to discuss your company's recent growth by showing examples of expansion in your presentation. In this situation, you could have a "talking head" video that shows a person relating expansion numbers from PowerPoint slides. However, one of the slides might explain that your company is constructing a new building to accommodate physical growth. In this situation, you might then insert a video file that shows the new building and its progress. This supporting video works to reinforce your message and give an example to supplement the "talking head" video and slides that discuss the company's growth.

Using digital media files in Microsoft Producer goes beyond audio and video files. For example, you can also switch between templates during the presentation. Continuing the previous example, you might have the "talking head" video play in a smaller display window while the slides are displayed in a larger window. However, when you show your supporting video of the building under construction, you might want to add a different template to the timeline so the supporting video plays in a larger display window while the slide then displays in the smaller window. When the supporting video is finished, you might then want to switch back to the original template.

By using digital media in this manner, where it has a specific purpose, you can greatly increase the effectiveness of your presentations. It gives your presentation a solid, coherent message rather than appearing as a random group of digital media files that were used in the presentation simply because they were available.

Chapter 9 shows you how to add new templates to the timeline, so the layout of your presentation can change while it plays in a Web browser.

Organizing Your Presentation

Closely related to the concept of using digital media files with a purpose, is that of organizing your presentation so the digital media files and their timing in the presentation make sense to your audience. Many times, this is one of the greatest challenges in creating a quality presentation. When you are using Microsoft PowerPoint slides, this becomes quite easy because your presentation will probably follow the order of the slides.

One way to show the organization of your presentation is through a table of contents. Microsoft Producer lets you create and edit a table of contents for your presentation. As mentioned in chapter 1, the presentation's table of contents functions much like the table of contents for a book. Just as a table of contents for a book shows how the book is organized and where certain information can be found, the table of contents for your presentation shows how your presentation is organized and provides links that your audience can click to see a specific part of your presentation.

You can edit the table of contents to add new entries, if necessary, when new digital media files are added to the presentation. Chapter 9 discusses how to create and edit a table of contents in Microsoft Producer.

Synchronizing Digital Media in Your Presentation

One of the best ways to increase the effectiveness of your presentation is to synchronize the timing of the digital media that you are working with. Microsoft Producer lets you do this when using audio only or both audio and video narration for slides, or when narrating a video screen capture in the **Capture Wizard**. However, you can also easily synchronize other digital media files by using the synchronize slides feature in Producer.

Continuing with the example presentation discussed previously in this section, you might want to have quiet background music playing with the video showing the new building because the construction video file does not contain any audio that adds to your presentation. In this situation, you would want the background music to start playing when the video begins and immediately end when you switch back to the PowerPoint slides and "talking head" video narration. When all of these events happen simultaneously, your presentation has a clean, dynamic, and professional appearance.

Chapter 7 discusses how to synchronize existing digital media using the synchronize slides feature.

Integrating Web or Intranet Sites

You might have content in Web sites or intranet sites that could add more information to the presentation. Integrating individual HTML pages or your entire Web or intranet site can help to increase the effectiveness of your presentation because it lets you add existing content to support the presentation. One of the added benefits of using a Web site is that it lets you work more efficiently because you avoid duplicating existing information.

In the example presentation on company growth, the presenter might mention the increase in the number of employees hired in the past year. However, you might already have this type of information available on your corporate intranet site. If this is the case, you could use these HTML pages in your Microsoft Producer presentation so these figures appear on screen when the presenter mentions the increase in the number of company employees.

Choosing Templates with Color and Style in Mind

When choosing the colors and templates for your presentations, think about a Web site that did not impress you because of the layout and colors used. Often, the layout and colors used in your presentation are one of the first things your audience notices.

For example, when choosing your presentation templates, think about how they will look with the existing Microsoft PowerPoint slides you have chosen for your presentation. The goal is to coordinate the templates used so they work together to add consistency and an appealing look.

On the Web, there are many sites that appear unprofessional because of the colors they use. Think about these unprofessional-looking Web sites and the effect the colors and appearance had on your opinion of the quality of the information contained on the site. The style and colors of your presentation can have that same effect on your audience. By choosing professional-looking templates with colors that work together, you can attract and keep your audience's attention.

For examples of color schemes and templates that work well together, see the CD that accompanies this book.

Making Your Presentations Interactive

Part of making a presentation dynamic and effective is to add interactivity to the presentation. Interactive presentations let your audience provide feedback and comments about the presentation they are watching.

When you publish a presentation, you can choose to enable Web discussions if you have a Web discussion server, which is available with Microsoft Office Server Extensions or SharePoint Portal Server. This server lets users enter comments and questions about the presentation in their Web browsers as the presentation is played back. When your audience provides their questions or comments, you or other users can provide feedback or answer the questions.

To participate in Web discussions, your audience must have the discussion server client installed on their computers. The discussion server client is installed with Microsoft Office 2000 and Microsoft Office XP. Furthermore, their security settings in Internet Explorer must be set to allow ActiveX controls to be downloaded to their computer.

Tips for Video Screen Captures

Video screen captures like the one shown in Figure 3.2 are commonly used in training presentations (although they can certainly be used for other presentations as well). By showing users the steps to accomplish a given task, the user can then watch the video and see the mouse clicks required to complete the described task. If you are explaining a procedure for a software application and the viewers have access to the program on their computers, they could then open the software application during the presentation and perform the described task themselves.

By using video screen captures in your training presentation, you can include another medium for teaching others how to perform a given task. Screen captures are helpful because they can reach all the different types of learners. Some people learn best by seeing how something is accomplished (visual learners), while others might learn best by hearing instructions (audio learners), while others learn best by doing the actual task themselves (physical learners). When you use Microsoft Producer to create training presentations, you can include different digital media elements that can help teach everyone, regardless of their learning style.

In part III of this book, there are specific instructions about how to record video screen captures in Microsoft Producer and how to create the training presentation itself. However, the following section is intended to give you a list of procedural guidelines to follow when recording the actual video screen capture for your training presentations.

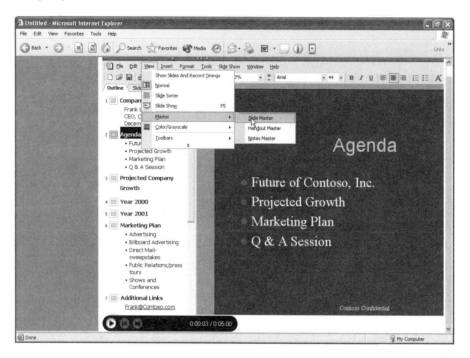

Figure 3.2 — Video screen capture in a training presentation.

Explaining What You Are Demonstrating

Before beginning the video screen capture, explain what you are going to show in the captured video. The way you explain it is up to you. You could use PowerPoint slides to explain the video screen capture, or you could add an audio or video narration to describe what you are going to show. The explanation helps the audience understand what to expect in the upcoming video screen capture.

Many times, when you are introducing the topic, you will only need a brief introduction, such as one slide or a short HTML file. The goal is to explain what is going to be shown in the video screen capture quickly and clearly.

Explaining When the Feature Is Used

After establishing what you are going to show in the video screen capture, the next step should be to describe one or more different scenarios in which this feature or task could be used. If the video is for internal training, try to give specific business scenarios that are familiar to your audience. This can help your audience understand more about the task or feature shown in the capture. However, perhaps more importantly, it provides a solid example of when they would do this task in their daily work.

Coming up with one scenario can be difficult because the task you are going to show can probably be performed in a variety of situations. In this case, you need to consider your primary audience and their needs. A helpful question to ask yourself is, "When and how would they use this feature or application in their daily work?" and then try to capture video of the computer screen in that situation, if possible.

Performing the Task

After introducing the task and possible scenarios, perform the task at a normal pace. By showing the task at a normal pace, you can give your audience an idea of how long the task will take.

Avoid rushing through the video screen capture and clicking through mouse movements too quickly because your users may feel rushed, and they will not be able to follow the steps. Conversely, avoid going through the task at an extremely slow pace because it may frustrate your users. In addition, if they see that this task takes an extraordinary amount of time, they might be intimidated and wary of performing the task themselves.

Paraphrasing What You Demonstrated

After you show the video screen capture, you might want to quickly review what was shown in the video screen capture. This type of quick review can help your audience understand, in everyday terminology, what was done during the screen capture.

When reviewing the video screen capture, it's a good idea to minimize the amount of technical terminology. By phrasing the review in everyday words, you can help your audience better understand what was done. Furthermore, by hearing the explanation in common language, the viewers will then be able to explain the task to others. By paraphrasing, you can quickly summarize the demonstrated task in order to help increase the effectiveness of the video.

Reviewing the Video and Practicing the Task

After the screen capture video has been played and reviewed, it is often helpful for users to be able to go back to the video screen capture and replay it if they choose. While some viewers will just continue with the presentation, others might choose to replay the video to see the steps again.

This is easy to do in Microsoft Producer, because users can pause, play, and replay the presentation as they choose. For example, if you added an entry for the table of contents in your presentation that starts the video screen capture, users can simply click that link and then watch the video again if they choose. Other viewers may find this helpful because they can pause your presentation, open the software application (if they have access to it from their computers), and then perform the same steps just shown in the video. After they are finished, they can then continue to play the presentation in their Web browsers from the point where they last paused the presentation. By providing an easy way for your audience to review the video screen capture as they choose, you let them learn at their own pace.

Soliciting Feedback

Finally, within your training presentation, you can provide a link for comments in order to see how you can make more effective presentations in the future. In Microsoft Producer, you can get feedback through a variety of methods. A simple way to get feedback is to provide an e-mail link that lets users send comments to you or to an e-mail alias. In addition to this, you could provide a link to a Web page that contains a form for users to send their feedback online.

CHAPTER 4

Setting up Hardware and Software

Microsoft Producer can interact with a variety of different hardware and software components. In order to interact with the various hardware and software components, you need to have installed or connected these devices properly.

It can be intimidating to start the process of purchasing, installing, and connecting hardware such as a Web camera, video camera, VCR, or video capture card. The goal of this chapter is to ease some of the anxiety that can come with purchasing and installing the different hardware and software components you can use with Microsoft Producer. This chapter will also explain the differences between the various types of video cameras and capture devices that you can use with Microsoft Producer.

Video Formats

The first step when choosing a camera that will fit your video recording needs is to understand the different available *video formats*. The video camera's format refers to the way that the video signal from the camera is recorded to tape. Each video camera uses one format for recording. This section introduces and briefly explains the different types of video cameras on the market today.

MiniDV

A digital video (DV) camera that records in the MiniDV format is capable of producing high-quality professional video. When video is recorded in MiniDV format by a DV camera, there is very little distortion in the recorded video and audio, and the video is of higher resolution than most other video formats. This lack of distortion is because the camera records through a precise digital signal rather than an analog signal used by the other formats such as Standard 8, Hi 8, VHS, and S-VHS.

A MiniDV camera is the highest-quality camera available for consumers on the market today. Because the video is recorded digitally, there is very little noticeable loss in quality when the video is transferred from MiniDV tape to a computer. The MiniDV format records video on 6-millimeter (mm) tape that is stored in a small cassette. These cassettes are smaller than those used by analog cameras.

Today, a vast majority of the MiniDV cameras have a digital output that lets you connect your camera, through an Institute of Electrical and Electronics Engineers (IEEE) 1394 connection (often called FireWire or iLink), to a computer that has an IEEE 1394 card or port. When digital video is transferred through this connection, the video is recorded on the computer at a high speed—approximately 400 megabits per second (Mbps)—with very little loss in quality. Using Microsoft Producer, you can record digital video from a MiniDV camera to a computer that provides an IEEE 1394 card or port, and then use the captured video in your presentations.

When comparing the cost of a MiniDV camera to an analog camera that may use Standard 8, Hi-8, VHS, or S-VHS, the MiniDV camera is usually more expensive. However, it also produces higher-quality video and audio than analog video cameras.

Digital 8

Digital 8 is a digital video format that records much like DV; therefore, the quality of the video is higher than Standard 8 or Hi-8, which are analog formats. Digital 8 uses the same video tapes as Hi-8. If you have Hi-8 video tapes, you can then play back these tapes in a Digital 8 camera.

Digital 8 cameras can provide an alternative to a MiniDV camera because they both record in a digital format. Usually, a Digital 8 video camera is less expensive than a comparable MiniDV camera.

Similar to MiniDV cameras, a vast majority of the Digital 8 cameras have a digital output that lets you connect your camera through an IEEE 1394 connection to a computer that has an IEEE 1394 card or port. Because the video is recorded digitally, there is very little noticeable loss in quality when the video is transferred from video tape to a computer.

Hi-8 and Standard 8

Standard 8 and Hi-8 are analog video formats that are recorded using 8mm video tapes. When compared to Standard 8 format, Hi-8 video cameras have a better recording system and use a high-quality metal tape that results in higher-quality video recording. Furthermore, Hi-8 video cameras have superior audio recording capabilities than Standard 8.

One of the drawbacks of using Standard 8 or Hi-8 format compared to the VHS analog standard is the durability of the tape. The 8mm-wide tape is more fragile than VHS tape, which makes the 8mm tape more prone to distortion that negatively affects the quality of your recorded video. However, compared to VHS, Hi-8 and Standard 8 video cameras are much smaller and more compact, and are much easier to handle.

An important distinction to remember between Hi-8 and Standard 8 video cameras is the type of tape they can use. A Hi-8 video camera can use both Hi-8 tape and Standard 8 tape, whereas a Standard 8 camera can only use standard 8mm tape.

If you have an analog capture device connected and properly installed on your computer, you can record from most Hi-8 or Standard 8 cameras using Microsoft Producer. Because Hi-8 and Standard 8 video is recorded with an analog signal, when you transfer the video to the computer, it will be of lower quality than that of MiniDV.

VHS and S-VHS

VHS and S-VHS cassettes are the same type of cassette that you use in a VCR. Just as Hi-8 has advantages over Standard 8, the newer S-VHS format has an improved recording system over its predecessor, VHS. Because these tapes are much larger, they are more durable and less prone to damage than the 8mm formats used by Standard 8 and Hi-8.

However, because these tapes are much larger, VHS and S-VHS cameras are larger than Standard 8 and Hi-8 cameras and also require larger batteries. Therefore, if you don't have the available resources to buy the high-quality MiniDV camera and you must choose between the different analog cameras, you might consider buying a Hi-8 or Standard 8 video camera if size and portability are concerns.

An S-VHS video camera can use either VHS or S-VHS cassettes. However, a VHS video camera can only use a VHS tape. Many new VHS video cameras use VHS-C or S-VHS-C cassettes. These cassettes contain the same tape in a smaller, more compact cassette. With these newer video cameras, the recording time per tape is shorter than the older VHS video cameras. However, the cameras are also more compact.

Video Sources

In Microsoft Producer, you can record from a variety of video sources. In general, the video source is the device, such as a camera or VCR, you use to record live video or to play back taped video. When you connect these video sources to a capture device on your computer, you can then record taped or live video from the device to your computer.

The following sections briefly explain the different video sources you can use to capture video to your computer if you have the appropriate capture devices installed.

Video Cameras

Analog video cameras use formats such as Standard 8, Hi-8, VHS, and S-VHS. When you record video from an analog camera or VCR to your computer, it must be converted from the analog signal to a digital signal. This conversion process can cause some distortion in the recorded video and audio when played back on your computer. However, the overall quality of the captured video is increased if the video is captured on a computer that has sufficient processing power.

A digital video camera, such as a MiniDV camera, records video digitally—that is, in the form of ones and zeroes. The main benefit that digital video provides over analog video is that the recorded digital video is already coded in a way that the computer can understand. Because of this, the data does not have to be translated into another format when copied to a computer. With DV and MiniDV, no translation is necessary. Therefore the data is passed from the DV camera or VCR to the computer through an IEEE 1394 connection, such as FireWire, with virtually no loss in quality. As long as you have a DV camera or DV VCR connected to an IEEE 1394 card or port, the video is easily transferred to your computer.

Web Cameras

A Web camera is a small camera that you can attach to your computer. As the name implies, these cameras are commonly used for Web sites that show live shots of people, locations, or objects. In Microsoft Producer, you can use a Web camera to record live video—and audio if the camera has a built-in microphone—to use in your presentations.

One of the main advantages a Web camera has over a video camera is the cost. Because Web cameras are generally less expensive than an analog or digital video camera, a Web camera is ideal if you are on a limited budget.

With a Web camera, you will not get the quality you would from an analog or digital video camera. Also, Web cameras do not allow you to record video to tape, and therefore you don't have the ability to fast-forward or rewind through the recorded video. All video you record with a Web camera is saved on the computer.

However, for some presentations, a Web camera can easily provide the quality you need. For example, you might create a *talking head* presentation that simply shows a stationary person in front of a static background—something like a news broadcast. By adjusting the lighting, focus, and setting for the recording, you can record video that is suitable for your presentations. Chapter 5 discusses adjusting lighting and settings to help you record quality video in an office setting.

Analog or DV VCRs

You can record your existing taped video into Microsoft Producer using an analog or digital VCR. In general, using a VCR is similar to using an analog or digital video camera to play back recorded video. Therefore, if you have either a camera or VCR attached to your computer, you can play back recorded video.

The differences between analog and digital VCRs are similar to the differences between analog and digital video cameras. A digital VCR lets you play back from and record to a DV tape, while an analog VCR lets you play back from and record to an analog tape, such as VHS. Connecting a VCR to your computer is discussed later in this chapter.

Satellite or Cable TV

Some organizations make satellite or cable TV available in office spaces. If this is the case with your organization, you can record video from the cable or satellite TV feed to your computer. As with recording from any video source to your computer, you need to have a video capture device installed, and you need to have a tuner to change channels.

When receiving a cable or satellite TV feed, there are two common ways to change channels: by using a VCR or by using a TV tuner card. One method you can use to change channels on your computer is to connect the cable or satellite TV feed to a VCR and use the tuner on your VCR to change channels. Connecting a satellite or cable TV feed to your computer so you can record video from it is discussed later in this chapter.

Another method is to have a TV tuner card attached to your computer. With a TV tuner card, you can change channels on your computer without using an external piece of hardware, such as a VCR. Connecting a TV tuner card to your computer and your satellite or cable TV feed is also shown later in this chapter.

Broadcasting Standards

Around the world, there are different standards used for TV broadcasts. These standards also affect the recording and playback of different video sources, such as video cameras and VCRs. These different standards can directly affect your work, especially if you have coworkers in other parts of the world who may need to play back your recorded tapes.

The following section gives you a brief overview of the different broadcasting standards and the countries or regions in which they are used. This distinction is important because if you are in a country or region that uses one standard and you try to send tapes to coworkers in a country or region that uses another standard, there is a good chance that they will not be able to play back your tape on their video cameras or VCRs. Today, there are a few video sources that play back all the dominant standards. However, these video devices are usually quite expensive.

In Microsoft Producer, you can record from a device that uses any of the three different broadcasting and recording standards described in this section. Because the video is converted when it is recorded to your computer, anyone around the world who has a computer and has access to your presentation can watch it. Not only can you share your presentations with audiences around the world, but you also eliminate the playback problems that arise when sharing video with people in countries or regions that use a different broadcasting standard.

National Television System Committee (NTSC)

The National Television System Committee (NTSC) standard is the broadcasting standard that is used in the United States, Mexico, Japan, and Canada. Because NTSC is the standard for broadcasting in these countries, most video cameras and VCRs record and play back video using the NTSC standard. The NTSC standard has a resolution of 525 lines per frame. The NTSC standard plays back at 30 frames per second.

Phase Alternate Lines (PAL)

The Phase Alternate Lines (PAL) standard is the broadcasting standard that is used in much of Western Europe, including the United Kingdom. A few other countries and regions, including China and Australia, also use the PAL standard. A vast majority of video sources, including TVs and VCRs, sold in these countries and regions only support play-back of video using the PAL standard.

In the areas where PAL is the standard, there may be slight variations. However, any PAL device can play back video recorded by any other PAL device, even if one of the devices use a slight variation of the PAL standard, such as PAL-M or PAL-N.

Compared to the NTSC standard, the PAL standard has a higher resolution: 625 lines per frame. The PAL standard records and plays back at 25 frames per second.

Sequential Couleur A Memoire (SECAM)

The Sequential Couleur a Memoire (SECAM) standard is the third dominant broadcast-ing standard. It is used in France and in many Eastern European and Middle Eastern countries and regions. The SECAM standard has a resolution of 625 lines per frame and plays back at 25 frames per second.

Though the resolution and frames per second for SECAM and PAL are the same, the for-mats are not compatible and video recorded by one type of device cannot be played back on the other type of device.

Understanding Capture Devices

A capture device enables you to record video from a video camera, VCR, or satellite or cable TV feed to your computer. The capture device is a piece of computer hardware that comes in a variety of forms. A majority of capture devices come in the form of a card that you install in your computer. This is true for both digital video and analog capture devices. However, there is a growing number of capture devices, such as those that attach to USB ports and video capture cards for use on a laptop computer.

The following section explains the basic aspects of capture devices and what they do. It includes information about the different interfaces you can use to connect a video source to a video capture card, as well as how to connect the devices to your computer. In addi-tion to explaining video and audio capture devices, this section gives general instructions about how to connect these devices to your computer so you can record video and audio to your computer.

Video Interfaces

An interface is a way of describing how one piece of hardware, such as a video camera or VCR, connects to another device, such as a computer. More specifically, the interface is the connector that attaches the different devices and the cables that allow video and audio to be transferred from one device to another.

Today, there a variety of different interfaces you can use to connect devices. For many devices, there are multiple ways to connect them. However, in many cases, the quality of the resulting video recorded to your computer will vary depending on which type of interface and connection you use.

The following sections briefly explain the different types of interfaces that you are likely to come across today. They also list the advantages and disadvantages of using the different interfaces. In addition, they include descriptions of how video is recorded using the different connections.

Composite Video

Composite video connections are for recorded and broadcast video using the NTSC, PAL, and SECAM standards. The coaxial cable that connects the cable outlet to your video source (such as a VCR or TV) has connectors at each end, called F connectors, shown in Figure 4.1. Audio and video are carried in a single signal, which is transferred through the coaxial cable.

F-connector

Figure 4.1 — F-connector on a coaxial cable.

Many analog and digital video cameras, VCRs, and capture devices have composite video inputs. These inputs often use RCA connectors. On a DV camera or VCR, the analog output is often a mini-jack. RCA and mini-jack connectors are shown in Figure 4.2.

RCA Connector

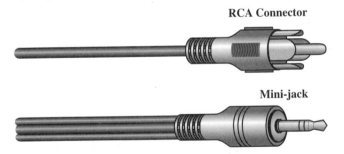

Mini-jack

Figure 4.2 — RCA and mini-jack connectors.

In composite video, the three main video colors—red, green, and blue (RGB)—are transferred by a single cable. When the colors are transferred in one cable, there is some loss in the sharpness of the video quality. In addition to combining the color in the video, the luminance (the brightness of the video), chrominance (the hue and saturation in the video), and the synchronization of your video are all transferred through one cable. As the information is transferred, there is a natural loss in video quality when using this composite video interface to connect a video source to your computer. The loss in video quality is slightly greater for NTSC than for PAL or SECAM.

S-Video

An S-Video connection will produce higher-quality video than a composite video connection. S-Video connections are usually found on digital video cameras and some analog video cameras, such as S-VHS and Hi-8 cameras. Some older analog cameras may not have S-Video connections. Sometimes, the term *Y/C connection* is used in place of S-Video.

An S-Video connection requires a special type of cable and connector, like the one shown in Figure 4.3.

S-Video Connector

Figure 4.3 — S-Video connector.

An S-Video connection produces a higher-quality video recording on your computer because the video's color information (chrominance) is kept separate from the video's brightness (luminance) information. Because these two types of information are carried separately, the resulting recorded video is sharper than that of composite video.

If the video camera or VCR and the capture device let you choose between using composite video or S-Video inputs, using the S-Video connection will result in a better quality video when recorded to your computer.

Component Video

Component video is usually found on higher-end video sources and capture devices. If your video camera and capture device allow you to connect to use component video, the resulting video will be of higher quality than both S-Video and composite video.

Component video produces high-quality video because it uses individual wires inside the cable to transmit information about the color and brightness of the video separately (see Figure 4.4). Unlike S-Video, where the color information is transferred in one wire, the three different colors in video—red, green, and blue—are kept separate in component video connections.

Component Video Connectors

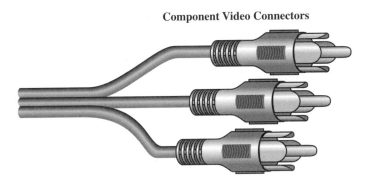

Figure 4.4 — Component video connectors.

IEEE 1394 (FireWire or iLink) Connector

An IEEE 1394 connector is used to link a DV source, such as a DV camera or digital VCR, to a computer. An IEEE 1394 link is a purely digital connection. As mentioned before, digital video is already in a format that the computer can immediately use. Because the computer can immediately use the data, the IEEE 1394 connection simply passes the digital video and audio from the device to your computer without having to convert the data. Therefore, the video and audio retain the high quality associated with digital video.

When connecting a DV device using a composite video or S-Video connection, there is a loss in quality (called degradation) in the video and audio because it must be converted to an analog signal, transferred to the computer, and then converted back to digital data. An IEEE 1394 connector is shown in Figure 4.5.

IEEE 1394 Connector

Figure 4.5 — IEEE 1394 connector.

Universal Serial Bus (USB)

One of the more popular connections used on computers today is Universal Serial Bus (USB). You may have USB connections for other devices that are attached to your computer, such as a scanner, digital camera, printer, or portable device. USB is also popular for video because of its plug-and-play capability, meaning that you simply connect the device to your computer and it is detected by Windows and installed on your computer.

USB is often used for Web cameras and video capture devices. USB allows data to be transferred at a maximum speed of 12 Mbps. Though the transfer rate is slower than IEEE

1394, it is still fast enough to provide another way for you to record video to your computer. Figure 4.6 shows the USB connector.

USB Connector

Figure 4.6 — USB connector.

A vast majority of today's computers have USB ports. Therefore, if you choose to buy and use USB video devices—such as a USB Web camera or USB video capture device—you usually will not have to install any additional video capture cards or hardware on your computer.

Video Capture Devices

With video capture devices, you can record video to your computer from your video source. These pieces of hardware allow video transfer from your video source, such as a camera or VCR, to your computer.

The role of a video capture device depends on what type of capture device it is, the connections, and the video source it is connected to. The following section explains the different types of capture devices. Keep in mind that these devices vary according to manufacturer. Therefore, the particular capture device you have may be different from what is described below. For complete information about your specific capture device, consult the documentation that was included with your device.

Capture cards are probably the most popular type of capture device today. A capture card is a video card that attaches to an expansion slot in your computer. These cards then have ports or inputs that you can then use to connect your computer to a video source.

You can also find USB capture devices that have a variety of inputs, and attach to your computer through a USB port.

IEEE 1394 DV Capture Cards

An IEEE 1394 video capture card enables you to record digital video from your DV device to your computer. Because the video is already in a digital format, the digital video and audio are left unchanged when the video source and device are connected through an IEEE 1394 connection, such as FireWire or iLink. When you record digital video through an IEEE 1394 card, the corresponding audio is also handled by the card and passed on to the computer with the video.

There is at least one—and sometimes more—IEEE 1394 port on an IEEE 1394 card. Some computers even come with a built-in IEEE 1394 port. If you have a laptop computer, you can also use an IEEE 1394 PC Card that you insert into the PCMCIA slot on your laptop computer. This PC Card functions the same way as a standard IEEE 1394 DV capture card.

Analog Capture Cards

An analog capture card is installed in your computer in the same manner as an IEEE 1394 card. However, the way the analog capture card works and the role it plays in transferring video to your computer is different. Because an analog camera records through an analog signal, an analog capture card converts the analog video to a digital format that your computer can understand. If you have a laptop computer, you can also use an analog PC Card that you insert into the PCMCIA slot on your laptop computer. This PC Card functions the same way as a standard analog capture card.

The inputs available on an analog capture card vary by manufacturer. Some cards only have composite inputs with RCA jacks for recording video. However, some cards may have more than one composite video input so you can connect multiple analog video sources to your computer. Furthermore, some capture cards also have a S-Video input, which is useful if you have an analog or digital video source that can output video through the S-Video interface.

In addition to specific video inputs, some analog video capture cards have a built-in audio capture card, enabling you to record audio directly through the card. If your video capture device does not have an audio input, you will need to use a separate audio card on your computer for recording the audio portion of your video. To find specific information about the connections available on your video capture card, consult the documentation that came with the device. Some newer capture cards on the market today provide flexibility because the capture card has both IEEE 1394 and analog ports.

TV Tuner Cards

A TV tuner card is a type of analog video capture card. With a tuner card, you can watch TV on your computer from an antenna, cable, or satellite TV feed. You can also view channels using the card's built-in tuner and the software that is shipped with the device.

If you plan to record in Microsoft Producer from cable or satellite TV, a tuner card enables you to capture video and change channels without any intermediary hardware. If you only have an analog capture card and you want to record from cable or satellite TV, you need to have an external tuner, such as a VCR, connected to your computer so you can change channels, watch, and record TV on your computer.

USB Capture Devices

Many USB capture devices have three RCA-type jacks—two inputs for audio (one for the left channel and one for the right), with another RCA jack for composite video. Some of these devices also provide an S-Video input. If you have a laptop computer, you can connect your analog video camera or VCR to your computer using a USB capture device.

Audio Sources

Up to this point, most of the discussion has focused on video. However, the video sources covered in this chapter, such as digital and analog video cameras and some Web cameras, also record audio along with the corresponding video. Most, if not all, digital or analog video cameras have a built-in microphone to record audio. The following sections describe additional audio sources you can connect to your video camera or computer in order to record audio.

Microphones

With a microphone, you can record speech and other audio to your computer. A number of cameras have an input for an external microphone. Many times, an external microphone used with a video camera can provide better quality audio than the camera's built-in microphone.

The microphone you choose to use for recording is up to you. Many good microphones are reasonably priced and can help you to record high-quality audio for your presentations. You can either plug an external microphone into your video camera or into the computer itself. If you are looking for a small microphone that is easy to connect to your computer, consider choosing a small lapel, or *lavaliere*, microphone. This type of microphone is small and unobtrusive, and it can be attached to the speaker's clothing to record audio for presentations.

Sound cards

You can use a sound card to record and play back audio on your computer. Most new computers are sold with a sound card already installed or with built-in sound recording connections and functionality.

Typically, a sound card has several inputs for you to attach a microphone for recording, speakers for playback, and a line input, also used for recording. For example, if you had the appropriate connectors (such as RCA cables) and you had a VCR attached to your computer, the video composite input could plug into your video capture card, and the audio line (or lines, depending on your connection cables and specific audio card) could plug into the line input jack (often a mini-jack) on the sound card.

Some video capture cards contain inputs for audio, while others only provide input for video connectors. To find out if your computer already has an audio capture card, consult the documentation that was included with the computer.

Configuring Capture Devices

Given the wide variety of capture devices and hardware manufacturers, it is nearly impossible to list all the different ways to attach a video source to your computer. Remember, when connecting capture devices and video sources, consult the documentation that came with your specific hardware. However, the following sections discuss software drivers and basic, common configurations for connecting your camera, VCR, or cable/satellite TV to your computer.

Device Driver Software

Many capture devices require some software to be installed before you can use the device. Usually, this software (called a driver) is provided with the capture device. This driver software enables the hardware and operating system to work together. For many devices, if these drivers are not installed correctly, the capture device will not work properly. Contact the device manufacturer for specific information about drivers.

Before you purchase or install a capture device, it is a good idea to research the different devices that are on the market. Some devices will not work correctly with all operating systems, or require a driver upgrade to work with a newer operating system.

The Microsoft Web site is a good resource to consult for a list of hardware that is compatible with the Microsoft Windows operating system. The hardware compatibility list, which can be found at *http://www.microsoft.com/hcl*, contains the latest information about devices that have been tested and verified to work within a given version of Windows. You can select the version of Windows you have or plan to use, and then verify that the capture device (or any other hardware you have or plan to purchase) is compatible with it.

You may have an older capture device that you want to install on a computer that has a newer version of Windows. In this situation, you may need to find new drivers for the device. Check the hardware manufacturer's Web site for updated drivers that you can download and install so that the device works properly.

Connecting Video Capture Devices

The following sections describe some basic configurations for connecting video sources to your computer or capture device. The sections are divided according to the type of connection described.

Digital Video Connections

Currently, the highest-quality consumer video connection is between a DV video source and an IEEE 1394 DV capture card. The port and connection shown in Figure 4.7 is similar whether you are connecting a DV source to an IEEE 1394 DV capture card on a desktop computer or to an IEEE 1394 PC card installed on a laptop computer.

A DV camera or VCR connected to an IEEE 1394 card helps you get the best quality video from your DV devices. For digital video, the video and audio is transferred through one IEEE 1394 cable, sometimes called FireWire or iLink. Figure 4.7 shows an example of this type of connection.

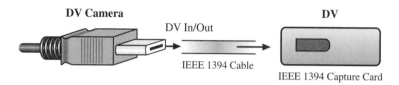

DV Camera

DV In/Out

IEEE 1394 Cable

DV

IEEE 1394 Capture Card

Figure 4.7 — Connecting a DV camera to an IEEE 1394 DV capture card.

Analog Video Connections

The most common connection you are likely to encounter is between an analog camera or VCR and an analog capture device. Although this provides lower video quality than an all-digital video chain, it will be sufficient for most situations. The most important differences between analog connections will be whether you use S-Video, composite video, or some other type of connection, and this will be dictated by the type of capture device installed on your computer.

Connecting to a Capture Device with Composite Video

To record video from your analog video camera or VCR to an analog capture device using composite video, your camera, VCR, and capture device must have composite inputs. This is the most common video connection type, and is likely to be available on most cameras, VCRs, and analog capture devices. For this type of configuration, you might need a separate connector for video and audio.

Figure 4.8 shows an example of how to connect an analog camera or VCR to an analog capture card.

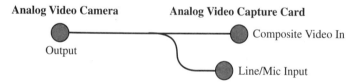

Analog Video Camera   **Analog Video Capture Card**

Output

Composite Video In

Line/Mic Input

Figure 4.8 — Connecting devices through a composite video connection.

Some analog cameras have separate video and audio connections. In this configuration, the inputs could look similar to the one shown in Figure 4.9.

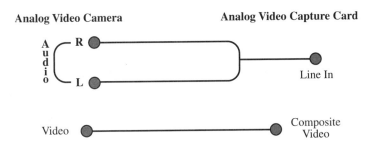

Figure 4.9 — Connecting devices through a composite video connection using separate video and audio connections.

Connecting to a Capture Device with S-Video

If your analog or DV camera or VCR has an S-Video output, your analog capture device has an S-Video input, and you have the appropriate S-Video cable, you can use this connection to copy video and audio to your computer. MiniDV, Digital 8, S-VHS, and Hi-8 cameras are more likely to have an S-Video output. Again, consult the documentation that came with your video camera or VCR to see if S-Video connections are possible.

If you have a choice between using an S-Video connection and a composite video connection, the S-Video connection results in higher-quality video than composite video.

Figure 4.10 shows an example of an analog or digital VCR or camera connected to an analog capture device through an S-Video connection.

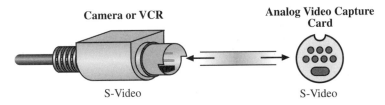

Figure 4.10 — Connecting devices through an S-Video connection.

Connecting to a TV Tuner Card

You can record a cable TV or satellite feed if your analog capture card has a built-in tuner. However, even if you do not have a TV tuner, you can still record cable or satellite TV by connecting your computer to a device that has a built-in tuner, such as a VCR. If you are using a TV tuner card, the connection will be similar to the one shown in Figure 4.11. If you make the connection through a VCR or cable box, you will probably use the composite or S-Video connections described earlier.

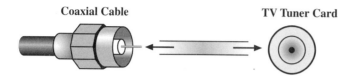

Figure 4.11 — Connecting to a TV tuner card.

USB Video Capture Device

You can easily connect a USB video capture device to your camera and computer through the USB connection. The capture device plugs into the USB port on your computer, while the camera's video and audio connection cables plug into the inputs on the capture device. These devices often provide RCA-type jacks for recording composite video and audio or S-Video connections.

Figure 4.12 shows the basic configuration for connecting a USB analog video capture device to your computer.

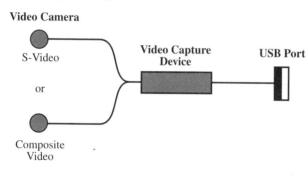

Figure 4.12 — Connecting a USB video capture device.

Hybrid Connections

The following configurations cover hybrid connections, in which a DV source is connected to an analog capture device. These types of connections are valuable because they allow you to record video from your DV source to your computer, even if you do not have an IEEE 1394 DV capture card. When you use these types of hybrid connections, however, there is a loss in the quality of the recorded video compared to when you record digital video to the computer through an IEEE 1394 connection.

Depending on the connection options provided by your video capture device, you can use S-Video or composite video connections to transfer video from a DV camera to your computer. By connecting a DV source to an analog capture device through S-Video, you can record video to your computer with some quality loss in the recorded video. This configuration results in poorer quality than component video, but better quality than composite video.

Most devices provide composite video connections, so you can always rely on this type of connection, even though the video quality may be compromised. Remember, depending on your specific video capture device, the audio input may be on the video capture card or on a separate sound card.

Web Cameras

The following sections describe possible configurations for connecting a Web camera to your computer. The type of connection you should use depends on the type of Web camera you are connecting. There are a variety of Web cameras and possible connections.

IEEE 1394 Web Camera

This type of Web camera has an IEEE 1394 connector that plugs into an IEEE 1394 port on your computer. As with a DV camera, an IEEE 1394 card or port is required for this type of camera to work properly. Figure 4.13 shows an IEEE 1394 Web camera connected to an IEEE 1394 port.

Figure 4.13 — Connecting an IEEE 1394 Web camera.

USB Web Camera

This type of Web camera has a USB connector that plugs into a USB port on your computer, as shown in Figure 4.14. This is one of the more popular types of Web camera.

Figure 4.14 — Connecting a USB Web camera.

Composite Web Camera

A composite Web camera can connect to an analog video capture device, as shown in Figure 4.15. Some composite Web cameras require a specific analog capture card created by the same manufacturer, while others can work with different analog capture cards created by a different manufacturer.

Composite Web Camera   **Analog Video Capture Card**

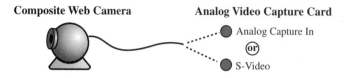

Figure 4.15 — Connecting a composite Web camera.

Web Cameras and Sound

The Web camera configurations listed previously assume that the Web camera has a built-in microphone, as is the case with many current Web cameras. However, if your Web camera does not have a built-in microphone, you can use an external microphone, such as a lapel microphone, to record sound.

CHAPTER 5

Preparing to Record Digital Media

Recording your video is easier if you plan in advance. If you establish what you want to record, and locate the tools and people involved before the recording date, you will find that recording will proceed much more smoothly. Advanced planning can also help you record better video and audio to use in your presentations.

Planning takes time; however, it can save you time in creating your project by preventing problems that could arise during recording. You will find that even a basic plan is better than attempting to throw everything together at the last minute.

The goal of this chapter is not to help you prepare to shoot a major motion picture using Microsoft Producer. Instead, the goal of this chapter is to help you prepare to record professional-looking, high-quality video, filmed in an everyday office setting, to use in your presentations.

Planning the Video in Your Presentation

Recording video for a rich-media presentation is quite different from filming a movie. In a standalone movie, the video itself tells the story. In a presentation, the video you record is used to enhance or explain other elements of the presentation, such as slides, still images, HTML files, and other digital media files you can use in Microsoft Producer.

You can determine what kind of video you need to record for your presentation by establishing the role of the video in your presentation. Before recording the video, you should consider the following questions in order to establish what video you need to record for your presentation.

What Type of Presentation Are You Creating?

One way to determine the type of video you need to record is to think about the type of presentation you are creating. For example, if you are creating a "talking head" presentation that features one person speaking, as is the case with many corporate presentations, the video you will need to record is usually of one individual in front of a stationary background. The video generally shows the person from the shoulders up. The reason that video is shot this way is because there is very little movement in the video other than the person's mouth moving and occasionally their eyes blinking. This lack of significant movement means that the video compresses well and that means the video file is smaller.

You might record a live software training event that you want to turn into an online training presentation using Microsoft Producer. The video you record might feature a speaker who is moving around a classroom. In addition, you might also want to include video screen captures of the software within the online training presentation.

When comparing the recording needs between these examples, think about how you would prepare for shooting this video. For the "talking head" video you might use a camera mounted on a tripod, with a solid color background behind the speaker. The speaker probably wouldn't need a microphone because the microphone on the video camera would suffice.

For the online training, you might want to have two or more video cameras set up so that you can videotape multiple angles. During production, you can cut between the different videos and use the best angle. To keep the audio level consistent no matter where the speaker is in the room, you may want the speaker to wear a microphone on his lapel. The audio from the lapel microphone would need to be captured and made available during production work so that it can be added to the presentation. You can use Microsoft Producer for all of this production work—cutting between various videos and adding a separate audio track.

These are just two of the many scenarios that illustrate the different types of video recordings you will need for different types of presentations.

What Role Does the Video Play?

Determining the role of the video in your presentation will help you decide what should occur in the video. Continuing with the software training presentation example from the previous section, the video in this type of presentation does a few things. It lets the online user see the training speaker and any examples he or she may use in class. The video provides a way for the viewers to see what is being accomplished during the training event.

So what should occur in the video? The video should show the trainer teaching the class and using any necessary props. In addition, video screen captures allow the audience to see what steps are needed to perform a given task with the software. The video screen captures you record should clearly show the steps for tasks described in the class.

Conversely, in the "talking head" example, the purpose of the video is not to show how something is done. The purpose is for the audience to see an individual speaking as he or she would in a face-to-face meeting. The role of this type of video is to make the presentation feel like a typical meeting.

The videos in these two presentations serve two different purposes, with some overlap. The video in the software training presentation shows viewers how to accomplish a task. The "talking head" video is intended to create speaker recognition. The speaker's face doesn't directly convey the speech's meaning; it's the audio that conveys the meaning. If the audience sees a face, especially one that is recognized, the words might be more meaningful to the user than if the presentation included the audio without the accompanying video.

How Long Is the Presentation?

When preparing to record video, consider the length of the overall presentation. By determining the approximate length of the presentation, you can determine how much video you will need. For example, if your presentation is only 15 minutes long, you probably do not need to create a shooting plan for an hour of video.

In other words, the amount of video you will need affects how you plan and eventually shoot the actual video. You always want to shoot enough video footage so that you can later edit the video to fit the allotted amount of time. So create a shooting plan or short script for the video that takes the overall length of the presentation into consideration.

Do You Have an Existing Slideshow?

One of the main differences between Microsoft Producer and other presentation software that features only video and audio is that Producer enables you to include Microsoft PowerPoint slides in your presentations. Because your presentations will often include PowerPoint slides, you should consider the slide content when recording video and audio for your presentation.

When recording video, you might simply narrate slides using video of a "talking head"-style speaker. However, you might also want to record additional video and audio to further stress your presentation's point. For example, if your "talking head" video introduces a slide and the point of the slide would be made even more clear by a testimonial from someone else—perhaps an expert, spokesperson, or customer—then include that additional video.

When you use additional video with your PowerPoint slides, remember that the slides and video need to work together. This will affect the type and amount of video you will shoot for your presentation.

Choosing a Recording Site

Before recording video, you need to decide where you want to record it. Sometimes, you may not be able to choose where you do the recording, as may be the case with training or product demonstration videos.

Regardless of whether you choose the recording site or the site is determined by the situation, one important thing to do before recording is to visit the recording site. By visiting the location before you record, you can avoid some undesirable surprises that may reduce the effectiveness of the video.

When you visit the site, you can see what limitations you may have to work with. For example, if the lighting is not appropriate, you might have to make arrangements to supply alternative lighting. You might also discover that the site is noisy, or too busy, or undesirable for some other reason.

If you do have the ability to choose a recording site, considering the following topics can help you choose a site that will accommodate your particular recording needs.

Accessibility

One consideration is the accessibility of the recording location to you and other people who will be working on the video. A location might seem ideal, but the lack of accessibility to the location might make the site impractical. For example, if you choose a location that is remotely located, people might need to coordinate transportation and travel time.

Try to estimate how long it will take to put your recording equipment together (including lighting, props, and any additional cameras and microphones) and to pack it up again. For example, if you are recording in a building that has several floors, and you need to make several trips upstairs in order to get all your recording materials unloaded and set up, your set-up and clean-up time will probably be substantial.

Budget

Budget constraints can often determine the types of video and audio you record, and can play a role in your overall presentation. You might be restricted in the amount of money you have to buy or rent recording equipment (for example, a video camera, tripod, lighting, external microphone, and so forth). If this is the case, you need to plan your video and its content around these circumstances.

In addition, you may also need to determine how much you will spend on the other aspects of the video, such as the salaries of the actors and any other people who are helping you to record the video footage.

Availability

Another aspect to consider when choosing a recording location is the availability of the site. For example, if you have a conference room in which you plan to record but that room is used throughout the day and is difficult to schedule, you might want to consider an alternative conference room or another location.

Scheduling may be difficult in some places and easier on others. If a location has limited availability, scheduling a location can be another important consideration to make before recording. Some locations, such as a professional recording studio, might need to be reserved days, or perhaps weeks, in advance. By scheduling in advance when necessary, you can prevent the problem that arises when you are ready to record the video and you cannot use that location.

Choosing Recording Accessories

Before starting to record, it is extremely helpful to have a few basic recording accessories. These accessories, along with your camera itself, can help you get the most out of your video camera. By purchasing or borrowing a few of the accessories, you may be able to increase the quality of your video.

These recording accessories can be found at most camera stores, some specialty online retailers, and though video camera catalogs. You can often do some comparison shopping to get the best price for the different accessories.

Many of these accessories are inexpensive compared to the initial cost of a video camera and computer. Buying some of the accessories mentioned in the following sections is a relatively inexpensive way to increase the quality of your video. In many cases, they will be a useful investment if you plan to record more video in the future.

Extra Battery and Charger

An extra battery or two can save you a lot of time when recording. When you purchase a video camera, consider buying an extra battery. Before your main battery runs completely out of power, you should rotate in the other batteries while recording so you use all of them evenly. Before beginning to record, make sure you charge all of your batteries fully. This lets you maximize the battery life and the time you have to record your video.

An extra battery is crucial, especially if you are recording outdoors or in an area where you cannot plug your video camera into an electrical outlet. If you know you are going to be recording in situations such as these, consider buying a battery with an extended life. Many cameras today come with a battery that will last for only a few hours when you are recording. If you have a battery with extended power and recording time, you can reduce the chance that you will run out of battery power while recording.

In addition to having extra batteries, you can purchase an external battery charger. An external battery charger plugs into an electrical outlet and charges the battery when it is not in use by your camera. If you have two batteries, a charger can be especially useful. Before you record your video, you could charge the first battery by plugging the camera into an electrical outlet (through the power adapter that came with the camera) and charge the second battery in the external battery charger. This lets you charge both batteries simultaneously, so you can maximize your battery power when it comes time to record the video for your presentation.

Tripod or Monopod

A tripod is a three-legged camera stand that can help you shoot better video because it helps hold the camera still. Although many video cameras are small enough to be held with one hand and contain features such as image stabilization, using a tripod will help you shoot better, more professional video. Also, a tripod can ease some of the strain on your arms that can occur when holding a video camera for a long period of time.

For recording video where your subject is rather stationary, such as video for a "talking head" presentation, a tripod can be invaluable because it enables you to focus the video camera on the speaker without worrying about your arm moving and disrupting the quality of the recorded video. In addition, many tripods have a swivel head or some rotation device that allows you to smoothly rotate the camera to follow a moving subject.

When buying a tripod, consider weight and portability. Many tripods are lightweight, which can make a big difference, especially if you plan on recording your video in a number of places. A lighter tripod is much easier to transport. Furthermore, many tripods today fold up, which helps to reduce its size during transport.

An alternative to a tripod is a monopod. As the name suggests, a monopod has only one leg. A monopod is lighter and more portable than a tripod. You might have seen a monopod used on television by sideline photographers at a sporting event or by a nature photographer. Because the monopod only has one leg, you still need to balance and stabilize the video camera when using the monopod to record. However, the monopod is still a good alternative because you aren't required to hold the camera completely still.

Monopods are often used because they are easy to move from one spot to another. Because they are smaller and more portable than tripods, a monopod is easier to transport, especially if you have to walk a distance to get to the recording location, as is often the case with nature photographers. If you are recording in a crowded area, a monopod is a better choice than a tripod because it is easier to set up, take down, and it takes up less space while filming.

Extra Videotape

A common annoyance during a recording session is running out of videotape. On a video shoot, this can tremendously slow, if not stop, the recording process. However, this problem is easily avoidable if you remember to bring extra videotapes for your camera.

External Microphone

As mentioned in the previous chapter, video cameras and some Web cameras have built-in microphones. However, the quality of audio that is recorded with the camera's microphone is not always the best possible audio you can record. Many cameras contain a connector for an external microphone. If you use a camera like this, you can use an external microphone and attach it to your camera when recording.

The two basic kinds of microphones are handheld microphones and lavaliere microphones. A lavaliere microphone, which attaches to the speaker's clothing, is especially useful because it is closer to the speaker and records better quality audio than the built-in microphone. Figure 5.1 shows and example of a lavaliere microphone. If you are planning on recording video for "talking head" presentations especially, a lavaliere microphone is a good choice because the microphone attaches to clothing, such as a tie or shirt, and can be easily hidden.

Figure 5.1 — Presenter with a lavaliere microphone.

Headphones

Many cameras also include a built-in headphone jack so you can hear the audio in your video, during recording, by listening through the headphones. If you review the recorded video on the camera, the headphones enable you to hear the audio more clearly than you would while listening to the audio through the small speaker on your video camera. Headphones that cover the whole ear are especially useful because they block out external noises. By listening to the audio immediately at the recording location, you can determine whether it has been recorded well enough for your presentation. If it isn't recorded correctly, you can do the recording again.

Camera Bag

As your collection of recording accessories grows, you will need to find a way to keep all these accessories together. A good basic accessory is a video camera bag or case that is small enough to carry, but that has a lot of pockets and storage room.

In addition to providing extra storage room, a video camera case or bag will also protect your camera when you move it from one place to another. Many camera cases and bags have built-in padding to protect the camera from damage. Furthermore, a camera bag will also prevent your camera from getting scratched or damaged. Considering the price of the video camera itself, the price of a camera bag is quite small.

Additional Accessories

You may need additional accessories while recording your video, including items such as clamps, duct tape, and tools. Duct tape can be used to attach foamcore (which is discussed in the next section) to a wall or other surface.

Small clamps, such as clothespins, can also be helpful to have when recording. For example, clothespins can be used to attach a gel (which is also discussed in the next section) to a light. Because clothespins are made of wood, they will not conduct heat from the light.

It is also helpful to have small tools, such as a small hammer, scissors, or a small battery-powered drill, to affix or repair sets and props you may use when recording. Because these tools can be easily lost, you will probably need some type of case to carry these different accessories, such as a lightweight toolbox or even a fishing tackle box. These makeshift carrying cases are relatively inexpensive, but they will help you organize the smaller recording accessories.

Preparing an Office for Recording

Many presentations will contain video featuring a presenter who is sitting in front of the camera behind a stationary background. These are called "talking head" videos. A popular place to record this type of video is in an office. When recording in an office, you can make some quick and simple changes to greatly improve the quality of the video. The following section helps you set up an office to record high-quality video and audio.

Lighting

When recording in an office setting, you should first adjust the lighting. Many offices have fluorescent overhead lights, which work well for recording. However, if you find that they do not supply enough light, you can add a light that is soft and diffused, such as a floor lamp.

You want the light to be diffused so that there are not concentrated bright spots where the light is shining. No matter what the color or pattern of the background is, if you have a direct light shining on something, then you'll see a white spot where the light is concentrated. A diffused light doesn't produce the white spot, but serves to brighten the room and not the subject, helping to create soft lighting, which is effective on video. See Figure 5.2 for an example.

Figure 5.2 — Diffused lighting on a presenter.

Another type of lighting is a small camera light. A camera light provides direct front light and typically attaches to a connector on the video camera. If you need to use a camera light, you can soften or diffuse the light by pointing the light at the ceiling instead of directly at your subject, or by taping a piece of frosted *gel* over the light.

A gel is translucent material that allows light to pass through it. Gels are sold in various sizes and colors at many camera stores and stores that sell equipment for theater productions and motion pictures. A small piece of frosted gel can be taped over a light, such as a camera light. When you tape the gel to the light source, be sure to leave an opening so the heat from the light can escape. Frosted gels can be re-used, and they are ideal for turning hard, directional light into soft, diffused lighting, which often results in better lighting and overall quality of the video.

If the office has windows, use the blinds to adjust the amount of sunlight in the office. If you would like to record the video with the setting outside the office still showing, you can adjust the blinds to reduce the amount of direct sunlight, but still allow the outdoor scenery to show through. However, it's best to reduce the amount of direct sunlight.

For example, if you are recording and your presenter is turned sideways and there is sunlight directly on the speaker's face, his or her facial expressions can be lost in shadow. In this case, reducing the amount of direct sunlight will help to accentuate the speaker's facial expressions. Many times, these non-verbal expressions help convey your presenter's message more effectively.

In general, you can improve the lighting by reflecting it off a white or light-colored surface, such as a ceiling or wall. If your office does not have light white surfaces or you wish to diffuse the light even more, you can use foamcore, which can be purchased from an art store. Foamcore is a quarter-inch sheet of Styrofoam situated between two sheets of white cardboard that you can clamp or tape to a surface. You can aim the light directly at the foamcore so the light bounces off it and diffuses the lighting throughout the office, rather than aiming the light directly at the presenter.

Improving Sound

In an office, you will most likely have external noises that can interfere with and degrade the quality of your recorded video and audio. Noise from external sources, such as fans, heaters, ventilation systems, air conditioning, and computers can be a distraction. If you can turn off these systems or machines, you may reduce background noise that will distract from your video. If you cannot turn these systems or machines off, try to find a way to at least minimize these noises.

Figure 5.3 — Hanging blanket to improve sound.

Any type of traffic outside of the office can also create unwanted background noise. Sometimes, this noise cannot be avoided. When choosing an office location, if at all possible, choose an interior office that is isolated from traffic. By reducing external noises, you can help eliminate background noise.

In addition to reducing or eliminating external noise, you want to maximize the quality of the audio you are recording in your video. To do this, you want to focus the sound directly toward your microphone. You can do this in a variety of ways. One quick way is to reduce the amount of audio that echoes off walls. Because audio will bounce off hard surfaces such as walls, creating an echo, you can hang sheets, blankets, or other material to reduce the echoing and improve your overall audio, as shown in Figure 5.3. Items like these absorb sound rather than reflect it. You can often arrange or hang these items in such a way so that they are not shown in the video itself. For example, if you record a speaker in front of a stationary background, you could cover three of the four walls, leaving the background as it is.

Using Microphones

As mentioned earlier, a popular and (usually) inexpensive recording accessory is an external microphone, such as a lavaliere microphone or a handheld microphone.

When using any microphone, either a lavaliere microphone or handheld microphone, you should try to eliminate unwanted microphone noise. Unwanted microphone noise is introduced into your audio when the microphone touches an object during recording. When placing the microphone, make sure it will not hit a surface, such as a table or desk. Also, make sure that the speaker does not tap the microphone with an object, such as a pen or pencil, during recording. By keeping the microphone free from contact and external noise, the recorded audio in your video will be more professional.

When you attach a lavaliere microphone to a piece of clothing, such as a shirt collar or tie, point the microphone away from the speaker's mouth. This prevents loud popping noises, such as when the presenter exhales. You can also help to prevent this unwanted occurrence by making sure that the microphone is not too close to the speaker's mouth.

When you are attaching the lavaliere microphone, also make sure that the person's clothing does not cover the microphone. If the microphone is completely or partially covered, the recorded audio will be unclear or muffled. You may also hear noises caused by clothing rubbing against the microphone.

Choosing a Background

When preparing an office for recording, choose a background that both complements and contrasts with the speaker. For example, if your speaker is wearing a blue shirt, you should avoid using a predominantly blue background when recording—there is not enough contrast between the speaker's clothing and the background.

In your presentation, the speaker might be introducing a new Web site or computer application. In this case, to build branding and name recognition, you might want to have the Web site or software application displayed on the computer monitor behind the presenter. You have probably already seen this done on television when a person is being interviewed in his or her office.

You might notice that, in some cases, the computer monitor may appear to flicker in your recorded video. This flickering occurs because of the rate at which the computer monitor refreshes. Although this is unnoticed by the human eye, the constant refreshing is sometimes captured on video.

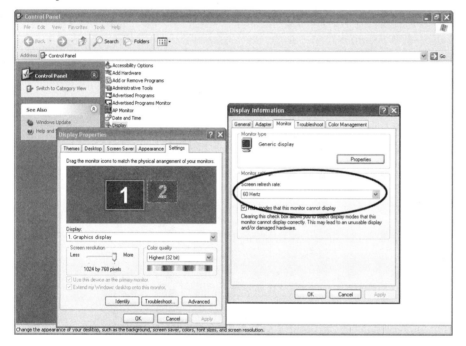

Figure 5.4 — Monitor set to refresh at 60 Hz.

To correct this, open the **Display** control panel in Windows and change the screen refresh rate to 60 hertz (Hz). This setting will reduce the flickering in the background of the computer monitor (see Figure 5.4). If you still see some flickering or a single line that scrolls up to the top of the monitor, reduce the refresh rate to a value less than 60 Hz.

Creating a Presentation Plan

You might find it helpful to outline your presentation and its contents. Unlike a simple text document, however, your rich-media presentations can contain a wide variety of digital media, which needs to be reflected in your outline and shooting plan. The following sections will help you quickly create a script and basic shooting plan for your presentation. This basic planning can help to ensure that you record the video you need for your presentation.

Creating a Basic Script

One of the first steps in creating a shooting plan is to develop a short script for the presentation. The script can contain such elements as the presenter's lines, dialog between two or more speakers, and directions for the speaker or speakers, if necessary.

For example, your video may feature a single speaker introducing a new software application. In your video, you may later record a separate video screen capture showing the software that the speaker is introducing. Your short script could include directions that instruct the speaker to discuss the application and then turn his or her chair to face the computer. During the editing phase, you could then add the video screen capture of the feature as it is used in the application.

By including dialog and brief directions, you can help to ensure that the video you are recording can be tightly integrated with the other digital media you plan to use in your presentation. Of course, if you are repurposing a previously recorded presentation, the "script" is already established for the most part.

Using Storyboards

A storyboard is a visual representation of the script and the overall presentation. The storyboard breaks your presentation into individual elements. Moviemakers use storyboards to plan the visual elements of a movie. You can use the same technique to envision how all of the elements of your presentation will come together.

In your storyboard, include the names of the different digital media files you plan to use and how and when you plan to use them in the actual presentation. This is not to say that every minute detail needs to be mentioned in the storyboard. However, by including basic information and key segments of your presentation, you can establish a working outline for your presentation.

If you are using Microsoft PowerPoint slides in your presentation, you may be able to use them as the storyboard for your presentation. For example, you could print your slides as handouts with three slides per page (see Figure 5.5), and then write basic information about the particular slide next to it on the printout. This information can include the names of accompanying video or audio files that you want to correspond to the particular slide or image in your Microsoft Producer presentation.

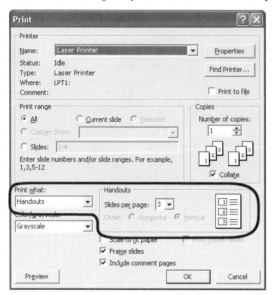

Figure 5.5 — Printing handouts with three slides per page.

Rehearsing the Presentation

Given the time constraints you will most likely face when recording original content for your presentation, time is often quite restricted. Therefore, gathering participants in advance to rehearse the presentation can be difficult. However, rehearsing the presentation, including any information contained in your scripts or storyboards, can actually save you time in the end. If you can schedule even one rehearsal, the actual recording of the video and audio is likely to go much more quickly.

Reducing the recording time is especially crucial if you plan to have different speakers in the video. Minimizing the time they are standing by or keeping on a recording schedule that enables the presenters to appear at a designated time will help ease frustration and keep the recording time to the absolute minimum.

When you are rehearsing, try to mimic as closely as possible the actual recording situation. This includes having the actors or presenters wearing the clothes they plan to wear for the actual recording, as well as adjusting the lighting conditions in the recording setting. You should also record video during rehearsal. This lets you test the current recording conditions, such as sounds and video quality, and then make any changes based on this test footage.

Perhaps more importantly, you might be able to use some of the video you recorded during rehearsal in your presentation. On some occasions, you might find that the presenter or presenters gave their best performances during rehearsal. Considering the cost of tape, it's easy to record extra video and then edit it later. By recording rehearsals, you maximize your chances for getting better video that will result in a more appealing and effective presentation.

In addition, by mimicking the actual recording situation, you can help to avoid last-minute problems. For example, if you are rehearsing and the presenter is wearing a striped shirt, you might notice that this does not yield the best-quality video. The striped colors on the shirt may "bleed together" on the recorded video or result in moiré patterns—small, distracting video artifacts which make it look like the lines are slowly crawling across the shirt. To eliminate the moiré patterns, the presenter could wear a different, solid-colored shirt during the actual video recording.

Furthermore, during the rehearsals you might realize that the audio that you have recorded is incomprehensible. During the actual recording, you could then have the speaker use a lavaliere microphone.

CHAPTER 6

Recording High-quality Audio and Video

For many presentations, the audio and video are the main ways your message is communicated to the audience. That is, the audio and video often become a focal point for your presentations. Therefore, you will probably want to make the best audio and video recordings possible, given the equipment available.

This chapter will explain some of the common features you will find on your video camera, and how to use the different features when recording video for your presentations. The more you know about your camera's features, the more likely you will be to record audio and video that enhances the overall presentation.

Video and Computers

Audio and video that you record on your video camera and transfer to a presentation will play back differently on a computer and in your final presentations. The audio and video play back differently because when you transfer the audio and video to a computer using Producer, the audio and video are compressed so that they are smaller and easier to distribute over networks and the Internet. As a result, you will need to make a few decisions about how you record audio and video and how you transfer it to your computer.

When you transfer or record video from your video camera to your computer in Producer, the video is saved as a file in Windows Media Format, a high-quality multimedia file format used by Microsoft Producer, Windows Media Player, and other Windows Media tools. These files have .wma (for audio only) and .wmv (for both audio and video) file name extensions.

Windows Media Format results in smaller audio and video files because the video and audio is compressed by *codecs*. Codecs are small pieces of software that contain mathematical algorithms used for encoding and decoding data. These algorithms analyze and compress the audio and video data to minimize file size while maximizing audio and video quality for the intended audience or distribution medium.

When the presentation is played back, the same codecs are used to decompress the audio and video. Your audience won't need to do anything to get these codecs since they are automatically installed with the software, such as Windows Media Player, that will be used to view your presentation. If your audience does not have the required codecs and they are connected to the Internet when watching your presentation, these codecs are automatically downloaded to their computers, without any need for user intervention.

How Video Works

In the next sections, there will be some discussion of video frames. This section provides a brief primer on video, particularly the concept of video *frames*. If you know what frames of video are, then you can skip this section. If you are not sure what video frames are, then you might want to read this section.

A frame of video is similar to a picture—a single picture in a series of pictures that shows motion. The quality of video is measured in frames per second, and the more frames per second you can display, the more smoothly the action in the video is shown. This is because the amount of movement between each video "picture" is smaller, so more detail of the movement is captured. The fewer frames per second there are in video, the more potential there is for the video to seem jerky because the amount of change between frames is greater. DVD-quality video is displayed at 30 frames per second.

For example, imagine a video of a ball rolling across the ground. If the ball moves 10 feet in the video and the video is shot with 10 frames per second, that means the ball moves one foot between frames. If you shot the video at 30 frames per second, then the ball moves four inches between frames. It would be much easier to tell that a ball moved one foot between frames than it would be to tell the ball moved four inches between frames, especially if you saw the two pictures flash before your eyes in a tenth of a second.

So why not shoot all video at 30 frames per second? Because the more frames per second, the larger the video file will be. As with everything you are going to use in your presentation, the quality of the video you use requires tradeoffs. Are you going to have a larger video file in your presentation because you want smooth video, or are you going to have a smaller video file and be content with video that is a little less smooth?

How Codecs Work

Codecs compress audio and video in a variety of ways. One common technique they use to reduce the file size is to look for and remove repetitive information. For example, if you make a recording of someone talking, the video recording probably won't contain much movement, especially in the background. This will be particularly true if you use a tripod when you are recording, which keeps the video camera still, thereby minimizing any changes to the background that would be introduced by the camera moving. Therefore, the video data needed to display the background is mostly repeated from one frame of video to the next.

A codec can analyze the video information and see that there is repeated information—the stationary background—in the video. Because the background does not change much, it does not need to be redrawn as the video plays on the computer, so the codec can eliminate the duplicated information. This helps to reduce the size of the Windows Media file that contains the video on your computer.

In Microsoft Producer, you have a number of different capturing profiles (which specify the codec to use and any necessary encoding options) to choose from. These profiles let you capture based on the video and audio content of your video. Your video might contain a lot of movement. When you capture this type of video, you will need to choose a capture profile that is specifically configured for high-motion video.

Capture profiles for high-motion video generally use a higher bit rate. Bit rate is basically how fast the bits need to be transferred in the audio and video to display properly on a computer. As the motion in your recorded video and audio increases, so does the bit rate needed to display the motion correctly. However, as bit rate increases, so does file size. More information about the different capture profiles and how they are used is provided in part III of this book.

Bandwidth Considerations

Aside from the profile you choose for recording, other factors also play a part. One important factor is your audience's connection speed or available network bandwidth. Bandwidth can be thought of as a pipe: if you have a larger water pipe, more water can flow through the pipe. However, if you have a smaller pipe, less water can flow through it at a time. The same concept applies to bandwidth and connection speeds for viewing video and audio.

If your audience is going to watch your presentation through a high-speed network connection, such as a corporate local area network (LAN), they have more available bandwidth than an individual who is watching your presentation over a 56.6 Kbps dial-up modem connection. In other words, the viewers on the LAN have a larger pipe than the viewers watching your presentation over a dial-up connection. The larger pipe lets bits of information travel at a faster pace, and this allows your viewers to watch a higher-quality video without bottlenecks that would interrupt smooth playback.

Of course file size and bandwidth are interconnected. More bandwidth means a larger file can be transferred to your audience more quickly. Likewise, a slower connection (and therefore less bandwidth) means that there will be bottlenecks—or else you need to scale back the quality (and therefore the size) of your files.

When recording audio and video, you need to consider your audience and the bandwidth or connection rate they will have when viewing your presentation. If your audience is going to be primarily connecting over dial-up modems, you would want to limit the amount of motion in your recorded video as a first step toward keeping file size down and video quality up. Conversely, if your audience is connecting over a LAN, the video you record for your presentation can contain more motion because the bandwidth will be available to transfer information at the increased bit rates needed for high-motion video.

In Microsoft Producer, you can choose to publish your final presentation based on your audience's connection method. Publishing presentations and choosing appropriate profiles will be discussed in part III of this book.

Recording Video

Obviously, the first thing you will need to start recording video is a video camera, usually called a *camcorder*. Most video cameras today are made so that they are easy-to-use, so you can immediately start recording. Before recording the video for your presentation, take a few minutes to familiarize yourself with the video camera. Also, consider reading the manual that came with it. The manual will explain what features your camera provides and how to use them.

Consider recording some practice video, so that you can get the shots you want when you are ready to begin recording the video for your presentation. Remember, you can easily erase or tape over the video you record when experimenting with your camera. After you understand how to use different features, you are ready to record the video for your presentation.

Basic Recording Steps

Though video cameras differ from one manufacturer to another, the same basic process applies when recording video with a video camera.

1. **Insert a battery**. Most video cameras come with at least one rechargeable battery. As mentioned in the previous chapter, make sure that the batteries are fully charged before you start recording. Most video cameras have a meter that shows the remaining charge on your battery.

   If you are recording indoors and using a power adapter, make sure the video camera is plugged in and properly connected.

2. **Insert a tape**. Open the compartment for the video tape cassette and insert the tape on which you want to record. After you have the video tape cassette inserted in the video camera, close the compartment.

3. **Turn the video camera to standby mode**. Video cameras have two different modes: camera and VTR. Camera mode is used when you want to record new video to the tape in your video camera. Therefore, when you are ready to record, switch the video camera to camera mode. You can then use the viewfinder or the LCD display panel (if your video camera has one), to see what the camera will record.

   In VTR mode, your video camera acts like a VCR—it lets you watch video you have recorded. You can use the transport controls, which are like the buttons on a VCR, to play, stop, pause, rewind, or fast-forward through the recorded video on your tape.

In camera mode, all you have to do is press the record button, which is usually red, when you want to start recording. The video recording functions are disabled and the camcorder goes into playback mode in VTR mode.

4. **Remove the lens cap and check your camera settings**. If all you see is black in your viewfinder, make sure the lens cap has been removed. Before you record, check the video camera and make sure the different settings are set on automatic such as focus, exposure, and gain (which will be discussed in the upcoming section). Make sure the battery is properly inserted and charged if you don't see the different lights on your camera. Now you can begin recording.

5. **Press the record button**. When you press the record button, video and audio is recorded to tape. You should see some indication that you are recording. This can be the word "Record" blinking on the viewfinder, a red light, or some other indication.

Common Video Camera Features

Many current video cameras have automatic features you can use when recording video. It's often best to use the automatic features for the video you are recording. However, if you have some experience with recording video, you might want more manual control over the video camera and the resulting video you record. Typically, more expensive video cameras will provide more manual override options than the less expensive cameras.

The following sections describe some common automatic settings that you can use with your video camera. Again, cameras differ from one manufacturer to the next, so consult the manual that came with your camera to learn about the specific features of your video camera.

Focus

Many current consumer video cameras have an automatic focus feature where a sensor in the lens detects an object and automatically focuses on the object. Usually, the video camera will correctly focus on the object you want the first time. This is what makes video cameras so easy to use and the quality of the video so good, even for inexpensive video cameras—all video that you shoot is in focus.

However, this feature can pose a problem because it can focus on a different object or person than what you want to record. For example, say you are recording a live training presentation. The presenter is speaking at the front of the room, but someone between the camera and the speaker gets up during the presentation and walks in front of the video camera. The video camera that was originally focused on the presenter would then incorrectly focus on the person passing in front of the video camera.

Switching to manual focus can correct this problem. Manual focus turns off the sensor, and then you can manually adjust the focus so that the correct object or person will be in focus for the video you record. However, switching off this automatic feature means that you have to do the work that the camera would do for you. So if the subject (such as the speaker in the previous example) is moving around, you would need to manually adjust the camera to keep your subject in focus. It requires practice to make this adjustment during a real video shoot.

A majority of today's consumer video cameras have both manual and automatic focus, so you can choose the setting that suits your needs.

Shutter Speed

Recording fast-moving subjects can sometimes be difficult. When you do record them, the objects may appear blurry and indistinct. Adjusting the shutter speed can help you to solve this problem. For example, if you use a shutter speed of 1/1000 of a second, the shapes of the fast-moving objects will become clear. However, if you slowed down the shutter speed to ¼ of a second, the object would become blurry again. By experimenting with the shutter speed, you can create interesting effects.

Exposure

Your video camera may also automatically adjust the exposure—the amount of light allowed to reach the camera's *CCD*—in the video you are recording. The CCD is a component within the camera that converts light into electrical signals. A sensor detects how much light is entering the lens and adjusts an iris in the video camera that works much like the iris in a traditional camera. If there is not enough light, the video you record will be dark, and details of your video will be lost. In this situation, the sensor will brighten the picture by opening the iris and letting more light reach the CCD. Conversely, if there is too much light in the video you are recording, the video will be extremely bright and *clipping* will occur. When clipping occurs, the video is overexposed.

The exposure feature of a video camera works to balance the amount of light reaching the CCD automatically so that you record a clear, detailed picture regardless of the lighting conditions. Most higher-end consumer video cameras have both automatic and manual exposure settings. A majority of the time, however, the automatic exposure feature will control the exposure correctly.

White Balance

The white balance feature of a video camera automatically adjusts the color of a scene so white objects appear white regardless of the type of lighting. Many video cameras have automatic features that can be used for achieving correct white balance whether you are recording indoors with incandescent lights or outdoors in sunlight.

Advanced Features and Effects

Except for some of the most basic video cameras, many current video cameras provide features that let you enhance the video you record. These effects are useful for creatively recording video, and using these features in moderation can help you to record more professional video for your presentations.

The following are brief descriptions of some additional features and effect that may be provided by your camera, and that you can use to enhance your video.

Titling

Perhaps you are recording video that you want to introduce with text. If so, the titling feature found on many video cameras lets you add text over your video. This text then appears in your video and is recorded to tape.

If you do not always want to have this title appear, consider recording without adding titling effects. Microsoft Producer enables you to produce similar results within your presentation.

Animation and Time-lapse

With some more advanced video cameras, you can set the recording so only a few frames or one frame is recorded at a time. This lets you create stop-motion animation. Some video cameras also provide time-lapse recording, where video is recorded at a given time interval. This lets you show the progression of a long-term project. You can often do this with some Web cameras by using the software that comes with the camera.

Transitions

Some video cameras allow you to add a transition, such as a fade out, when recording is stopped and then started again. Similar to when you add effects and titling with your video camera, the transitions you add with your video camera are recorded to tape with your video. This makes it impossible to hide or remove the transition later.

In Microsoft Producer, you can choose from a wide variety of different video transitions that you can add while editing your project. Adding transitions in Microsoft Producer, rather than while you are recording, is often easier because you can easily remove or change these transitions. It's impossible to remove transitions that were created by the video camera during the original recording.

Night Shot

When using the night shot feature of a video camera, you can record objects or people in dimly lit settings, such as at night. When you record video using night shot, the eyes of animals and people may appear to glow. However, this feature can be useful for recording in dimly lit situations where there is not an alternative light source.

Still Images

Most MiniDV cameras have a feature that lets you take still images. These still images are often saved as JPEG format files (with a .jpg file name extension) that you can import and use in your Microsoft Producer presentations. How the still images are stored on your video camera depends on the particular camera. Some video cameras have a floppy disk adapter that lets you save the images to disk, while some other video cameras store the images to removable media. For many of the MiniDV cameras, you can use the IEEE 1394 connection to transfer still images to your computer.

Video Effects

Video effects include a variety of features that let you change the way your recorded video looks. For example, some cameras enable you to record in black and white. The "negative" effect switches colors to their opposites (like a color film negative). Some effects, such as solarize and mosaic, digitally distort your video.

Note, however, that these features are not provided on all cameras, and your particular camera may provide other effects not described in this book.

You can choose to record video as usual and then add these effects to your video when it's recorded to your computer in Microsoft Producer. Using the video effects while recording can limit the use of your video because the effects are recorded to tape; therefore, they cannot be removed from the tape. Microsoft Producer includes a variety of video effects that you can add to your video after it has been transferred to your computer. Therefore, if you plan to reuse the video you are recording, you may want to record without effects, and then add an individual video effect when needed for your presentation in Microsoft Producer. If you choose to reuse the video later in the presentation or in a different presentation where the video effects are not well suited, you still have the original video without any added effects.

Some Basic Shots

When recording video, you can use the different features of your video camera to get the video you need for your presentation. When using your video camera, there are basic shots you can use to record the video you want. Each shot becomes a small story within the overall presentation. Individual shots are the basic elements of the entire video you record.

Each of the following sections describes a basic shot you might use.

Static

The first basic shot for recording video is a static shot. The video camera remains stationary and only the people or other objects that are being recorded move. A tripod or monopod is especially useful for static shots because it helps to keep the video camera still, which results in smooth video.

Pan

When you pan, the video camera moves along a horizontal plane. If you are using a tripod, all you need to do is move the video camera with the handle of the tripod. If you are not using a tripod and hand-holding the video camera, you can follow the action by moving the camera. Panning with a video camera on a tripod will result in better, smoother video because a tripod moves with a smoother motion.

Panning the video camera is most effective when your subject is moving. Our eyes do not pan naturally; they tend to jump from one point to another. The jumps are not smooth moves like panning. However, when an object is moving, our eyes move to follow that object or person. If you pan along with a moving object, the movement is more realistic because it duplicates what we do with our eyes.

Another shooting technique that is similar to panning is tilting. The only difference is that the video camera moves on a vertical plane rather than a horizontal plane. However, though tilting is an unnatural movement, the same rules apply to tilting as to panning—if you do shoot the video by tilting the video camera, move the video camera slowly up and down.

Zoom

The zoom control on your video camera enables you to make an object appear either closer or farther away, without having to move the camera. We would normally move closer to an object or person to get a better view. Zooming in on an object or person lets your audience see the object more closely, just like they might if they were there at the scene. Likewise, zooming out increases the distance between the video camera and the subject you are recording.

Although physically moving the camera closer to or further from the object creates a more realistic picture than using the zoom, many times moving closer or further from an object is not possible. In that case, zooming in or out is the best way to record video that will convey the message in your overall presentation.

Setting up Shots

Individual shots work together to form the scenes that make up a complete video. A shot is taken when you turn on the video camera, record video and audio, and then stop recording. The different shots work together to form a scene.

Setting up a shot requires some planning. You should have basic instructions or a script for your video, but don't be afraid to let your "actors" improvise at times and explain the topic or subject as they see or understand it. This often leads to more natural and compelling video because it lets your subjects relax and explain the topic or subject in their own words and using genuine emotion.

When you are shooting video, there are some basic steps you can take to get better shots.

Of course, these are only the very basic elements of recording video. Whole books have been written on filmmaking techniques. However, the goal is not for this to be an exhaustive reference on recording video, but to help you quickly learn basic techniques when recording video. Using these techniques to block and compose shots should help you record better-quality video quickly and easily.

Blocking the Shot

In a sense, every shot is a mini-story in itself in terms of the overall video. You will probably find that you do not always record extremely long, continuous segments of video. Instead, you might find yourself recording many shorter segments, or shots. Blocking the shot helps you determine how you will create the shot. Blocking the shots also helps you determine the focal point of each video segment you are going to record.

Think about what each shot covers. For example, if you are recording a sales presentation, the first shot might focus on the presenter, because he or she is speaking and introducing the product. Then you'd want to focus on the product itself. The first shot establishes the presenter, and then the second shot shows the product the presenter is discussing.

Composing the Shot

Composing a shot requires you to study the object or persons you are recording. If you can control the setting, you may be able to move the subjects you are recording. However, if you cannot control the setting, study what you have to work with to determine what will make the best video.

When composing a shot, do the following:

- **Select a subject**. A shot should only have one subject. The subject can be two people talking, one person speaking, a single product, or whatever you like. However, determine what the subject is and focus on that subject. Sometimes there is a tendency to try to record everything that is occurring rather than concentrating on the main subject. Concentrating on one subject lets you focus your audience's attention on what you consider important.

- **Find a frame for the subject**. After selecting your shot, look at what else is in the shot. If you are recording a person talking in a room and you want to record what's going on in front of the speaker, find an angle that lets you capture all this. For example, you might want to zoom out from the speaker so that the audience, who are facing away from the camera, can also be seen. Framing the shot as they would see it live and in person can help improve the realism and effectiveness of the video because the camera becomes the eyes for your online audience.

- **Find a balanced composition**. Balance the shot to help keep it from looking lopsided. If one part of the frame is empty, while the other half is completely full, the shot will look unbalanced. At times, you will not want to include more objects in the shot, you might want to simply zoom in on the subject to balance the shot more evenly.

- **Zoom in and check the shot**. Zoom in on the subject you are recording and then check the focus. Zooming in and checking the focus provides a way for you to check the video you are recording to get the best shot possible.

- **Change the depth of field**. The depth of field is the area in front of and behind the subject that is in focus. It changes when you zoom in or out from the subject you are recording. When you change the depth of field, you can focus your audience's attention on the subject you are recording. For example, you can stand about 20 feet from a person you are recording and then zoom in. When you do this, people in front of the person and the people behind them appear out of focus and are blurry while your subject remains in focus. This helps to focus your audience's attention on the main subject in the shot. Figure 6.1 shows an example of a subject that is isolated by narrowing the depth of field.

Figure 6.1 — Using depth of field to focus attention on the subject.

- **Use the rule of thirds**. The rule of thirds is a guideline used by photographers that is also applicable to shooting video. Basically, according to the rule of thirds, your subject should not appear directly in the middle of the frame. To establish where the subject should be positioned in the frame, the frame should be divided into thirds, with two horizontal lines and two vertical lines. The subject should then be framed at one of the four points where the lines intersect. Figure 6.2 shows a frame divided using the rule of thirds.

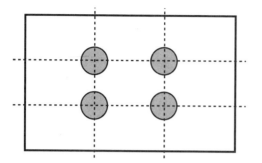

Figure 6.2 — A frame divided using the rule of thirds.

- **Lead the eyes and movement of your subject**. When people are watching a moving person, there is a tendency to look at the person or the moving object and then look at where they are heading. Recording video with this in mind can help you capture a person's or object's movement in a realistic way as it would normally be seen live. If a person is standing on the left and then moving right, frame the person on the left side and leave room on the right side of the frame for the person to move to. This is often called *leading* the subject.

- **Adjust focus and exposure**. After you line up the shot and zoom in on the subject, you might find the lighting is unnatural, too bright, or too dark. Adjusting the exposure on your video camera can correct these lighting problems. However, if you have control of the lighting and the setting you are recording in, you might want to make adjustments to the lighting on the "set."

Recording Video to Edit

Recording video and audio that you are going to edit and then distribute is often different from simply recording video and distributing it in its entirety without editing. Because you are most likely going to edit the video for your presentation, think of your video in terms of the entire presentation and the pieces of video you need. This can help you determine how small pieces of video work together to form one complete coherent presentation. This means that when you are recording your video, you may record small segments of video, with differing shots and settings as discussed earlier in this chapter.

Recording video that you are going to edit lets you take chances and keep recording where you would normally stop recording. Because you can remove unwanted footage in Microsoft Producer, you can keep recording video even if you think it will not be usable in your presentation. The biggest temptation is to stop recording once the shot or scene is finished. However, there are times when you might want to keep recording because you can get some unexpectedly good video that you can use in your presentation. If you stop recording immediately, you might miss footage that you could really use. Video tape is relatively inexpensive, and you can always tape over existing video if you like. However, if you stop recording video early, that valuable video is missed and difficult (if not impossible) to record on tape.

You'll find that the proportion of the recorded video you have, compared to the amount of usable video for your presentation, is quite large. That's why it is a good idea to keep recording even before the main video shoot, such as during rehearsal, if applicable. The more video you get, the more you have to work with for your final presentation. If you establish a basic shooting plan, as discussed in chapter 5, and then combine this when recording video, your chances of recording quality video that will truly enhance your presentation are greatly increased.

Recording High-quality Audio

Chapter 5 discussed how to prepare an office or other setting for recording quality audio. Many times, the sole source of audio will be from the built-in microphone on your video camera. However, the audio that it records can be quite different from the audio recorded with an external microphone, such as a lavaliere or other professional microphone. This is due to the position and quality of the microphone.

Because a built-in microphone is mounted directly on the video camera, it records audio that is near the video camera itself. This might be your own voice if you are trying to give instruction or are speaking to someone else rather than the words from the presenter. However, if you are using an external lavaliere microphone that is attached to the speaker's clothing and connected to the microphone input on the video camera, the audio that is recorded will be what is closest to the microphone, which is the speaker's voice and words. You will capture more of the sound you want, and less of the sound you don't want.

An external microphone is easy to use, and often rather inexpensive to purchase. Most of all, it helps to improve the quality of the audio in your video so that your audience can not only clearly see the speaker, but will understand what the speaker is saying as well.

Headphones can help you to improve the quality of the audio you record as well. Many video cameras have a jack so that you can plug headphones into your camera. This lets you hear exactly what is being recorded to tape. You can also play back the recorded video and audio and hear the audio that was recorded.

By using headphones, especially if you have a set that cover the entire ear, you can block out external sounds and hear only the audio on tape. Listening to recorded audio played back over the video camera speakers does not do this. If you listen to the audio and determine that adjustments need to be made to the setting or room, you can then make those adjustments and immediately record the shot again, if necessary. However, if you wait to get back to your computer, capture the video and audio to Microsoft Producer and then determine that the quality is insufficient, it may be difficult to gather the actors, prepare the setting, and then record the video and audio once again.

Part III

Creating Presentations Using Microsoft Producer

Chapter 7: Starting a New Presentation

Chapter 8: Capturing Video, Audio, and Still Images

Chapter 9: Editing on the Timeline

Chapter 10: Microsoft PowerPoint Presentations In Producer

Chapter 11: Publishing Your Presentation

Starting a New Presentation

After gathering the content you want to include in your presentation, you can now import your content into Microsoft Producer and start creating your presentation. The first step is to start Producer and begin your new project. You will see a dialog box like the one in Figure 7.1.

The method you use to begin your project is up to you. When you first start using Producer, you might find it helpful to use the **New Presentation Wizard** because it walks you through the process of starting a new presentation step-by-step. However, as you become more experienced with Producer, you might want to begin your presentation by starting with a new, blank project.

Figure 7.1 — The dialog box that appears when you first start Microsoft Producer.

In this chapter, you will first create a new project using the **New Presentation Wizard**. Then later in the chapter, you will see how to build a project from scratch by starting with a new blank project.

Using the New Presentation Wizard

The **New Presentation Wizard** helps you start a new presentation by walking you through the following steps. By going through the **New Presentation Wizard**, you can quickly create a new project, which you can later publish as a presentation.

While working in the **New Presentation Wizard**, you can click **Cancel** at any time. When you click **Cancel**, the wizard ends and any steps you completed to that point will be discarded.

On the other hand, you may decide that you want to complete a few steps in the wizard and then continue creating your project on your own. You can do this by clicking **Finish** at any time in the wizard. If you click **Finish**, any steps you have completed up to that point will be applied to your project. For example, let's say you completed both the **Choose a Presentation Scheme** page and the **Presentation Information** page in the **New Presentation Wizard**, and then clicked **Finish**. In this situation, the presentation template you chose would be added to the timeline, and the font and colors would be selected for your presentation. You would then need to import digital media files and add them to the timeline outside of the wizard in order to continue creating your presentation, just as you would if you were starting with a new blank project.

The companion CD includes a sample presentation that was created using Microsoft Producer. You can watch this presentation by opening the file \Samples\Chapter7\Interview.htm.

The **New Presentation Wizard** proceeds as follows. You can complete each of the following steps on the individual pages of the wizard:

1. Read the introduction page that briefly outlines the steps and pages of the **New Presentation Wizard**.

2. Choose a presentation template for the presentation you are creating.

3. Choose a presentation scheme for the presentation.

4. Enter information about your presentation.

5. Choose a Microsoft PowerPoint presentation or individual still images that you want to include in your presentation.

6. Choose existing audio and video files that you want to include in your presentation, or capture new content using Microsoft Producer.

7. Specify whether you want to synchronize your slides and still images with the selected audio and video immediately after completing the wizard.

8. Complete the wizard so the selected content is imported into the current project and added to the timeline.

Choosing a Presentation Template

The **Presentation Template** page of the **New Presentation Wizard** lets you choose which presentation template you want to apply to the current project. The presentation template you choose determines the layout and appearance of the content in your presentation, as well as which items are displayed. For example, if you plan on using slides and still images for a presentation that contains audio without video, you would choose an audio presentation template that displays slides and still images, such as one of the following presentation templates that are installed with Producer:

- **Clouds Audio – Fixed Slides and HTML**

- **Globe Audio – Resizable Slides and HTML**

- **Organizational Audio – Resizable Slides and HTML**

- **Standard Audio – Resizable Slides**

Even if you have only completed the audio portion of your presentation, you could choose any one of these presentation templates and then import and add HTML files or Web links at a later time.

Many times, your presentations will also contain video with accompanying audio. In these instances, you would choose a presentation template that displays slides and still images, as well as video (with accompanying audio), such as one of these templates:

- **Clouds Video (240x180) – Fixed Slides and HTML**

- **Globe Video (240x180) – Fixed Slides and HTML**

- **Organizational Video (240x180) – Resizable Slides and HTML**

- **Standard Video (320x240) – Resizable Slides and HTML**

The numbers in parentheses describe the size of the video display area, in pixels, in the presentation template. The particular presentation template you choose depends on the display size of the video you want to playback in the presentation template. Capturing video, display size, and its relation to choosing a presentation template is discussed in chapter 8.

All of the templates just described are part of the predefined set of templates that are installed with Producer. You can add to this set by creating your own custom templates. When you copy the new templates into the default template folder, they will appear in the contents pane and you can add them to your project. Creating and customizing Microsoft Producer templates is discussed in chapter 12 of this book.

The presentation template you choose is applied for the current project and added to the timeline after you click **Finish** in the **New Presentation Wizard**. If you later decide you want to change the template or use multiple templates in your presentation, you can easily do so at any time by adding them to the timeline.

Understanding Presentation Template Styles

By using different presentation templates, you can change the look and feel of your presentation. When choosing a presentation template, it is helpful to understand the basic presentation template styles and what they contain.

The following list describes the presentation templates installed with Producer and briefly explains the appearance of each style:

- **Standard**. The Standard template style contains solid colors without background images. This lets you display solid colors in your presentation. For example, you could create a color scheme that is compatible with that of your organization, logo, or campaign.

- **Clouds**. The Clouds template style contains one large background image. Audio and video content is displayed on the right side in these templates. If slides or HTML are displayed in a presentation with a Cloud template, the slides and HTML do not resize, meaning that if the window is resized, the slides and HTML remain the same, fixed size.

- **Globe**. The Globe template style displays a background image and a header image at the top of the page. This presentation template style often contains small, tiled images in the presentation background.

- **Organizational**. The Organizational template style contains one large background image. If slides or HTML are displayed in a presentation with an Organizational template, the slides and HTML resize. Therefore, if the window is resized, the slides and HTML also resize.

Step-by-Step: Selecting a Presentation Template

To choose a presentation template:

1. Click the name of the template in the **Templates** list box.

2. Click **Next** to proceed to the **Choose a Presentation Scheme** page.

Choosing a Presentation Scheme

The **Choose a Presentation Scheme** page of the **New Presentation Wizard** lets you choose the font and colors to use in your presentation. By choosing a scheme for your presentation, you can select which font, font size, font color, and background colors you want to use in your presentation.

In Microsoft Producer, you will notice that you can accomplish the same task in different ways. This is the case when choosing a presentation scheme. The information that you specify on this page of the wizard can also be selected through the **Presentation Scheme** dialog box. Therefore, if you create your presentation through the **New Presentation Wizard** and then later decide you want to change the selected colors or font, you can do so without going through the **New Presentation Wizard** again.

When choosing a presentation scheme, you can change the appearance and colors for the table of contents and the slides area of your final published presentation. Figure 7.2 shows which parts of your final presentation are affected by the choices you make when selecting options for the presentation scheme.

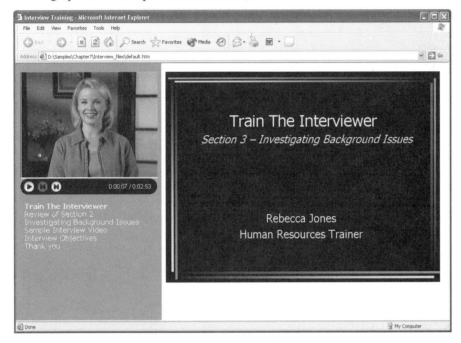

Figure 7.2 — A published presentation showing the table of contents and slides area.

Selecting the Font and Colors for the Table of Contents

The table of contents provides an outline or guide to your presentation. It lets your users see a list of topics that are covered in your presentation. The topics are clickable links that the audience can use to navigate through your presentation. Therefore, if an individual watching your presentation in his or her Web browser wanted to watch a specific part of the presentation, he or she could do so by clicking the corresponding table of contents entry. Chapter 9 discusses the process of creating and editing a table of contents for your presentation.

The fonts that you can select for table of contents entries consist of a list of fonts that will display properly in most Web browsers. These are fonts that are common and are likely to be installed on your audience's computers. This is important because your audience must have the selected font installed on their computers in order to see the font in their Web browsers when they watch your published presentation. In addition to specifying the font for the table of contents, you can select the font size (which determines how large or small the font will appear in the table of contents area of your presentation) and the font color.

After selecting the font, font size, and font color for entries in the table of contents, you will also want to specify a background color for the table of contents. When choosing a background color, keep in mind the importance of color and contrast. For example, if you selected a lighter font color for the table of contents, you should choose a background color that contrasts with the table of contents text color. If you choose two colors that are similar and do not provide sufficient contrast, the table of contents entries will be difficult to see in your presentation.

Selecting the Background Color

The **Slides area background** setting determines which color is displayed in the area behind your slides. When choosing this color, consider the color used in your Microsoft PowerPoint slides, as well as the color you selected for the table of contents. This will help you choose a background color that is suitable for your presentation.

When choosing background colors, consider what look you want for your presentation. For example, your organization might have a standard set of colors that are used in corporate communications or on the company's Web site. You can choose colors to give your presentations a uniform look and feel or to associate that presentation with your company's colors and logos.

For example, your organization might use a specific shade of blue. If you know the color's RGB value, which is a standard for specifying colors, you could click the **Define Custom Color** button, type the RGB values in the **Red**, **Green**, and **Blue** boxes of the **Color** dialog box, and then add the color to the list of custom colors. This allows you to choose the exact shade or color that is used throughout other corporate communications and use it in your presentation. This custom color would be available in the current presentation as well as in future presentations. You could select this custom color for other parts of your presentation as well, such as the font color or background color for the table of contents.

Differences Between Templates and Schemes

The presentation scheme determines the font and colors that can be used by the presentation template or templates you choose. If you apply one of the Standard templates to your presentation, the font, font size, and colors you choose will display in your presentation. However, if you apply one of the presentation templates which contain background images, such as the Clouds, Globe, or Organizational templates, the font and colors that display are determined by the presentation template itself rather than by the font and colors you select for the presentation scheme.

After completing the **New Presentation Wizard**, you can apply one or more additional templates to the timeline. This allows you to switch presentation templates throughout the presentation. This feature is helpful because you may want your presentation scheme colors and fonts to appear during some parts of your presentation, but not during other parts. By switching presentation templates and styles, you can dynamically change the appearance of your presentation as your audience watches it in their Web browsers. Chapter 9 discusses editing a project and switching presentation templates.

Step-by-Step: Selecting a Presentation Scheme

To choose a presentation scheme:

1. Select the font name from the **Font** drop-down list. These fonts are listed because they can be viewed in a Web browser, and they are most likely already installed on your audience's computers.

2. Select the font size from the **Font Size** list for the table of contents entries in your presentation. The font size is specified in points.

3. Click **Font color** to choose a color from the **Color** dialog box. You can instead click **Define Custom Color**, enter values in the **Red**, **Green**, and **Blue** boxes for the color, click **Add to Custom Colors**, and then click **OK** to choose the new custom color.

4. Click **Background** to choose or define a background color.

5. Click **Slides area background** to choose or define a color for the background.

6. Click **Next** to proceed to the **Presentation Information** page.

Entering Information About Your Presentation

It may be helpful to provide your audience with information prior to them viewing your presentation. To effectively communicate the purpose and other pertinent background information about your presentation, Microsoft Producer creates an introduction page. Figure 7.3 shows an example.

The introduction page is useful because it can help to set your audience's expectations and to state the goal or purpose for the presentation. For example, if you are creating a presentation that discusses quarterly corporate earnings, you could provide this information on the introduction page along with information about the presenter. Furthermore, you can display an image, such as a corporate logo.

The presentation information is optional. However, by taking a few minutes to complete this page, you can convey important details to your audience that can help to increase the overall effectiveness of your presentation. This information displays on the introduction page in the viewer's Web browser while your presentation is loading. By clicking **Preview** in the wizard you can see what the introduction page will look like to the viewer. That way, you can make any necessary adjustments before you complete the **New Presentation Wizard**.

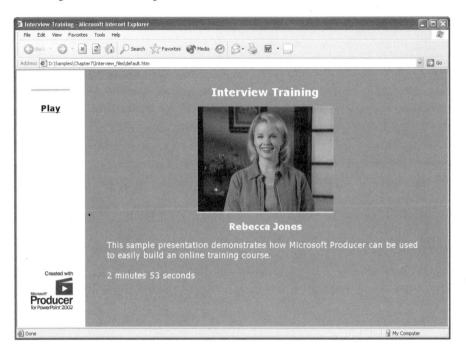

Figure 7.3 — The introduction page for a published presentation.

Step-by-Step: Entering Presentation Information

To specify the information for the introduction page:

1. In the **Title** box, type a descriptive title for your presentation. This title should describe the main point or purpose of your presentation. Specifying a title is not required, but strongly recommended.

2. In the **Presenter (optional)** box, type the presenter (or presenters) name.

3. In the **Introduction page image (optional)** box, enter the path and file name for the image you want to appear on the introduction page. Or click **Browse** to find the still image, which can be located on your computer, on a shared network location, on a CD, and so on.

4. In the **Description (optional)** box, type a brief description for your presentation. This description should briefly describe the presentation or provide background information about the presentation.

5. Click **Next** to proceed to the **Import Slides and Still Images** page.

Using PowerPoint Slides or Still Images

The **Import Slides and Still Images** page lets you choose which Microsoft PowerPoint presentations or still images you want to include in your presentation. These are the slides and still images that you synchronize with audio and video content.

You can choose the slides or still images from a variety of locations. The slides, PowerPoint presentations, or still images can be located on your local computer, on a shared network location, on a CD, or on another type of storage device, such as a CompactFlash card for a digital camera.

The following file types can be imported in this page of the wizard. These file types include Microsoft PowerPoint presentations and still image files with the following file name extensions:

- **Microsoft PowerPoint presentations**. .ppt and .pps

- **Still image files**. .bmp, .dib, .emf, .gif, .jfif, .jpe, .jpeg, .jpg, .png, .tif, .tiff, .wmf

Microsoft Producer lets you import these file types, as well as a wider variety of other digital media file types. A complete list of all supported file types is discussed later in this chapter.

When you are selecting your PowerPoint presentations or still images, you may already know the order in which you would like these slides and still images to be added on the timeline. If so, you can quickly organize the slides or still images you select in this page of the wizard. After completing the **New Presentation Wizard**, the slides and still images are added to the timeline in the order that they appear in the **Files** box.

You can save time by arranging the slides and still images in the order that you think you want them to appear. If you already know the path and file name of the slides or still image you want to add, you can type it in the **Path** box, and then click **Add**. To change the position of a file in the **Files** box, simply click the file and use the **Move Up**, and **Move Down** buttons. If you change your mind about including a particular file, you can use the **Remove** button to delete the file from the list. If you decide you want to reorder the slides or still images after completing the wizard, you can easily do so at any time by rearranging them on the timeline.

Step-by-Step: Importing Slides and Still Images

To add slides and still images to your presentation:

1. If you know the path and file name of the still image or Microsoft PowerPoint slide or presentation that you want to import, type that location, and then click **Add**.

2. If you want to locate and select the Microsoft PowerPoint slide or presentation or still images, click **Browse**, locate the slides and still images you want to import into your current presentation, and then click **Open**.

3. To select multiple Microsoft PowerPoint presentations and/or still images, you can press the Ctrl key and click multiple still images and Microsoft PowerPoint presentations to include in your Producer presentation.

4. After selecting multiple files, click **Move Up** or **Move Down** to specify the order that the slides and still images should be added to the timeline.

5. To remove an item from the list of files to be imported, click **Remove**.

6. Click **Next** to proceed to the **Import or Capture Audio and Video** page.

Choosing Audio and Video for Your Presentation

If you want to include audio or video content in your presentation, the **Import or Capture Audio and Video** page lets you specify these digital media files. If you included Microsoft PowerPoint slides or still images on the previous page, the audio and video files you choose will usually relate to those slides and still images.

The audio and video you want to use in your presentation may be on your computer already. If the audio and video has been saved as digital media files, you can choose the files you want to use. Like slides and still images, these files may be located on your local computer, on a shared network location, or on a CD. On this page of the wizard, you can choose to import audio or video files with the following file name extensions:

- **Audio files**. .aif, .aifc, .aiff .asf, .au, .mp2, .mp3, .mpa, .snd, .wav, .wma

- **Video files**. .asf, .avi, .m1v, .mp2, .mpe, .mpeg, .mpg, .mpv2, .wm, .wmv

If the audio and video content that you want to use for your presentation is not saved to your computer, network, or a CD, you can go from this page directly to the **Capture Wizard** in order to capture the video, audio, or still images you want to include in your presentation. For example, you may have recorded video with a camcorder, but not yet transferred it to your computer and saved it as a video file. In this situation, you can start the **Capture Wizard** to save this recorded video footage to your computer. The video, audio, or still images you capture and save are then added to the list of files that can be imported on the **Import or Capture Audio and Video** page of the wizard. Chapter 8 discusses capturing content through the **Capture Wizard** in Producer.

If you plan to narrate slides with video or audio, continue working in the **New Presentation Wizard**. After you complete the wizard, you can start the **Capture Wizard** and narrate the slides. Narrating slides is discussed in chapter 8.

Just as you can organize the slides and still images, you can also determine the order for the corresponding audio and video you want to synchronize with the slides. Therefore, when arranging the list of audio and video files to be imported, make sure that the order corresponds roughly to the order of the slides and still images you selected. You can then easily synchronize the different elements after completing the wizard.

Step-by-Step: Importing or Capturing Audio and Video

To add digital media files to your presentation:

1. If you have recorded audio or video that you want to capture on your computer, or if you want to capture live video, audio, or still images, click **Capture** to start the **Capture Wizard**.

   On the main page of the **Capture Wizard**, you can choose which type of content you want to capture. After you capture the content and save it as a file, the **Capture Wizard** ends, and the video, audio, or still image is added to the list of files to be imported in the **Import or Capture Audio and Video** page of the **New Presentation Wizard**. For more information, see chapter 8.

   Still images captured from the **Import or Capture Audio and Video** page are added to the **Video** track of the timeline. This means that these images show in the video display area of the presentation template, not the slide display area.

2. If you know the path and file name of the audio or video file that you want to import, type that location in the **Path** box, and then click **Add**.

3. If you want to locate and select the individual audio or video files, click **Browse**, locate the audio or video file you want to import into your current presentation, and then click **Open**.

   Video and audio content you select will be added to the **Video** and **Audio 2** tracks, respectively, on the timeline after you have completed the wizard. You can later synchronize the slides or still images with the audio and video you select on this page of the wizard.

   To select multiple audio and video files, you can press the Ctrl key and click each video or audio file that you want to include in your presentation. If the files appear contiguously, you can press the Shift key, click the first file in the list, and then click the last file in the list while still pressing the Shift key.

4. After selecting multiple files, click **Move Up** or **Move Down** to specify the order in which the audio and video will be added to the timeline.

5. To remove an audio or video file from the list of files to be imported select the file in the **Files** box, and then click **Remove**.

6. Click **Next**. Depending on the content you selected, you will either proceed to the **Synchronize Presentation** page or the **Complete Presentation** page.

Synchronizing Slides—Now or Later

The **Synchronize Presentation** page lets you determine when you want to synchronize your slides. You can choose to synchronize your slides immediately after completing the **New Presentation Wizard,** or you can choose to synchronize your slides at a later time.

If you have captured live or taped audio and video to synchronize with your slides, and imported your slides and digital media files in the correct order, you will probably want to synchronize your slides immediately after completing the wizard. In this case, click **Yes** on the **Synchronize Presentation** page before proceeding.

There are times when you would not want to synchronize your slides with the audio and video content immediately after completing the **New Presentation Wizard**. For example, you might have used the Microsoft Producer PowerPoint add-in program (which comes with Microsoft Producer) to track slide timings when the original, "live" presentation was recorded. Since the slides were already synchronized, you would not need to synchronize them again. The Microsoft Producer PowerPoint add-in program is described in chapter 10 of this book.

As you work with the **New Presentation Wizard**, you may notice that this page does not appear in the following situations:

- No slides or still images are selected.

- No audio or video is selected.

- No audio, video, slides, or still images are selected.

If any of these situations are true, you will go directly to the last page of the **New Presentation Wizard,** which lets you complete the wizard.

Step-by-Step: Choosing When to Perform Synchronization

To specify whether to synchronize slides immediately or not:

1. If you want to synchronize your presentation immediately after the files are imported and the wizard has completed, click **Yes**.

2. If you do not want to synchronize your presentation immediately after the files are imported, click **No**.

3. Click **Next** to proceed to the **Complete Presentation** page.

Completing the Wizard

The **Complete Presentation** page lets you finish the wizard and import the content you have selected to the presentation timeline. When you click **Finish**, any content you have selected and any information you have entered is then applied to the current project. The content is then added to the appropriate track on the timeline. This lets you immediately begin editing your project.

If you chose to synchronize your slides with audio and video on the **Synchronize Slides** page of the **New Presentation Wizard**, the **Synchronize Slides** dialog box opens after you click **Finish**.

If you change your mind about the presentation you are creating and decide to start over, you can easily do so by clicking **Cancel** on this page or any other page of the **New Presentation Wizard**.

Step-by-Step: Completing the Wizard

To finish creating your presentation:

- Click **Finish** to close the wizard and import the files you selected and create the presentation project, or click **Cancel** to end the wizard and discard your work.

After completing the **New Presentation Wizard**, one of the following will occur, depending on the choices you made in the wizard.

- If you click **Finish** and you chose to synchronize your presentation after completing the **New Presentation Wizard**, the selected files are imported into the current project and added to the timeline. In addition, the **Synchronize Slides** dialog box appears. You can then synchronize your slides and still images with the audio and/or video files you selected. After synchronizing your presentation, you can then preview it using the **Preview Presentation** tab.

- If you click **Finish** and you chose not to synchronize your presentation after completing the **New Presentation Wizard**, the files you selected are imported into the current project and added to the appropriate tracks on the timeline. The **Preview Presentation** tab is selected for you, and you can then preview your presentation.

Synchronizing Slides and Still Images

You may already have many Microsoft PowerPoint presentations or other types of still images that you have created. You may even have video or audio that accompanies these slides. You can use the synchronize slides feature in Microsoft Producer to put these elements together. With this feature, you can synchronize your slides so a specific slide, slide animation, or still image corresponds to the correct part of your video or audio content. In order to do this, each slide or other still image must appear on the **Slide** track of the timeline. For the remainder of this section, the term "slide" will refer to all types of still images or slides on the timeline.

You can synchronize your slides with video or with audio only, depending on the type of content you choose, and the goal of your presentation. For instance, you might have a video recording of an instructor teaching a class (which naturally includes an audio track), or you might have only an audio narration without a video image. Regardless, the process for synchronizing slides is basically the same. The main difference you will notice is that a video display appears when you are synchronizing with video.

Step-by-Step: Synchronizing Slides with Video and Audio

The following procedure describes the step-by-step process for synchronizing slides with video or with audio only. Whether you synchronize your slides after completing the **New Presentation Wizard** or later in the process of creating your presentation, the synchronize slides feature functions in the same way.

1. Open the **Synchronize Slides** dialog box. There are two ways to do this:

   - In the **New Presentation Wizard,** click **Yes** on the **Synchronize Presentation** page, and then click **Finish** to complete the wizard. The **Synchronize Slides** dialog box automatically opens after the files you selected are imported and added to the timeline.

   - On the **Tools** menu, click **Synchronize** to open the **Synchronize Slides** dialog box. The **Synchronize** command is only enabled when you have added content to both the **Slide** track and either the **Audio 2** or **Video** track.

2. If you want to preview the current slide timings with the audio and video content, select **Preview slide timing,** and then click the **Play** button. This lets you see the slide timings as they currently appear on the timeline.

   It is a good idea to preview the presentation and observe the current slide timings before making any changes, especially if you are unfamiliar with the content you are synchronizing. This lets you familiarize yourself with the content and see how the slides, still images, video, and audio work together. You may discover that you need to click **Cancel** in the **Synchronize Slides** dialog box so you can rearrange the order of the audio, video, slides, or still images you are synchronizing. No changes are made to the slide timing when you preview the current slide timing.

3. To begin synchronizing, select **Set slide timing,** and then click the **Play** button. The video or audio begins to play as the current slide or still image is displayed in the **Slide** window. From this point forward, Producer will record your actions in real time, so pay close attention to the progress of the presentation. When you want the presentation to move to the next slide, click **Next Slide** to set the slide timing.

4. If your slide contains slide animations, they are displayed in the **Slide** window. You can then click **Next Effect** to play the next slide animation or effect and to synchronize that animation or effect with the particular part of the audio or video.

   Whether slide animations or slide transitions are displayed depends on the options that you set in Producer. If the options **Disable slide transitions on import** or **Disable slide animations on import** are selected when the Microsoft PowerPoint presentation is imported into Producer, slide animations or slide transitions will not display when you are synchronizing slides, when you preview your presentation in Producer, or when the published presentation is viewed in a Web browser. Therefore, if those options are selected, the entire slide will be displayed in the **Slide** window rather than a particular slide animation. Furthermore, slide transitions will not be displayed in your synchronized presentation.

5. If necessary, use the controls to navigate through the video or audio file. You can use these controls to skip ahead in the presentation, which might save time if you have slides that remain static for long periods. You can also rewind the presentation, but be careful—once you rewind past slide timings you've already set, the timing information is lost and you will have to redo the synchronization from that point forward.

6. After you have synchronized your slides and still images with video or audio, do one of the following:

   - Click **Finish** after you have completed synchronizing your presentation. The slide timings you set are then shown on the respective tracks on the timeline.

   - Click **Cancel** if you want to discard the slide timings you just set.

Starting a New, Empty Project

You can accomplish the same result by creating a presentation from a new blank project as you can by using the **New Presentation Wizard**. After you become familiar with working in Microsoft Producer, you may decide that starting a presentation from a new blank project is quicker than working through the **New Presentation Wizard**. Although the **New Presentation Wizard** takes you through the process step-by-step, you may find that you prefer to create your presentation on your own.

At times, it may be helpful to start a new blank project, especially if you are unfamiliar with the slides, audio, video, HTML, or other digital media files you are working with. Using a new blank project allows you to import and preview slides, audio, or video before beginning to create your presentation. You can also easily edit and rearrange content on the timeline before synchronizing your presentation. Editing your project and individual items in your project is discussed in detail in chapter 9.

Table 7.1 shows the page of the **New Presentation Wizard** and the equivalent menu command you can select to accomplish the same step if you create your presentation starting with a new blank project instead.

Table 7.1 – Project Creation Commands.

New Presentation Wizard page	Producer command
Welcome to the New Presentation Wizard	None
Presentation Template	Choose a presentation template and then, on the **Clip** menu, click **Add To Timeline**.
Choose a Presentation Scheme	On the **Edit** menu, click **Presentation Scheme**.
Presentation Information	On the **Table of Contents** tab, enter the information in appropriate boxes in the **Introduction page** area.
Import Slides and Still Images	On the **File** menu, click **Import**.
Import or Capture Audio and Video	On the **File** menu, click **Import**. Or, on the **Tools** menu, click **Capture**.
Synchronize Presentation	On the **Tools** menu, click **Synchronize**.
Complete Presentation	None

Step-by-Step: Starting a New Project

The following steps will help you start a new presentation using a new blank project:

1. On the **File** menu, click **New**.

2. Import the individual digital media files you want to use in your presentation.

3. Add existing digital media files to the timeline or capture any new video, audio, or still images you want to include in your presentation.

4. Arrange any slides, still images, audio, video, or HTML content on the timeline.

5. Synchronize your presentation.

Importing Digital Media Files

When creating a new presentation, the first step is to import existing digital media files into Microsoft Producer. These digital media files can then be added to the timeline and arranged appropriately.

Producer supports a wide variety of digital media file formats. This helps to ensure that a majority of your existing digital media files can be used in your presentation. The following is a list of digital media file types and file formats that can be imported into Producer and used in your presentations:

- **Audio files**. .aif, .aifc, .aiff .asf, .au, .mp2, .mp3, .mpa, .snd, .wav, .wma

- **HTML files**. .htm, .html

- **Image files**. .bmp, .dib, .emf, .gif, .jfif, .jpe, .jpeg, .jpg, .png, .tif, .tiff, .wmf

- **PowerPoint files**. .pps, .ppt

- **Video files**. .asf, .avi, .m1v, .mp2, .mpe, .mpeg, .mpg, .mpv2, .wm, .wmv

Microsoft Producer keeps your digital media files organized by storing them in folders according to file type. This makes it easy to find your captured or imported video files, audio files, Microsoft PowerPoint presentations, HTML files, and other digital media files when you are creating your presentation. These folders appear in the **Media** tab of Microsoft Producer. Using the **Media** tab to create and edit your project is discussed in detail in chapter 9.

When you import a file into Microsoft Producer, the source file remains unchanged in its original location. You can edit the original source file outside of Microsoft Producer and any changes you make to the source file will be reflected in the file shown in your current project. On the other hand, any editing you perform in Microsoft Producer does not change the source file. To ensure that Producer can locate all the necessary files for a project, it is strongly recommended that you do not rename, move, or delete the original source files.

Microsoft Producer lets you set many options to customize Producer for your own use. These options relate to different aspects of creating a presentation in Producer. One of these customizable aspects involves importing digital media files. The following sections discuss the different options associated with importing files into Producer.

Importing Microsoft PowerPoint Presentations

Your Microsoft PowerPoint presentations may include slide animations and slide transitions. You can add these types of effects when creating the original PowerPoint presentation. In Microsoft Producer, you can specify whether you want PowerPoint slide animations or slide transitions to be displayed.

Whether slide animations or transitions are displayed in Producer depends on whether the **Disable slide animations on import** and **Disable slide transitions on import** check boxes on the **General** tab of the **Options** dialog box are selected when the Microsoft PowerPoint presentation is imported. This is true whether you import slides by using the **Import** command or the **New Presentation Wizard**.

For example, if the **Disable slide animations on import** check box is selected when you import your PowerPoint presentation, slide animations in this presentation will not display in Producer or in your final Producer presentation. If you later decide that you want the slide animations to display, you need to re-import the PowerPoint presentation into Producer after clearing the **Disable slide animations on import** check box. This is true for slide transitions as well.

You can also choose whether any audio and video that is already added to your PowerPoint presentation is separated from the slides when the PowerPoint presentation is imported. This option can be set using the **Separate audio and video from slides on import** check box on the **General** tab of the **Options** dialog box. For example, you might have already incorporated audio and video into your PowerPoint presentation. If so, you may want to separate audio and video when you import the PowerPoint presentation into Producer so you can use the audio and video in other parts of your presentation.

By default, when a PowerPoint presentation is imported, slide animations and transitions are displayed and audio and video in the PowerPoint presentation is separated from the slides. The default settings for importing PowerPoint slides are shown in Figure 7.4.

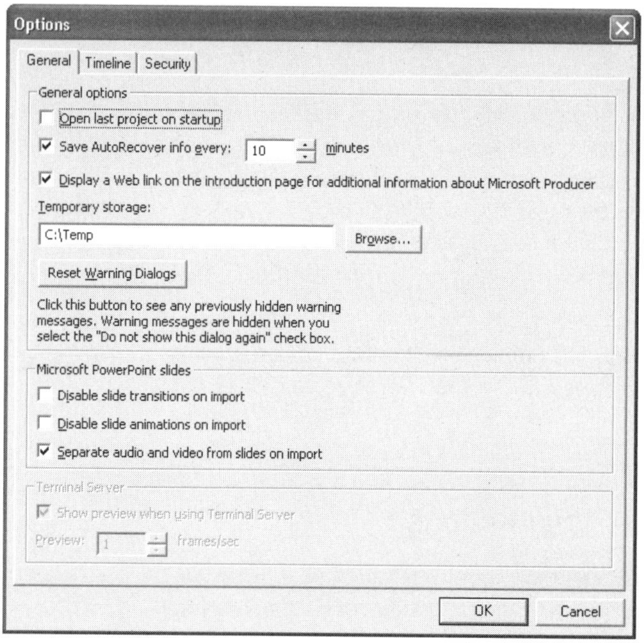

Figure 7.4 — Settings for importing a Microsoft PowerPoint presentation.

Step-by-Step: Setting PowerPoint Import Options

The following procedure describes the step-by-step process for setting the import options for Microsoft PowerPoint slides. For these settings to take effect, they must be configured before the PowerPoint presentation is imported into Producer.

1. On the **Tools** menu, click **Options**, and then select the **General** tab.

2. In the **Microsoft PowerPoint slides** area, do one or more of the following based on the settings you want:

- If you do not want slide transitions to display and play back in Producer, select the **Disable slide transitions on import** check box.

- If you do not want slide animations to display and play back in Producer, select the **Disable slide animations on import** check box.

  For example, if you selected this check box, imported the slides, and then synchronized your slides to audio and video you imported, the entire slide will be displayed at once, rather than each individual slide animation.

- If you want video and audio to be separated from your slides when a PowerPoint presentation is imported into Producer, select the **Separate audio and video from slides on import** check box. When the slides are imported, the separated audio and video files are imported and added to the **Audio** and **Video** folders that display in the **Media** tab in Producer.

3. Click **OK** to close the **Options** dialog box and save the new settings.

Importing Audio and Video

Producer lets you import a variety of audio and video files for use in your presentations. When importing video files, you can choose to have the file separated into smaller, more manageable clips. For example, if you had a video file that was 30 minutes long, but you only wanted to use a three-minute portion of the file, you could select the **Create clips for video files** check box in the **Import File** dialog box, and then import the selected video file. The file would then be broken down into smaller clips, so you could more easily find the particular portion of the video that you want to use in your presentation.

How the video files are separated into smaller clips depends on the type of video file that you select. This is discussed fully in chapter 9.

Step-by-Step: Importing Digital Media Files into Producer

The following procedure describes the step-by-step process for importing existing digital media files into Producer. You can import files regardless of whether you are creating a presentation with a new blank project or you have already started a presentation using the **New Presentation Wizard** and need to import additional digital media files.

1. On the **File** menu, click **Import**.

2. Locate and select the digital media files you want to import. These files can include still images, video, audio, HTML files, and Microsoft PowerPoint presentations.

   You can import multiple digital media files at one time. To do this, press the Ctrl key, and then click each file you want to import into your current project. If multiple files are listed contiguously in the **Import File** dialog box, you can press the Shift key, click the first file you want to import, and then click the last file in the list that you want to import.

3. Do one of the following:

- Select the **Create clips for video files** check box if you want any video files you select to be separated in to smaller clips using clip detection. Remember, the original file is not changed in any way.

- Clear the **Create clips for video files** check box if you do not want any selected video files to be separated into clips.

  If you later decide that you want the video file to be separated into clips, you can do so after the files are imported by choosing the **Create clips** command from the **Tools** menu. Likewise, if this check box is selected and you later decide you want the clips to appear as one file, you can combine the clips. Clip detection and combining clips is discussed in chapter 9.

4. Click **Open** to import the selected digital media files into Producer.

    When the files are imported into Producer, they are automatically added to the appropriate folder in the project. For example, still images are added and stored in the **Images** folder, video files are stored in the **Video** folder, and so forth.

Saving Your Project

After you start a presentation using the **New Presentation Wizard** or a new blank project, you will want to save the project. A project is made up of all the files you have imported and captured in Microsoft Producer. This includes any audio, video, or still images you have imported or captured in Microsoft Producer, as well as any HTML files or Microsoft PowerPoint presentations you have imported.

The arrangement of these items on the timeline is also saved in your project. Therefore, you can later open the project and then continue editing from where you left off when you last saved your project. A Microsoft Producer project file has an .MSProducer file name extension.

After completing your project, you are then ready to publish the project as a presentation. This is the presentation that your audience will watch in their Web browsers on their computers. You can publish the presentation to a variety of locations, including an internal intranet site, a shared network location, a Web site, an e-service provider's Web site, or a recordable or rewriteable CD. Chapter 11 discusses the publishing process and publishing your presentation to these different locations.

Saving Project Archives—Pack and Go

With time constraints in the working environment, things are always changing. Even after you publish the project as a presentation, you might need to make changes later on. For example, you might create and publish a presentation containing marketing information for a product line that you know you will change several times a year.

So that you do not have to create the entire presentation again, you might want to *pack* the project, meaning that all the source files and the actual Microsoft Producer project file are stored in one file—a Microsoft Producer project archive with an .MSProducerZ file name extension. This way, when the updated information is available, you can simply insert the new information and then publish the presentation again without starting from the beginning.

Packing a project to create a project archive is helpful because it lets you put all the necessary source files in one file. When you import source files, such as video, audio, still images, and so forth, Producer links to the source files in their original locations. Unfortunately, if the original source file is moved, renamed, or deleted, the link in the project file is broken—Producer will not be able to locate the files. As you can probably see, this could be a problem if you need to move your project from one computer to another or if you think you will need to make changes to the project later on. By packing your project, you can avoid this potential problem.

After you pack a project, you can then open the packed project archive on another computer. Copies of all of the associated source files are also unpacked to the folder or location you specify, along with the Producer project file.

This feature can be especially useful for those who spend a lot of time traveling. For example, you might start a presentation on a computer in your office, where you import files located on your office computer or a network location into your project, but you do not have the time to complete the project and publish it in while you are in your office. You could take the CD that contains the packed project archive and then unpack it on another computer, such as on a laptop computer. This allows you to work on your project while you are on the road without having to worry about broken links from source files that were originally located on a network or on your office computer.

Step-by-Step: Packing and Unpacking a Project Archive

The following procedure describes the step-by-step process for packing a Microsoft Producer project archive. These first steps describe how to create a project archive.

1. On the **File** menu, click **Save Project**. If you have not saved the project yet, type a project name in the **File name** box, and then click **Save**.

2. On the **File** menu, click **Pack and Go**.

   The **About Pack and Go** page appears and provides information about using **Pack and Go** to create a project archive.

3. On the **About Pack and Go** page, click **Continue**.

4. In the **Pack Project As** dialog box, click the location where you want your project archive to be saved.

When choosing the location for your project archive, choose a location that has enough available disk space. Depending on the source files and contents of your project, the project archive file can become quite large.

5. In the **File name** box, type a new name for the archive or accept the default project archive name (which is the same name as the Microsoft Producer project file). Click **Save** to create the project archive.

The time it takes for the project archive to be created depends on the size of the project and the source files used in the project. For example, if you have longer video or audio files in your project, the time it takes to create the project archive will be greater than if you had shorter video and audio files. Furthermore, your connection speed to a corporate network can also play a role if some of your source files are located on the network. A project archive cannot exceed 2 gigabytes (GB) in file size.

This second set of steps describes how to unpack the project archive.

1. On the **File** menu, click **Open**, and locate the project archive file. Click **Open**.

   The project archive can be saved on a shared network location, on your local computer, on a recordable or rewriteable CD, or on a compressed media disk.

2. In the **Browse For Folder** dialog box, locate the folder to which you want your project file and the associated project files to be unpacked, or click **Make New Folder** to create a new folder. Figure 7.5 shows an example of selecting a location to unpack a project.

Figure 7.5 — Selecting the folder where the project files will be stored.

3. Click **OK** to begin unpacking the project archive.

The time it takes for the project to be unpacked depends, as before, on the size of the files in the project.

The files are unpacked to separate subfolders based on the file types in the project. For example, Figure 7.6 shows the resulting project and folders created for a sample interview training presentation.

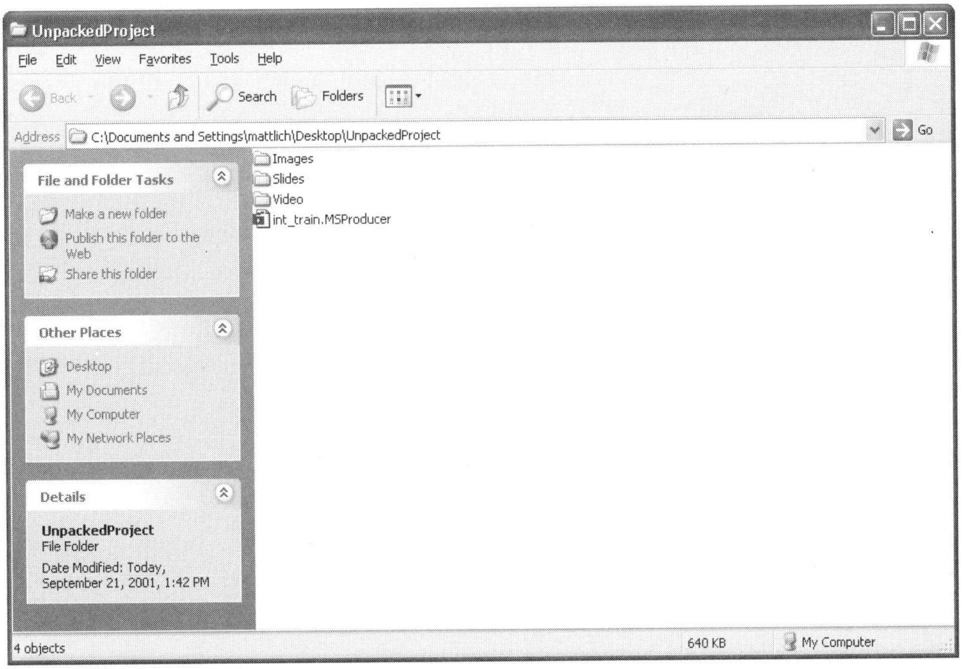

Figure 7.6 — The folders created for unpacked project files

CHAPTER 8

Capturing Video, Audio, and Still Images

Using the **Capture Wizard**, you can record audio, video, and still images from a variety of sources to your computer. This process is often referred to as *capturing* content. The video sources from which you can capture content range from the mouse actions on your computer screen to audio and video recorded on tape or captured live in Producer.

After you connect your video source, such as a video camera, Web camera, or VCR, to a capture device on your computer, you are ready to start capturing video, audio, or still images to your computer using Microsoft Producer. When you capture content to your computer, the video, audio, and still images are transferred from the specified source and then stored as a digital file on your computer.

The **Capture Wizard** can be used for the wide variety of video, audio, or still images you may want to include in your presentations. The **Capture Wizard** walks you through the step-by-step process of capturing content to your computer for use in a presentation. The process the wizard walks you through changes depending on the capture option you choose on the first page of the **Capture Wizard**.

Before You Begin Capturing Content

Chapter 6 discusses how to record high-quality content using your Web camera, analog video camera, digital video (DV) camera, or external microphone. However, whether you are using the **Capture Wizard** to record content live or from a tape, you can take certain steps to maximize the quality of content you capture in Microsoft Producer. The following tips can also help you work more quickly and efficiently when capturing content in Microsoft Producer.

Closing Unused Programs

Quitting unused programs can help preserve system resources on your computer. Capturing video and audio on your computer requires that you have the necessary computing power and available system resources. Quitting unused, open programs can help free up valuable resources, such as RAM and video memory.

Furthermore, quitting unused programs that are not part of the video, audio, or still images you want to capture can make the content you capture more effective. For example, if you are capturing still images or video from your computer screen, your audience sees what is on the computer screen. This means that any icons, open programs, or even sensitive data on your computer screen could be captured and seen in the video or still images. By taking a few seconds to quit any unused programs, you can avoid these problems and save yourself a lot of time when you edit the captured video and audio.

Closing Other Video-related Programs

Many current capture devices come with accompanying software that you can use with the capture device. Before starting the **Capture Wizard**, make sure that these programs are closed. This precaution helps to avoid errors within the **Capture Wizard**.

Microsoft Producer cannot capture video and audio if another program is using the device. For example, if you have a Web camera and a standalone program that lets you record from the Web camera, the program is using the video device even if you are only viewing the video and not recording it. Therefore, you cannot use the Web camera to capture video in Microsoft Producer until the standalone program is closed and the device is no longer in use. This applies to other capture devices or recording devices, such as a digital or analog video camera, microphone, or TV tuner card you may have attached to your computer.

Preparing the Office

Chapter 5 discusses how you can prepare your office for recording video and audio. You can apply many of the suggestions listed there before you capture content in Producer. By following these suggestions, you can save time and increase the quality of the captured content.

If you are recording in an office and it is feasible, try to avoid events that could interrupt you if you are recording content live into Producer. Place a note on the door informing people that you are recording. This may help to avoid interruptions. Other occurrences can interrupt your recording, such as a ringing phone or sounds from your computer. Avoiding these interruptions or distractions can help you work more quickly, so you can avoid unnecessary retakes when you are recording your video and audio into Producer.

Making Sure Capture Devices Are Working Properly

As discussed earlier in this book, there are many different devices you can use to capture video and audio in Producer. Make sure that these devices are connected and working properly before you start capturing video. By ensuring that the capture and recording devices, such as a Web camera, analog camera, or DV camera, are working properly, you can avoid issues that could arise during the capturing process. For more information about how different recording devices and capture devices can be connected and installed on your computer, see chapter 4.

Checking Network Permissions

After capturing any video, audio, or still images in Producer, you will be required to save the captured digital media file. If you are working on a corporate network and you plan to save the captured digital media files on a shared network location, make sure you have sufficient network permission to save and view the file from the shared location.

A good way to do this is to open My Network Places, add the shared network location, and make sure you can open that location and save files to it. This way, when you want to save your captured content in one central location, you can then simply save the files to that shared network location. Of course, you will probably want to save the files to a location on your hard disk as well. Saving files on your local hard disk can prevent performance issues that you may encounter when editing the project where the files are stored on a shared network location. Network traffic can interfere with performance when you are editing a project and later publishing it as a presentation.

When creating a project in Microsoft Producer, it is a good idea to keep the Microsoft Producer project (which has an .MSProducer file name extension) and the associated source files in one location. This can help you keep your projects better organized.

Starting the Capture Wizard

You can begin capturing video, audio, or still images in Microsoft Producer by first starting the **Capture Wizard**. You can access this wizard in two different places in Producer: through the **New Presentation Wizard** or through the **Tools** menu. Each way offers its own advantages.

Starting the Capture Wizard through the New Presentation Wizard

The **Capture Wizard** can be started from within the **New Presentation Wizard** if you click **Capture** on the **Import or Capture Audio and Video** page. This option lets you capture new content to your computer while you are creating a new project through the **New Presentation Wizard**. Therefore, if you have existing audio and video files that you want to import into the new project but you also want to capture new content, you can do both while creating a new presentation through the wizard.

Figure 8.1 shows the page in the **New Presentation Wizard** from which you can start the **Capture Wizard**.

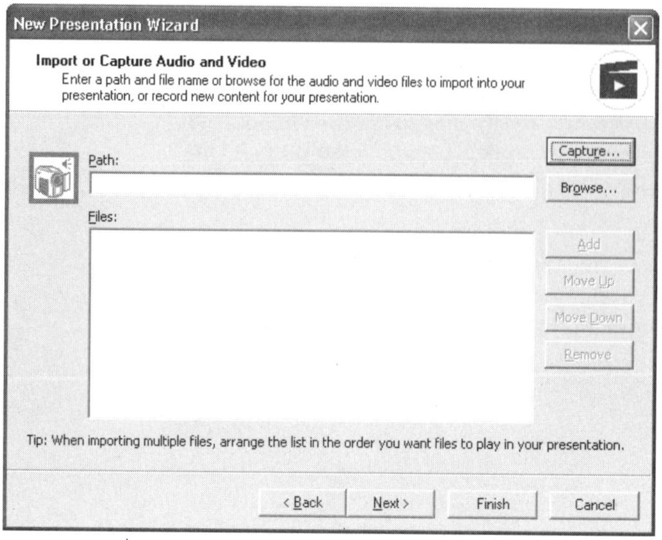

Figure 8.1 — Starting the **Capture Wizard** in the **New Presentation Wizard**.

The main benefit of using the **Capture Wizard** through the **New Presentation Wizard** is that you can start and create a project by using the **New Presentation Wizard**, regardless of whether the audio, video, and still images are already stored on your computer. As mentioned in the previous chapter, when you complete the **New Presentation Wizard**, all the content you capture or select is automatically imported into the current project and added to the timeline. You can then immediately start editing the contents on the timeline to continue working on your new project.

This is not true when you start and use the **Capture Wizard** by clicking **Capture** on the **Tools** menu. The video you capture is imported into the current project, but it is not automatically added to the timeline unless you narrate slides with video or audio. Therefore, you must add any other video, audio, or still images to the timeline before you can begin using them in your project.

Starting the Capture Wizard through the Tools Menu

The **Capture Wizard** can also be started by clicking **Capture** on the **Tools** menu. This launches the same **Capture Wizard** that is launched through the **New Presentation Wizard**. However, if you choose to create a new project without using the **New Presentation Wizard**, this is the method you must use to capture video, audio, or still images to use in your project. As you become more familiar with Microsoft Producer, you may find that you can begin to create a new project more quickly on your own rather than by using the **New Presentation Wizard**.

Figure 8.2 shows how you can start the **Capture Wizard** by using the **Capture** command on the **Tools** menu.

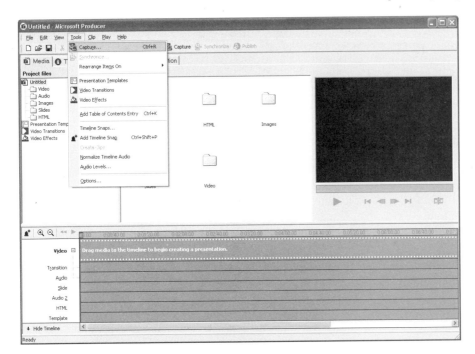

Figure 8.2 — Starting the **Capture Wizard** from the **Capture** command on the **Tools** menu.

Starting the **Capture Wizard** from the **Tools** menu enables you to capture new content to your computer for an existing project. For example, you may be editing a project on the timeline and realize that you need to capture additional content to complete the presentation. Instead of having to start your project over (which is what you would have to do if you wanted to use the **New Presentation Wizard**), you could start the **Capture Wizard** and then capture the desired content for your project. You would then need to add the new content to the timeline. Except for when you narrate slides with video or audio, captured content is not automatically added to the timeline as it is when you capture audio, video, or still images through the **Capture Wizard** in the **New Presentation Wizard**.

Using the Capture Wizard

The capture option you choose depends on the type of content you want to capture and use in your presentation. Your presentations will often contain a variety of recordings. The capturing options are based on the different types of presentations you can create in Microsoft Producer and the content you need for each.

To help you determine which capture option to use, a brief description of the selected capture option appears in the **Description** area on the **Capture Video, Audio, or Still Images** page of the **Capture Wizard**.

Figure 8.3 shows the first page of the **Capture Wizard**. This page appears whether you start the **Capture Wizard** through the **New Presentation Wizard** or through the **Capture** command on the **Tools** menu.

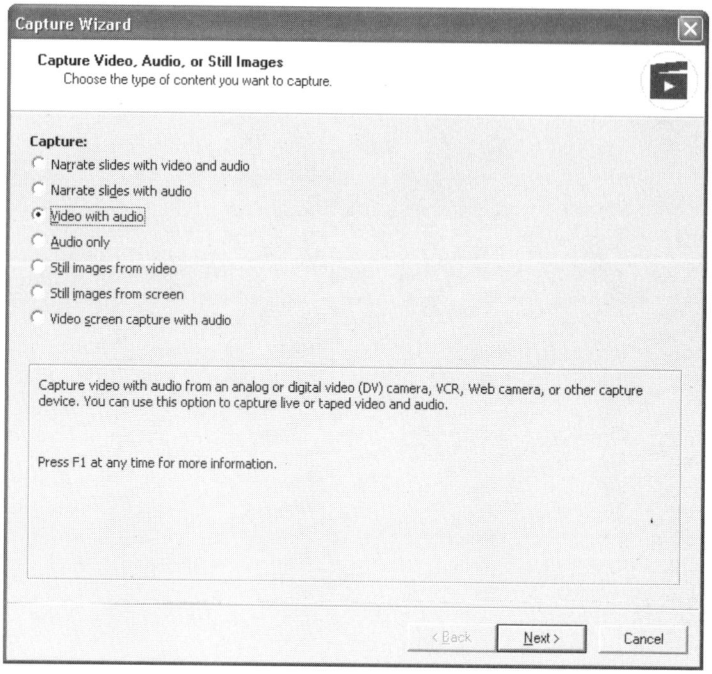

Figure 8.3 — The first page of the **Capture Wizard**.

As you use the different capture options, you will notice that several pages within the **Capture Wizard** are repeated, often with only slight differences. This helps make the capturing process simpler because many of the same tasks apply regardless of the capture option you choose. This occurs for common tasks you perform when capturing, such as choosing your capture settings, choosing capture devices, and capturing the actual video and audio to your computer.

Most likely, you will use the **Capture Wizard** more than once while creating a presentation. For example, you may need to first capture audio and video from a Web camera using the **Video with audio** option. You may then need to capture still images from your computer screen.

After you save a captured file, you can then capture more content by using the **Back** button on the **Capture Wizard** to go back to the **Capture Video, Audio, or Still Images** page and selecting the appropriate capture option.

On the first page of the **Capture Wizard**, some capture options may be shaded and cannot be selected. This occurs if you do not have the capture device that is necessary for that specific type of capture. For example, if you do not have a video recording device installed on your computer, the capture options which include video, such as **Narrate slides with video and audio**, **Video with audio**, and **Still images from video** are shaded and cannot be selected. These options may also appear shaded if you have a capture device attached to your computer, but it is not detected by Producer.

The following sections include detailed information about the different capture options you can choose in the **Capture Wizard**. These sections are organized by the different types of content you can capture. In each of the sections about capture options, you will find the following:

- Information about the capture options.

- Brief usage scenarios that provide examples of how the captured content could be used in different types of presentations.

- Detailed information about the specific page of the wizard with which audio, video, or still images are captured.

- Step-by-step procedures for using the **Capture Wizard** to capture the specified type of content.

Narrating Slides with Video and Audio

Microsoft Producer lets you narrate your slides with audio and video or with audio only, depending on the type of content you want to include in your presentation. When you narrate slides, the narration content is separated into clips that correspond to the individual slides.

To use either the **Narrate slides with video and audio** or **Narrate slides with audio** capture options, you must first import the slides or still images and add them to the **Slide** track on the timeline.

The video and audio you capture to narrate the slides is synchronized with either the entire slide or an individual slide animation or transition that appears within the slide. You can synchronize the audio and video with the entire slide—without animations or transitions—by clearing the slide animations and transitions check boxes in the **General** tab of the **Options** dialog box before importing the PowerPoint presentation.

If you capture video with audio for a narration, your captured file is saved as a Windows Media Video (WMV) file with a .wmv file name extension. If you capture audio only for the narration, then your captured file is saved as a Windows Media Audio (WMA) file with a .wma file name extension. Video clips and their associated audio clips appear on the **Video** and **Audio** tracks above the corresponding slide or still image on the **Slide** track. Likewise, if you narrate your slides with audio only, the corresponding audio clips appear below the slide on the **Audio 2** track of the timeline.

If you later decide that you need to rearrange the order of the slides, audio, or video on the timeline, you can quickly determine where you need to move the corresponding video, audio, or slides so that all the different elements remain synchronized after they are moved.

Figure 8.4 shows how the audio of a speaker's voice that is narrating slides is separated into pieces of audio that correspond to the slides.

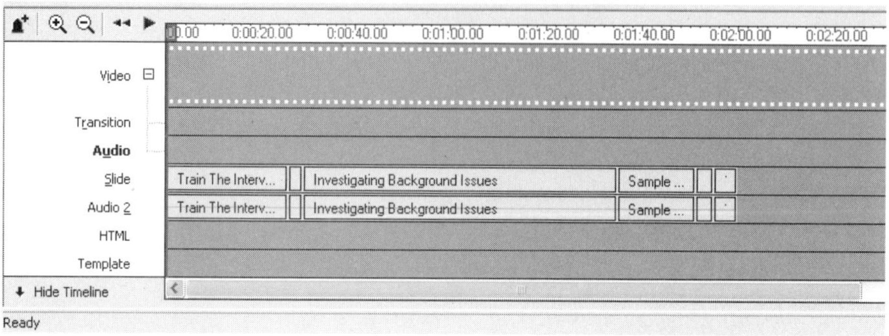

Figure 8.4 — An audio track used to narrate slides.

You can capture audio and video content for narration purposes from a variety of capture and recording devices, such as a Web camera, analog or DV camera, standalone microphone, or VCR. While you are capturing the content, it can be synchronized with the slides on the timeline.

The following are some examples of when you might choose this capture option.

- **Educational courses**. Distance learning is becoming more prevalent at many universities. Often, the presenter has a set of Microsoft PowerPoint slides that he or she uses to conduct and teach the class. The presenter may decide to record video or audio of the presentation. The instructor, or presenter, could then quickly create an on-demand presentation of the class and synchronize the audio or video with any PowerPoint slides used during the original class.

    Therefore, if any students were absent or unable to attend the class, they could play the on-demand presentation of the class they missed. Students who were at the class, but wanted to hear the lecture (or parts of the lecture) again could also play back the presentation to review the class.

    In addition to distance learning, corporations could create online training courses. The process is the same; you could capture video of a training session, and then use the video and audio to narrate the slides. This enables employees to watch the online training from their desktop computers at any time.

- **Corporate communications**. Many enterprises span cities, states, and even countries. Because of this, it can be impossible to gather all employees together at one time so that an employee, manager, or CEO can deliver a corporate message. In this situation, you could capture video of the manager speaking and using any slides, which may contain charts or graphs, and synchronize the audio and video with the appropriate slides.

You could then post the presentation on a corporate intranet site for employees to watch. You can even use network permissions to control access the intranet site, thereby protecting sensitive company information. This lets employees view important information regardless of time or location.

Step-by-Step: Narrating Slides with Audio and Video

The following procedure describes the step-by-step process for narrating slides with video and audio.

In the steps below, narrating slides with both video and audio or with audio only are explained simultaneously, because they follow the same basic steps in the wizard. The only difference is that video is not captured (and, therefore, not displayed) if you choose the audio-only option.

1. Import and add the slides or still images you want to narrate to the **Slide** track on the timeline.

2. Depending on the capture device you have connected to your computer and the content you are capturing with your slides, do one of the following:

   - If you are using a DV camera or analog camera to narrate slides from previously taped video and audio, turn on the device and switch the camera to the playback mode (usually labeled VCR or VTR).

   - If you are using a VCR to capture video and audio from tape, make sure the VCR is on.

   - If you are using a DV camera, analog camera, or Web camera to capture live video or audio, turn on the device and switch the DV or analog camera to the correct position to record live video.

   - If you are using a standalone microphone to capture live audio, make sure the microphone is connected to your computer. The input jack is usually labeled "Microphone" or "Mic."

3. On the **Tools** menu, click **Capture**.

4. On the **Capture Video, Audio, or Still Images** page of the **Capture Wizard**, choose one of the following capture options, and then click **Next**:

   - Click **Narrate slides with video and audio** if you want to narrate your slides with both video and audio.

   - Click the **Narrate slides with audio** option if you want to narrate your slides with audio only.

If you are using a DV camera and are narrating slides, the audio is not played back on your computer. Therefore, make sure the volume on the camera is set high enough that you can hear the audio to properly narrate and synchronize the audio with the slides.

5. If video or audio already appears on the timeline, one of the dialog boxes shown in Figures 8.5 and 8.6 appears. Do one of the following:

   • Click **Yes** if you want to clear the **Video** track (or **Audio 2** track, if you captured audio only). The narration you capture will then be added to the appropriate track of the timeline after completing the wizard.

   • Click **No** if you do not want to clear the **Video** track (or **Audio 2** track). The narration will be imported into the project, but it will not be added to the timeline.

   • Click **Cancel** to return to the **Capture Video, Audio, or Still Images** page of the **Capture Wizard**.

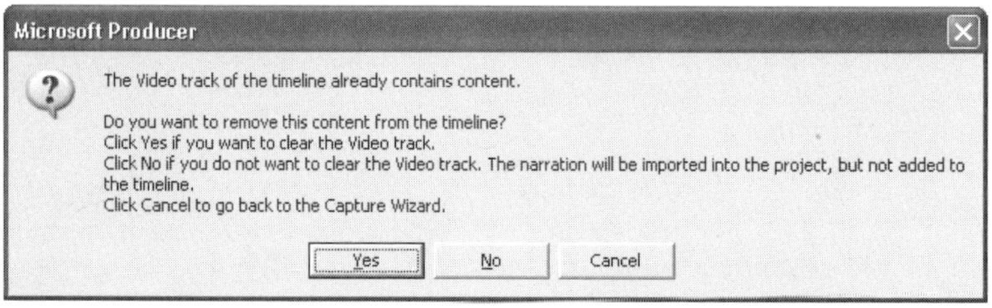

Figure 8.5 — This dialog box appears if video is already on the **Video** track.

Figure 8.6 — This dialog box appears if audio is already on the **Audio 2** track.

6. The next page depends on whether you chose to capture video or just audio. The two different pages that can appear are as follows. After you choose the capture setting, click **Next**.

   • If you chose to narrate your slides with video and audio, the **Capture Video and Audio** page appears, and you can choose capture settings for capturing video with audio.

   You should choose your capture settings based on the type of video you are capturing and the connection rate that your audience will most likely use to watch your final presentation. For example, if your presentation contains a stationary speaker—a "talking head" video, or someone standing at a podium—and you plan to use a presentation template with a small video display (240x180), you could choose the **Typical** capture setting.

If you are unsure about the presentation template you will use, choose a capture setting that displays the video at a larger display size. If you later choose a presentation template that has a smaller display size, the video will still display correctly. Guidelines for choosing capture settings are discussed later in this chapter.

- If you chose to narrate your slides with audio only, the **Capture Audio** page appears, and you can choose capture settings for recording audio only.

  Like choosing the capture setting for video, you should choose your audio capture settings based on the type of audio you are capturing and the connection rate that your audience will most likely use to watch your final presentation.

  For example, if your presentation contains a speaker who is talking, and you plan to use an audio-only presentation template, you could choose the **Typical** capture setting. This lets you capture audio that is well-suited for voice and mixed audio. Again, guidelines for choosing capture settings are discussed later in this chapter.

7. The options available on the **Choose Capture Devices** page depend on whether you chose to narrate slides with video or with audio only. The options also depend on the types of capture devices that are connected to your computer.

   Whether a separate input source for video can be selected depends on the type of video capture device you are using and its software drivers. Details about video capture devices and the combination of video and audio sources you can select are discussed later in this chapter.

   Click **Next** after you have selected and configured your capture devices.

8. Choose the appropriate options in the **Capture Wizard** as follows before capturing the video or audio to narrate your slides.

   - Select or clear the **Show preview** check box. This check box only appears if you have chosen to narrate your slides with video and audio.

     To preserve your computer's system resources when capturing video and audio, it is recommended that you clear the **Show preview** check box. This can help improve the overall quality of the video and audio that is captured. Many DV or analog cameras have built-in LCD panels and speakers that let you see the video and hear the audio you are capturing. You can use the LCD panel and built-in speaker to preview the content instead.

   - Select the **Mute speakers** check box if you are capturing live video and audio. Muting the speakers prevents audio from being played back on the speakers, which can distract from the audio you are capturing for your narration.

- Move the **Input level** slider up or down to increase or decrease the volume of the captured audio.

  When adjusting the **Input level** slider, try to avoid reaching the red levels while you are recording. You can test the volume by speaking into the audio device and seeing how the levels move up or down on the **Input level** meter. If the meter reaches the red levels when recording, the captured audio will be unclear and distorted. Try to avoid low volume levels as well (readings on the lower third of the meter) because the volume of the captured audio may be too low and difficult to hear.

  If you are using a DV camera for capturing, the **Input level** slider does not appear.

- Click **Previous Slide** or **Next Slide** until the first slide you want to narrate appears in the **Slide** window.

9. Depending on whether you are capturing live or taped audio and video to narrate your slides, do one of the following:

   - If you are capturing taped video or audio, make sure the playback device is set to the playback mode (often labeled VTR or VCR on a camera), cue the tape to the part you want to capture, and then press the play button.

   - If you are using a DV camera connected to an IEEE 1394 port, you can use the **Digital video camera controls** to locate the section of video and audio on the tape that you want to capture to narrate your slides. When you click **Capture**, the tape plays back automatically.

   - If you are capturing live video, focus the camera on the subject you want to capture.

10. Click **Capture** to begin capturing video or audio.

    As you narrate your slides, click **Next Slide** to go to the next slide on the timeline after you have finished narrating the slide currently displayed in the **Slide** window.

    If your slides contain animations, click **Next Effect** when you have narrated the current part of the slide and you want to move to and narrate the following animation.

11. After you have finished narrating your slides, click **Stop**. If you are capturing taped video or audio from an analog camera or VCR, press the stop button on your camera or VCR as well.

    If you are using a DV camera, the tape will stop playing back automatically when you press the **Stop** button in the **Capture Wizard**.

12. In the **File name** box, type the name for the captured Windows Media file. Click **Save**, and then click **Finish**.

    The narration will be saved as a WMV file if you captured video, or it will be saved as a WMA file if you captured audio only.

13. After you complete the **Capture Wizard**, video and audio is separated into clips and added to the timeline. The video or audio clips have the same names as the slides they narrate. Click **Finish** to end the **Capture Wizard**.

Clips are added to the project as follows:

- If you narrated slides with video, the captured video file is separated into clips and added to the **Video** track on the timeline.

- If you narrated slides with audio only, the captured audio file is separated into clips on the timeline and added to the **Audio 2** track.

- If you had video and audio content on the timeline before you captured the audio or video narration, and you did not choose to clear the timeline when prompted by the wizard, the audio and video is imported into the current project, but it is not added to the timeline.

   If you captured video, it is separated into clips that have the same names as the slides they narrate, and then stored in the **Video** folder.

   If you captured audio only, the audio file is stored in the **Audio** folder. To match the slides with the audio narration, add the audio file to the **Audio 2** track of the timeline so that it starts at the same point as the first slide that was narrated.

Capturing Video and Audio

Choosing the **Video with audio** capture option lets you record live or taped video and audio to your computer. The video sources you can record from include a Web camera, DV camera, analog video camera, or an analog or digital VCR. The video sources you can choose depend on the capture devices installed on your computer.

Choosing the **Audio only** capture option lets you record live or taped audio to your computer. You can capture from audio-only sources, such as a microphone, or you can capture audio from a video source.

The video you capture is stored on your computer as a WMV file. When you finish the **Capture Wizard**, the saved WMV file is automatically imported into your current project. It is stored in the **Video** folder on the **Media** tab.

If you choose **Audio only**, the audio you capture is stored on your computer as a WMA file. The saved WMA file is automatically imported into your current project. It is stored in the **Audio** folder on the **Media** tab.

The following are examples of scenarios in which you might choose to use the **Video with audio** or **Audio only** capture options.

- **Video of a recorded or live training course**. If you are creating a training presentation, whether it is computer-related or not, you might choose to record video of the trainer so you can use the footage in your online training presentation.

- **Video from a recorded or live presenter**. You might record a live presentation directly into Producer. This presentation could feature someone introducing a new product or service, an internal corporate event, an earnings statement, or an online company meeting. The video or audio captured at the event could later be supplemented with PowerPoint slides.

- **Capturing supporting video for your presentations**. Your live or recorded video footage might support the message you are trying to convey in your presentation. For example, an automobile maker might want to show video of a new car.

Step-by-Step: Capturing Video or Audio

The following procedure describes the step-by-step process for capturing video or audio. These two options follow the same basic steps in the wizard.

1. Depending on the capture device you have connected to your computer and the content you are capturing, do one of the following:

   - If you are using a DV camera or analog camera, turn on the device and switch the camera to the playback mode (usually labeled VCR or VTR).

   - If you are using a VCR, make sure the VCR is on.

   - If you are using a DV camera, analog camera, or Web camera to capture live video or audio, turn on the device and switch the DV and analog camera to the correct mode to record live vidco.

   - If you are using a standalone microphone to capture audio, make sure the microphone is plugged into the appropriate line on your computer, usually labeled "Microphone" or "Mic."

2. Do one of the following to start the **Capture Wizard**:

   - On the **Import or Capture Audio and Video** page of the **New Presentation Wizard**, click **Capture**.

   - On the **Tools** menu, click **Capture**.

3. On the **Capture Video, Audio, or Still Images** page of the **Capture Wizard**, choose one of the following capture options, and then click **Next**:

   - Click **Video with audio** if you want to capture video with audio.

   - Click **Audio only** if you want to capture audio only. You can use this option to capture only the audio portion of a video source, if necessary.

4. The next page depends on whether you chose to capture audio and video or audio only. The two different pages that can appear are as follows. After you choose the capture setting, click **Next**.

   - If you chose to capture video, the **Capture Video and Audio** page appears, and you can choose capture settings for capturing video with audio. You should choose your capture settings based on the type of video you are capturing and the connection rate that your audience will most likely use to watch your final presentation.

For example, if your presentation contains high-motion video, you plan to use a presentation template with a large video display (480x360), and your audience will watch your presentation over a LAN or broadband connection, you might click **More choices**, and then select the **Large video display (480x360) for delivery at 300 Kbps** capture setting. Guidelines for choosing capture settings are discussed later in this chapter.

- If you chose to capture audio only, the **Capture Audio** page appears, and you can choose capture settings for capturing audio only. As with video, choose your audio capture settings based on the type of audio you are capturing and the connection rate that your audience will most likely use to watch your final presentation.

  For example, if you plan to use an audio-only presentation template and your audience will most likely watch your final presentation over a LAN or broadband connection, you could then click **More choices** and select the **High quality audio for delivery at 128 Kbps** capture setting. Guidelines for choosing capture settings are discussed later in this chapter.

5. The **Choose Capture Devices** page depends on whether you chose to capture video or audio and the types of capture devices you have connected to your computer.

   Whether a separate input source for video can be selected depends on the type of video capture device you are using and its software driver. Details about video capture devices and the combination of video and audio sources you can select are discussed later in this chapter.

   Click **Next** after you have selected and configured your capture devices.

6. Choose the appropriate options in the **Capture Wizard** as follows before capturing your audio and video or audio only:

   - To preserve system resources when capturing video and audio, clear the **Show preview** check box. This can help preserve valuable system resources and can help to improve the overall quality of the video and audio that is captured. Many DV or analog cameras have built-in LCD panels and speakers that you can use to preview the content.

   - Select the **Mute speakers** check box if you are capturing live audio. Muting the speakers prevents the audio from being played back on your computer's speakers, which can distract from audio you are capturing.

   - Move the **Input level** slider up or down to increase or decrease the volume of the captured audio.

     When adjusting the **Input level** slider, try to minimize the volume sensitivity so that the recording levels do not go into the red. You can test the volume by speaking into the audio device and seeing how the levels move up or down on the **Input level** meter.

If you are using a DV camera for capturing, the **Input level** slider does not appear.

- Select the **Capture time limit** check box to set the amount of capturing time. After the time limit expires, capturing stops automatically.

- Select the **Create clips** check box if you want your video to be separated into clips after you save the WMV file and it is imported into the current project.

7. Depending on whether you are capturing live or taped audio and video, do one of the following:

   - If you are capturing taped video or audio, make sure the device is set to the playback mode (often labeled VTR or VCR on a camera), cue the tape to the part you want to capture, and then press the play button.

   - If you are using a DV camera connected to an IEEE 1394 port, you can use the **Digital video camera controls** to locate the section of the video and audio that you want to capture. The tape begins playing automatically when you click the **Capture** button.

   - If you are capturing live video or audio, focus the camera on the person or thing you want to record.

   - If you are capturing live audio from a standalone microphone, make sure the microphone is attached properly.

8. Click **Capture** to begin capturing.

9. After you have finished capturing video or audio, click **Stop**. If you are capturing taped video or audio from an analog camera or VCR, press the stop button on your playback device as well. If you are capturing from a DV camera, the tape stops playing automatically.

   If you selected the **Capture time limit** check box, capturing stops automatically once the time limit has expired. Therefore, you do not need to click **Stop**. However, you can click **Stop** to end capturing at any time.

10. In the **File name** box, type a name for the captured Windows Media file. Click **Save**, and then click **Finish** to complete the **Capture Wizard**.

    The file will be saved as a WMV file if you captured video, or as a WMA file if you captured audio only.

    After you complete the **Capture Wizard**, the video and audio is imported into the current project. If you captured video with audio, the video is stored in the **Video** folder. If you captured audio only, the audio is stored in the **Audio** folder.

Capturing Still Images from Video

With taped or live video, you may have some individual shots that illustrate the point or message you are trying to convey to your audience. For these shots, you can capture a still image from a video source to use in your presentation. You may also find that you want to capture still images from your video and narrate them along with your slides. The **Capture Wizard** enables you to capture these still images from a video source.

Still images are saved as JPEG image files with a .jpg file name extension. Because the still images are captured as JPEGs, you can edit them in most image editing programs.

Step-by-Step: Capturing Still Images

The following procedure describes the step-by-step process for capturing still images from video.

1. Depending on the capture devices you have connected to your computer and the content you are capturing, do one of the following:

   - If you are using a DV camera or analog video camera to capture still images from taped video, turn on the device and switch the camera to the playback mode (usually labeled VCR or VTR).

   - If you are using a VCR to capture still images from tape, make sure the VCR is on.

   - If you are using a DV camera, analog camera, or Web camera to capture still images from live video, turn on the device and switch it to the correct position to record live video and audio.

2. Do one of the following to start the **Capture Wizard**:

   - On the **Import or Capture Audio and Video** page of the **New Presentation Wizard**, click **Capture**.

   - On the **Tools** menu, click **Capture**.

3. On the **Capture Video, Audio, or Still Images** page, click **Still images from video**, then click **Next**.

4. The **Choose Capture Devices** page appears, and you can select the capture device (and the appropriate input source, if available) to use. Click **Next** after you have selected and configured your capture devices.

5. Depending on whether you are capturing still images from live or taped video, do one of the following:

   - If you are capturing still images from taped video, make sure the playback device is set to the correct playback mode (often labeled VTR or VCR on a video camera), cue the tape to the part you want to capture, and then press the play button.

Press the pause button on the camera when you see the frame you want to capture as a still image.

- If you are using a DV camera connected to an IEEE 1394 port, you can use the **Digital video camera controls** to locate the frame of the taped video that you want to capture, and then click **Pause**.

- If you are capturing live video, focus the camera on the subject you want to capture in a still image.

6. Click **Browse** to select the location to which you want to save your captured still image. The path and file name for the saved image is displayed in the **File name** box.

   The default name for the first image you capture is Picture_0001.jpg and the second image you capture is saved as Picture_0002.jpg, and so forth. However, you can replace the prefix of the file name, Picture, with any name you want to help you find and organize your still images.

7. For each still image you want to capture, click **Capture Image**.

8. Click **Finish** to complete the **Capture Wizard**. The captured still images are imported into the current project and stored in the **Images** folder.

Capturing Images from Your Computer Screen

Still images you capture from your computer screen are saved as Portable Network Graphics (PNG) files with a .png file name extension. PNG files are bit-mapped images that are well-suited to display images that have similar blocks of color. This is often the case with different parts of the Microsoft Windows operating system, such as dialog boxes, title bars, menu bars, and so forth.

This capture option can be used for software-related presentations ranging from software training to marketing a new software application. The following list provides some brief examples of how you could use still images captured from your computer screen in your presentations.

- **Software training**. During software training, the instructor shows different features of a program. The training presentation might even contain "tutorials" that students can use to learn the program. In your Producer presentation, you could include a screen shot of the correct settings in a dialog box for successful completion of the task, or some other appropriate user interface item.

- **Marketing new software**. Screen shots are often used when new software is being sold or marketed. Think about some new software you may have purchased or seen advertised on the Web. Many times the packaging or advertising has some screen shots to show the user interface. You can use Producer to capture these types of still images to show a new product and the basic elements of the user interface.

- **Introducing a new or revised Web site**. You can capture screen shots of a Web site as it displays in a Web browser. This is useful if you have a new Web site or intranet site that you want to introduce to potential users. You can take screen shots of the Web site and explain what its features are used for.

Step-by-Step: Capturing Screen Images

The following procedure describes the step-by-step process for capturing still images from your computer screen.

1. Do one of the following to start the **Capture Wizard**:

   - On the **Import or Capture Audio and Video** page of the **New Presentation Wizard**, click **Capture**.

   - On the **Tools** menu, click **Capture**.

2. On the **Capture Video, Audio, or Still Images** page, select **Still images from screen**. Click **Next**.

3. Do one of the following in the **Capture Wizard**:

   - To capture an image of an area of the screen, click **Select Region**. Your cursor changes to look like crosshairs. Use the crosshairs to click and drag a box to specify the area of the screen you want to capture.

   - Drag the **Capture icon** over the area of the screen you want to capture as shown in Figure 8.7. You can resize the capture window to adjust the area you want to capture.

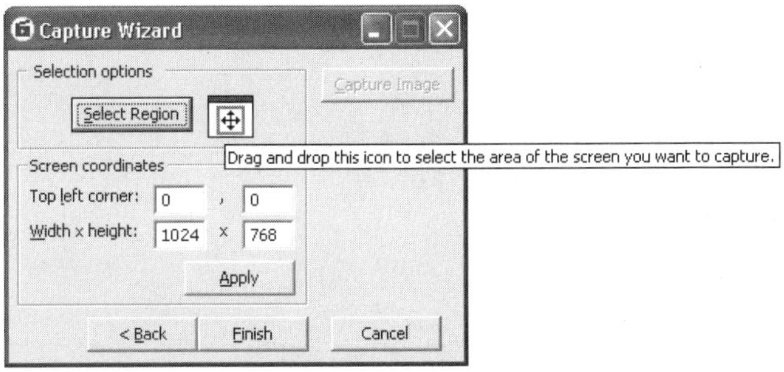

Figure 8.7 — The **Capture icon**.

When you select an area of the screen by using the **Capture icon**, individual elements in the screen are selected in a rectangular box. For example, if you wanted to capture an image of a toolbar, drag the icon on the toolbar you want to capture and drop it on the toolbar. If you wanted to capture the entire window of a software application, drag the icon over the title bar of the application window and drop it.

- Type the screen coordinates of the area you want to capture. Enter the top-left corner coordinates in the **Top left corner** boxes, and then type the width and height of the area you want to capture in the **Width x height** boxes. Click **Apply** to select the specified are of the screen.

4. Click **Capture Image** to capture the selected area of the screen. When you click **Capture Image**, the **Capture Wizard** dialog box is minimized so it is not included in the image.

5. In the **File name** box, type a name for the captured image, and then click **Save**. The captured image is saved as a PNG file and then imported into the current project and stored in the **Images** folder.

6. You can repeat steps 3 through 6 to capture and save additional images from your computer screen. Click **Finish** to complete the wizard.

Capturing Video from Your Computer Screen

Screen capture videos let you show your audience what is occurring on your computer screen. This enables you to demonstrate tasks on a computer that would be difficult to describe solely with words and text.

You can use the following types of capture devices to capture the audio:

- Standalone microphone

- Web camera with a built-in microphone

- Analog video camera

A DV camera cannot be used to capture audio when you are capturing video from your computer screen.

The video screen capture is saved as a WMV file. Like other video you capture in Microsoft Producer, the video screen captures are added to the current project.

This capture option is often used for software-related presentations ranging from training to marketing. The following list provides some brief examples of how you could use video screen captures with audio in your presentations.

- **Software training**. In this type of presentation, you may be focusing on how several of the program's features can be used to complete tasks. Capturing video of your computer screen while demonstrating the keystrokes or mouse actions needed lets you both show and describe how to complete common tasks.

  Your organization might create and distribute a CD that contains licensed software that the students or employees need in order to connect to the organization's network. This type of CD could also contain a Microsoft Producer presentation that shows how to install, configure, and use the software.

- **Marketing a new application**. Software marketing presentations come in many forms and at different points in a product's development cycle. Many times, marketing personnel may be showing software that is not yet available for public distribution. However, you can create a presentation to show the prospective customer what the user interface will look like and how the software can be used. This could be more useful than just showing static images.

- **Product support and customer service**. Product support departments may encounter commonly asked questions or problems. You could create presentations that focus on the solutions to these common issues and then direct users to these presentations as a first resource for solving problems. These presentations could use video screen captures to demonstrate common configuration or troubleshooting tasks.

Tips for Successful Video Screen Captures

When capturing video from your computer screen using Microsoft Producer, keeping a few simple guidelines in mind can increase the effectiveness and the quality of the video you capture.

- **Quit unused applications**. Each open software application uses system resources. Just as when you capture video or audio from a capture device, you should close any unnecessary software applications that are not part of your video screen capture.

- **Hide bitmap images when possible**. Bitmap images, such as images that might appear on the desktop, may not appear optimally in a video screen capture. This occurs because there is a reduced number of colors that can be captured and displayed properly in a video screen capture. You can avoid this issue by setting your desktop background to a solid color.

- **Avoid unnecessary mouse movements**. Unnecessary or quick mouse movements may not be displayed correctly in your video screen capture due to the low number of frames per second (fps) that are captured (approximately 5 to 10 fps; other video is captured at 15 or 30 fps). Objects move more smoothly and with greater clarity when video is captured at a higher number of frames per second. Therefore, as you move an object during a video screen capture, the object may display unevenly if it is moved quickly. When you type or select check boxes or option buttons, do these actions slowly to improve the overall quality of the video screen capture.

- **Match the video display size with the appropriate presentation template**. As mentioned earlier in this chapter, you can improve the quality of the video in your presentation by applying a presentation template that displays video at the size it was captured. This is especially true when working with video screen captures.

Step-by-Step: Capturing Video from Your Computer Screen

The following procedure describes the step-by-step process for capturing video from your computer screen.

1. Do one of the following to start the **Capture Wizard**:

   - On the **Import or Capture Audio and Video** page of the **New Presentation Wizard**, click **Capture**.

   - On the **Tools** menu, click **Capture**.

2. On the **Capture Video, Audio, or Still Images** page, click **Video screen capture with audio**. Click **Next**.

3. On the **Choose Capture Devices** page, select the audio capture device (and input line if necessary) to use for capturing the audio with your video screen capture. Drag the **Input level** slider up or down to increase or decrease the recording volume level. Click **Next** to continue.

   For example, if you have a microphone attached to your sound card, you would select the sound card as the **Audio device** and select **Microphone** as the **Input source**.

   Note that audio from a DV camera cannot be used when capturing video from your computer screen. Therefore, if you have a DV camera connected to your computer, it will not be displayed in the **Audio device** box.

4. In the **Capture Wizard** dialog box (shown in Figure 8.8), do the following:

   - Select the **Minimize while capturing** check box if you want the dialog box to minimize to an icon on the taskbar while you are capturing your video screen. This prevents the dialog box from appearing in the video you capture.

   - Select the **Mute speakers** check box if you are capturing audio with your screen capture. Muting the speakers prevents audio from being played back on the speakers, which can distract from the audio you are capturing.

   - Drag the **Input level** slider up or down to increase or decrease the volume of the captured audio.

   - In the **Capture setting** box, select the capture setting that best matches the display size of the area of the screen you want to capture and the connection rate your audience will most likely use to watch your presentation.

     The capture area is shown as a square on you computer screen, and the size changes based on the capture setting you select. The area of the computer screen is a fixed size based on the capture setting you selected. Therefore, the width and height are also size based on the current capture setting.

5. Drag the box so it appears on the area of the screen you want to capture, and then click **Capture**.

   If you selected the **Minimize while capturing** check box, the dialog box appears as an icon on the taskbar and the rectangle that shows the selected area does not appear. If this check box is cleared, the **Capture Wizard** dialog box will appear in your screen capture if it appears in the selected area.

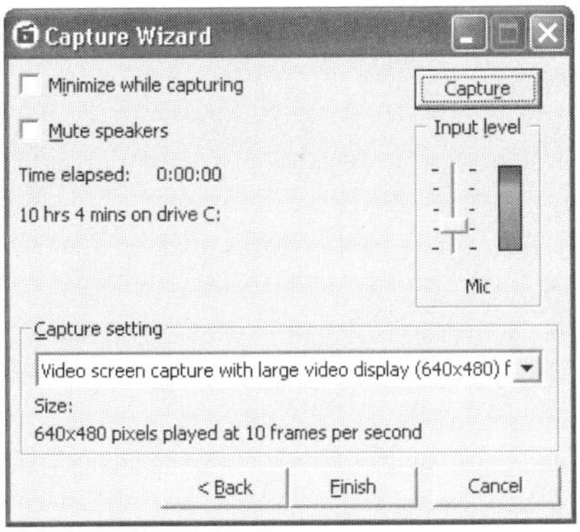

Figure 8.8 — Capturing video from your computer screen.

6. Perform the actions on your computer that you want to record for your video screen capture. If sound capture equipment is available, you can narrate the screen capture and your narration is saved as the audio portion of the screen capture video file.

7. After you have completed you screen capture, do one of the following:

   • If you selected the **Minimize while capturing** check box, click the **Stop Capturing** icon on the taskbar to stop capturing.

   • If the **Minimize while capturing** check box was cleared, click **Stop** to stop capturing.

8. In the **File name** box, type a file name for your video screen capture, and then click **Save**. Click **Finish** to complete the **Capture Wizard**.

   The video screen capture is imported into your current project, and it is stored in the **Video** folder for the current project.

Understanding Capture Settings

As you proceed through the **Capture Wizard**, you are prompted to select the capture settings for video and audio. This step occurs when you select any one of the following capture options on the first page of the **Capture Wizard**:

• **Narrate slides with video and audio**

• **Narrate slides with audio**

• **Video with audio**

• **Audio only**

• **Video screen capture with audio**

The quality of the video in your final presentation depends on the quality of the video and audio you capture. Because of this, selecting appropriate video and audio capture settings is important. The options in Producer affect the following aspects of the video and sound you capture:

- The number of video frames per second.

- The video bit rate, which is the speed at which the pieces of video, called *bits*, transfer in your video.

- The quality of the audio.

- The audio bit rate, which is the speed at which the audio transfers.

- The quality of the video and audio when the audience plays your final, published presentation.

For example, you can choose to capture video at different bit rates by using different capture settings—even though the settings use the same video display size. The number of frames per second that are captured at a higher capture setting (such as **Medium video display (320x240) for local playback**) is greater than the number of frames per second that are captured at one of the lower capture settings with the same display size (for example, **Medium video display (320x240) for delivery at 300 Kbps)**.

The higher capture setting (**Medium video display (320x240) for local playback**) captures 30 fps, whereas the lower capture setting (**Medium video display (320x240) for delivery at 300 Kbps**) only captures 15 fps. In general, as you increase the number of frames per second, motion in your video is displayed more smoothly. However, more frames per second also increases the size of the video file. Audio quality is greater when you use the higher capture setting because the audio bits transfer at a higher rate than they do with the lower capture setting.

The quality of the video and audio in your final published presentation directly depends on the quality of the original captured video and audio. As a general rule, it is always better to choose a higher capture setting when you capture the original audio and video. If you choose to capture at a lower capture setting, and you then publish your final presentation at a higher capture setting, the quality of the video and audio in your published presentation will not increase. If you then wanted to increase the quality of the video and audio in your published presentation, you would have to recapture the content at a higher capture setting, add it to the appropriate place on the timeline, and then publish your presentation again at a higher capture setting. This is especially important to remember if you need to publish your presentation audiences that may connect at different rates in order to play back your presentation.

For all profiles, you will notice that the information in the wizard changes if you choose to record video with audio or audio only. For example:

- **Best used for**. This information provides examples and suggestions for the type of capture that is best-suited for the selected setting. This information includes the recommended audience connection rate.

- **Size**. This setting identifies the display size and the number of frames per second for the selected video and audio capture setting. This setting is not displayed when you choose to capture audio only.

Considerations for Choosing Capture Settings

Chapter 7 briefly discusses capture settings and how they affect the video and audio you capture on your computer. The following are some questions you should consider, along with guidelines to help you choose the appropriate capture setting in Producer.

What Kind of Content Are You Capturing?

If you are capturing high-motion video, you would probably want to use a capture setting that has a higher bit rate, such as one of the profiles that are designed for delivery at 300 Kbps or for local playback, rather than a capture setting designed for delivery at 100 Kbps. If you use a lower capture setting, the movement of the objects might appear uneven and jerky because there is not enough video information being captured to accurately display the rapid movement. In addition, any audio captured with the video will sound better if you select the capture setting with a higher bit rate. The display size you choose depends on how you want to use the video in your presentation.

Conversely, if you have video that does contains some movement or variable noises such as a recording of person sitting and talking, but you want the video to display at a smaller display size, you can probably safely use the **Typical** capture setting.

Which Presentation Templates Are Used in Your Presentation?

Producer includes different templates that provide a variety of display sizes for video in your final published presentation. The display size is based on the template or templates that are applied to the presentation. Choose a presentation template that has the same or similar display size as the captured video, so the video does not appear stretched and distorted in the published presentation.

For example, if you capture video using the **Small video display (240x180) for delivery at 300 Kbps** capture setting, which has a display size of 240 pixels by 180 pixels, and you apply a presentation template that displays video at 640 pixels by 480 pixels, the video you captured would not be displayed correctly. The descriptions of the presentation templates include the size of the video display for the given template.

What Is the Connection Speed Viewers Will Use?

The connection speed used by your audience plays an important role in choosing the capture settings for your video and audio. If you capture video with a large display size and high bit rate, and then publish it at a higher quality setting, your audience will experience a long wait while your video and audio downloads. If your presentation is streamed and your audience has slower connection rates, the video and audio may be interrupted due to buffering.

Choosing Video and Audio Devices

Choosing the correct video and audio devices is essential to capturing high-quality content in Microsoft Producer. You must choose both the correct device and the correct source inputs. If either of these settings is incorrect, your video and audio will not be captured successfully.

The **Choose Capture Devices** page appears when you choose one of the following capture options:

- **Narrate slides with video and audio**

- **Narrate slides with audio** (Only audio devices appear)

- **Video with audio**

- **Audio only** (Only audio devices appear)

- **Still images from video** (Only video devices appear)

- **Video screen capture with audio** (Only audio devices appear)

The following sections describe common configurations when choosing the video and audio device settings on the **Choose Capture Devices** page of the **Capture Wizard**. Remember, the connections on your computer may be different due to the variety of available hardware.

Capturing Audio and Video from Analog Tape

Video device: Video capture card

Audio device: Default audio device

Input source: Line In

Capturing Audio and Video from DV Tape (IEEE 1394 Capture Card)

Video device: DV camera or VCR

Audio device: DV camera or VCR—you will need to increase the volume of you camera or VCR to hear the audio of your video. You will not hear the audio on your computer.

Input source: Already selected or not applicable

Capturing Audio and Video from DV Tape (Analog Video Capture Card)

Video device: Video capture card

Audio device: Default audio device

Input source: Line In

Capturing Live Video and Audio from a Web Camera with a Built-in Microphone

Video device: Web camera

Audio device: Web camera microphone (this must be chosen as the audio device)

Input source: Already selected or not applicable

Capturing Live Video and Audio from a Web Camera with No Microphone

Video device: Web camera

Audio device: Default audio device

Input source: Microphone or Mic (if you have a microphone attached to your computer)

Capturing Still Images from an Analog Video Camera, Web Camera, or DV Camera

Video device: Video capture card, Web camera, or DV camera

Audio device: None

Input source: None

Capturing Video from the Computer Screen with Audio

Video device: Computer screen (selected by default)

Audio device: Default audio device

Input source: Microphone or Mic (if you have a microphone attached to your computer)

Even if you do not have any capture devices, you can still use Producer. However, you will not be able to capture directly into Producer; you can only import existing digital media files to use in your project.

Video Device Drivers

For current video capture devices, two basic driver standards exist: Microsoft Video for Windows (VFW) drivers and Windows Driver Model (WDM) drivers. The only difference you are likely to see is the choices provided when you are configuring the device. A device that uses WDM drivers will have a dialog box with an extra video source input option if the device has multiple inputs, whereas a device that uses VFW drivers (or a WDM device that has only one input) will not provide this option. Figure 8.9 shows the page in the **Capture Wizard** that is displayed if your capture device uses WDM drivers and has multiple inputs.

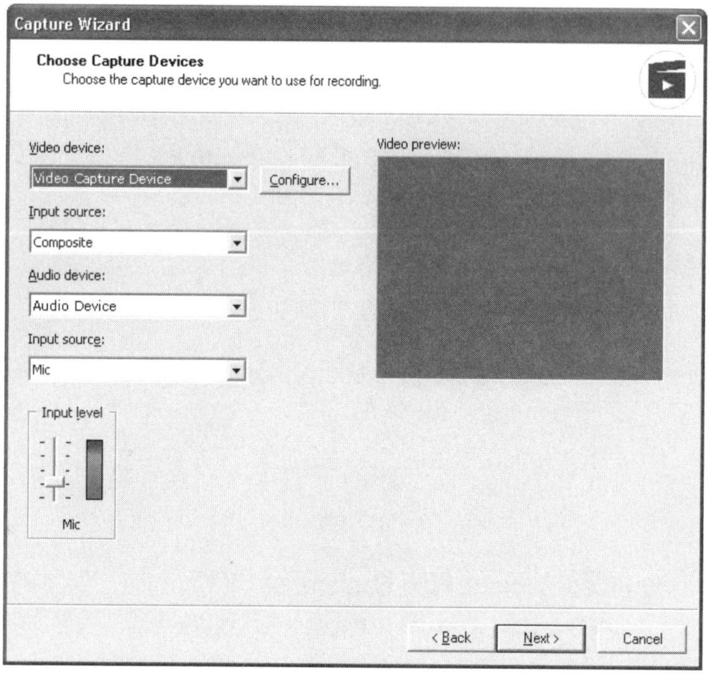

Figure 8.9 — Options for a device that uses WDM drivers and has multiple inputs.

The next two step-by-step procedures describe configuring capture devices that use VFW and WDM drivers. The capture device might be a Web camera or an analog camcorder connected to an analog capture card.

Step-by-Step: Configuring a Video Device with VFW Drivers

1. On the **Capture Video, Audio, or Still Images** page of the **Capture Wizard**, choose one of the following capture options, and then click **Next**:

   - **Narrate slides with video and audio**

   - **Video with audio**

   - **Still images from video**

2. If you chose to capture video, choose the capture setting, and then click **Next**. If you chose the **Still images from video** option, the capture setting page does not display.

   The **Choose Capture Devices** page, shown in Figure 8.10, appears.

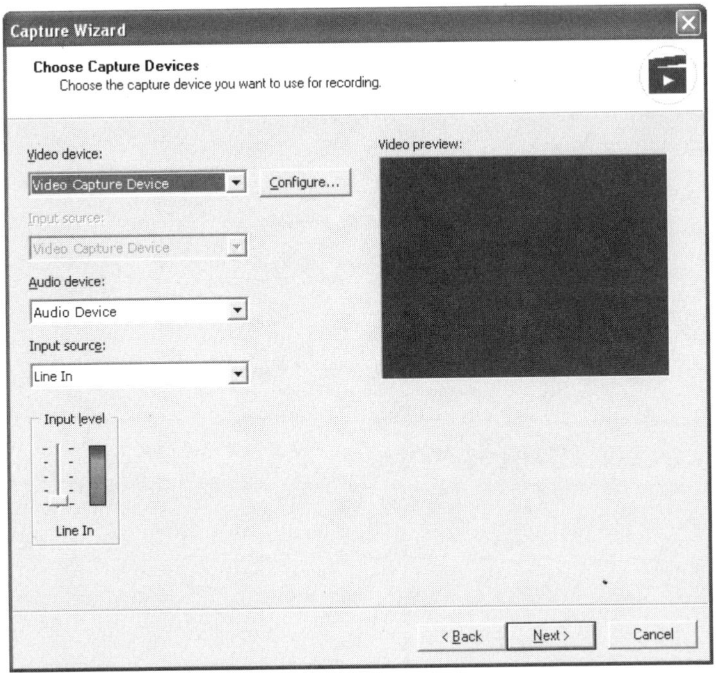

Figure 8.10 — The **Choose Capture Devices** page for a device that uses VFW drivers.

3. In the **Video device** box, select the device you want to use, and then click **Configure**.

4. The resulting dialog box depends on the manufacturer of your capture device and the accompanying software. Typically, in this dialog box you can control capture settings such as:

   - Video connection to use

   - Image size

   - Standard to use, usually NTSC or PAL

   - Image format

   - Brightness, contrast, hue, and saturation

5. After you apply the changes, move the **Input level** slider up or down to increase or decrease the volume of the captured audio.

6. After you have made these changes and other changes, click **Next** to continue the **Capture Wizard**.

Step-by-Step: Configuring a Video Device with WDM Drivers

1. On the **Capture Video, Audio, or Still Images** page of the **Capture Wizard**, select one of the following capture options that lets you capture video from an attached recording or video capture device, and then click **Next**:

   - **Narrate slides with video and audio**

   - **Video with audio**

   - **Still images from video**

2. If you chose to capture video, choose the capture setting for the video content you want to capture, and then click **Next**. The **Choose Capture Devices** page, shown in Figure 8.11, appears.

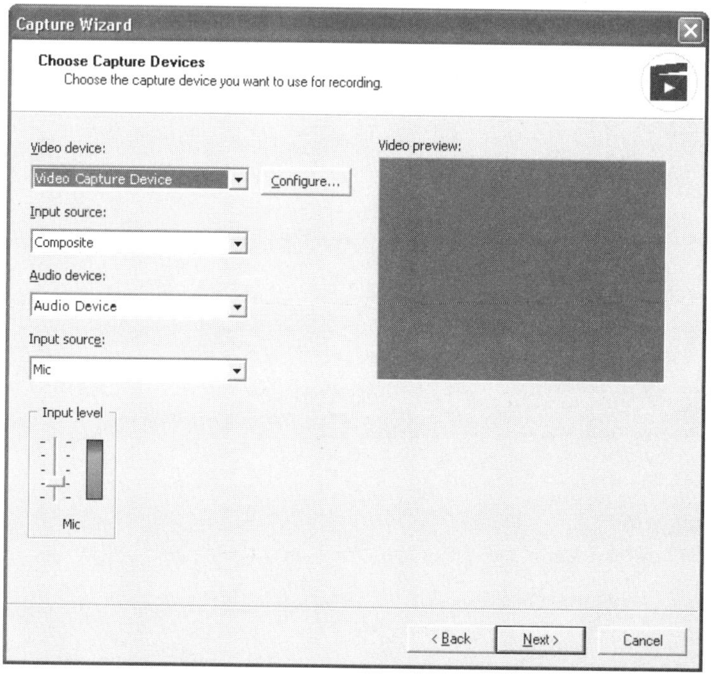

Figure 8.11 — Selecting a capture device that uses WDM drivers.

3. From the **Video device** box, select the device you want to use.

4. From the **Input source** box, select the **Input source** for the video, and then click **Configure**. The dialog box shown in Figure 8.12 appears.

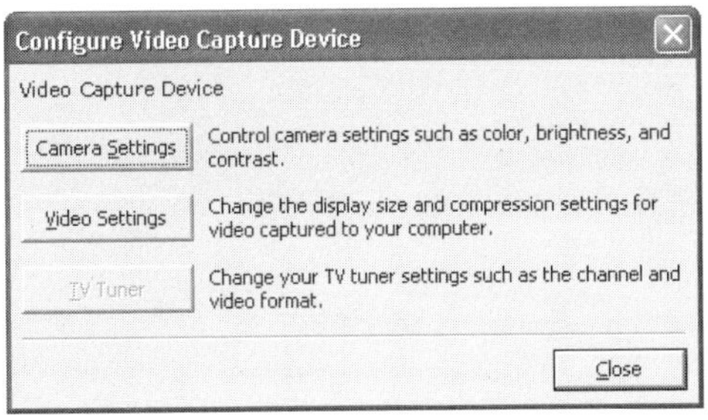

Figure 8.12 — Configuration options for a device that uses WDM drivers.

5. In the **Configure Video Capture Device** dialog box, click **Camera Settings**. The resulting dialog box depends on the manufacturer of your capture device and the accompanying software. Typically you can control settings such as:

- The video standard to use, usually NTSC or PAL

- Camera controls such as pan, tilt, and so forth

- Settings such as brightness, contrast, hue, and saturation

6. In the **Configure Video Capture Device** dialog box, click **Video Settings**. Again, the resulting dialog box depends on the device manufacturer and the accompanying software. Typically, you can control video settings such as:

- Frame rate

- Compression size

- The display size of the captured video

As a general rule, you should leave these settings as they appear by default and change the settings only if you are experiencing problems with the capture device.

Some Web cameras will default to a smaller display size. Therefore, when you capture video or a still image using the Web camera, it may appear distorted. You should set the display size to a larger size to avoid this issue.

7. If you have a TV tuner card installed on your computer, you can click **TV Tuner** to change settings such as the current TV channel.

8. After you have selected the appropriate **Audio device** and **Input source** settings, click **Next** to continue the **Capture Wizard**.

CHAPTER 9

Editing on the Timeline

After you have added digital media files to your Microsoft Producer project, whether it is by using the **New Presentation Wizard**, importing files from your computer or network, or capturing content, you are ready to begin editing your presentation. To edit your presentation, you arrange and synchronize digital media elements on the timeline. When you are satisfied with the choice of digital media and the arrangement of the elements on the timeline, you can then publish the presentation in a final form that can be viewed by your audience in their Web browsers.

The types of edits you can make in Producer range from altering individual files in the project to rearranging the contents of the entire project on the timeline. The edits you make directly affect the final message that is communicated to your audience in the published presentation.

To create a presentation, you will probably follow an editing process. First, you add digital media files to the timeline, and then edit the items on the timeline. After you make one or more edits, you play back what you have done, and then you edit again or add more digital media files. You continue adding, editing, and viewing until you are finished. Then you publish your final presentation. Publishing is discussed in chapter 11.

As you build and synchronize the elements of your presentation on the timeline, the following three tabs provide you with different views of your project. The tab you use depends on what you are doing.

- You use the **Media** tab when you are adding digital media to the timeline.

- You use the **Table of Contents** tab when you want to edit the table of contents and the introduction page.

- You use the **Preview Presentation** tab when you want to see and hear how all the elements on your timeline play together.

You can change between the tabs at any time during the editing process. For example, you can add some digital media files on the **Media** tab, view the results with the **Preview Presentation** tab, and then go back to the **Media** tab and add more digital media.

This chapter discusses the editing process in Microsoft Producer. The topics covered range from editing your overall presentation to editing individual elements, such as video and audio files. The goal of this chapter is to explain the editing tools and overall editing process in Producer.

The first step in editing is adding digital media to the timeline. The digital media items you can use on the timeline come from the **Media** tab.

Working with the Media Tab

In Microsoft Producer, editing starts from the **Media** tab. As discussed in chapter 7, the files you import or capture in Producer are stored in different folders according to the file type. This helps you to find the type of file you want to use in your presentation. The **Media** tab contains two panes: the tree pane and the contents pane. The tree pane contains the folders. When you select a folder, the digital media files contained in it are displayed in the contents pane. For example, Figure 9.1 shows a project with **Video** and **Slides** folders. The **Video** folder is selected, displaying the four video files that it contains in the contents pane.

Figure 9.1 — The **Media** tab, which contains the tree pane and contents pane.

The **Media** tab contains all the different files that are available in the current project—the individual elements of the project you can add to the timeline and arrange to create your presentation. You can add digital media files to the **Media** tab at any time by importing the files into the appropriate folders.

Adding Files to the Timeline

You can add digital media files to the timeline in several different ways. Digital media files can be added automatically, such as when you start a presentation by using the **New Presentation Wizard**. Files are also automatically added to the timeline if you choose to narrate your slides with video or with audio only by using the **Capture Wizard**.

You can also add digital media files manually to the timeline in a variety of ways:

- Selecting **Add To Timeline** on the **Clip** menu.

- Right-clicking the file and selecting **Add To Timeline** on the shortcut menu.

- Dragging the file to the timeline.

- Using the **Copy** and **Paste** commands.

The way you choose to add the file is up to you. You should choose the method that is the most comfortable and efficient for you.

When adding video files to the timeline, you can add the entire video file by selecting and adding the file from the tree pane. You can also add clips from the file by selecting the file in the tree pane. When you select the file from the tree pane, the clips are displayed in the contents pane. You can then add the whole file or individual clips from the contents pane.

The same holds true for Microsoft PowerPoint presentations. If you, for example, click and drag a PowerPoint presentation file from the tree pane, all the slides are added to the timeline with their associated timings. If you want to add slides individually, you can click and drag the slides from the contents pane.

Creating Clips from Video Files

You can choose to have your video files separated into smaller video clips. In chapter 7, you saw that clips can be created when video files are first imported into a Producer project. However, you can also choose to create clips from your video files after the video has been imported. This option enables you to create clips at any time.

You can have your video files separated into smaller clips by using an automatic process called *clip detection*. Clip detection is especially useful if you have a long video file, say 30 minutes, but you want to add only a five-minute segment from the middle of the video file. You could run clip detection to separate the video file and help you find the clip or clips you are looking for rather than having to search the video file manually.

Clips are created in a variety of ways. How clips are created depends on the video source and where you select the file in Producer. The following list briefly explains how clips are created in relation to the video file and source when you use clip detection from the tree pane:

- **Windows Media video files**. Clips are created based on file markers that are automatically inserted in Windows Media files. For example, as discussed in chapter 8, when you narrate slides using video with audio, the video is automatically broken down into smaller clips that correspond to the timings of the slides on the **Slide** track. The clips were created using markers that were added to the video file when slide changes were inserted. This applies to all Windows Media video files that have a .wmv or .asf file name extension. If file markers do not appear in the Windows Media file, then clips are created the same way as with video from an analog video source.

- **Video from an analog video camera or Web camera**. Video from an analog source is separated into clips based on changes in the video. When Producer detects a new frame of video, a new clip is created. For example, if you focus the camera on your speaker and then abruptly change the focus of the camera to a computer in the office, a new clip is created at that point, because there is a significant change in the video content.

- **Video from a DV camera**. When you use a DV camera to record video, the DV camera inserts time stamps into the video. In Producer, clips are created based on these time stamps.

You can also create clips from video files after selecting them in the contents pane. Using this method, clips are created in the same way as when you select analog or Web camera video files from the tree pane, or when the video source is an analog video camera or Web camera. In other words, clips are created based on significant changes in the video file, regardless of the video source.

When you run **Create Clips** from the contents pane, the clips are separated and named according to the original file name followed by an incremented number (in parentheses) that indicates the order in which the clip appeared in the original video file. For example, if you created clips from a video file named Speaker.wmv in the contents pane, the resulting clips would be created in the contents pane and named Speaker.wmv (2), Speaker.wmv (3), and so forth.

Determining Where Files Are Added on the Timeline

By default, digital media files are added to the beginning of the timeline when the timeline is empty. However, there may be times when you want to add video or still images to the **Video** track or audio to the **Audio 2** track of the timeline so they display at a different time. You can do this by copying a file or clip from the **Media** tab, and then pasting it in the appropriate track of the timeline at the time you want, based on the position of the time indicator.

In Producer, a digital media file is added by default to its associated track on the timeline. Which track the content appears on by default depends on the file type and the track that is selected when the file is added to the timeline.

The digital media types and the tracks to which they are added by default are shown in Table 9.1.

Table 9.1 — Default timeline tracks for various file types.

Digital media type	Default timeline track
Video	**Video**
Audio track of a video file	**Audio**
Audio (not part of a video file)	**Audio 2**
Images	**Slide**
Slides	**Slide**
HTML	**HTML**
Presentation template	**Template**
Video transition	**Transition**
Video effect	**Video**

In Microsoft PowerPoint, you can choose to save your slides as a Web page. If you do this, you can use the PowerPoint presentation (with an .htm file name extension in this case) in your Producer project. Although the PowerPoint presentation and the individual slides have .htm file name extensions, the slides are still added to the **Slide** track by default and stored in the **Slides** folder of the current project.

You can add some digital media file types to tracks other than the default ones, depending on how you want to use that type of digital media for your presentation. For example, you might have a video file that contains accompanying audio in it, and you only want the audio to play back in your presentation without displaying the video. To do this, you could add the video file to the **Audio 2** track of the timeline rather than to the **Video** track. In your final presentation, the audio would play back, but the video portion of the file would not.

Table 9.2 shows which types of digital media files can be added to more than one timeline track.

Table 9.2 — Digital media files that can be added to more than one track.

Digital media type	Possible tracks
Video	**Video** or **Audio 2**
Images	**Video** or **Slide**

Setting Default Durations for Digital Media Files

As you add elements to the timeline, you will see that the digital media files that have no set duration are given default durations. You can view and modify these default duration times on the **Timeline** tab of the **Options** dialog box, shown in Figure 9.2.

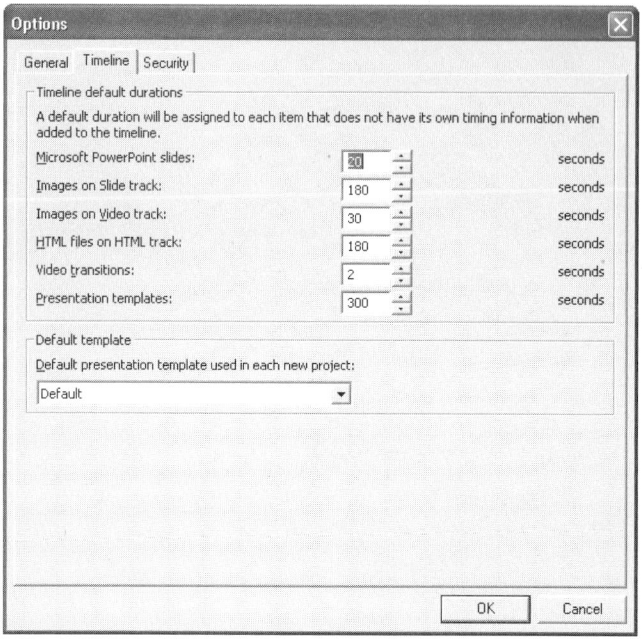

Figure 9.2 — Setting the default durations for files added to the timeline.

For example, if you used the Microsoft Producer for PowerPoint add-in program to record slide timings, or if you used the **Rehearse timings** feature in PowerPoint to time your slides, the timing information is retained for the slides and the slides appear on the timeline for the amount of time specified in the recording. This is also true for slides you narrate or synchronize with video or with audio. However, if you have imported Microsoft PowerPoint slides that do not have any timing information associated with them, the slides appear on the **Slide** track for the amount of time specified for the **Microsoft PowerPoint slides** option on the **Timeline** tab.

When you choose the default durations for the different file types on the **Timeline** tab, think about how the files will be used in your presentation. This will help you estimate a default duration. Remember, you can always increase or decrease the amount of time the files appear on the designated track after you have added them to the timeline. Trimming files and adjusting playback duration are discussed later in this chapter.

Adding Web Links

Your Microsoft Producer project can contain a variety of digital media files combined to make a dynamic presentation. You can also include existing Web content in your presentation by adding a Web link.

Live Web links let you display Web content in your presentation. You can choose to display the actual Web page or simply provide a link that your audience can click to go to the specified site.

The Web site (or link) you choose to display can be an internal intranet site or an external Web site. As long as your audience has the required permissions to view the specified Web site, they will be able to see it in your presentation. For example, if you create a presentation to introduce a newly designed intranet site and you publish the presentation on a shared network location, company employees could watch the presentation and see the new Web site by using the link, provided they have the necessary network permissions to connect to that intranet site.

Whether the actual live Web page or just a link displays in your presentation depends on the options you select in the **Add or Replace Web Link** dialog box, shown in Figure 9.3. For example, the Web link shown here will display the main page of the Microsoft Web site in the presentation.

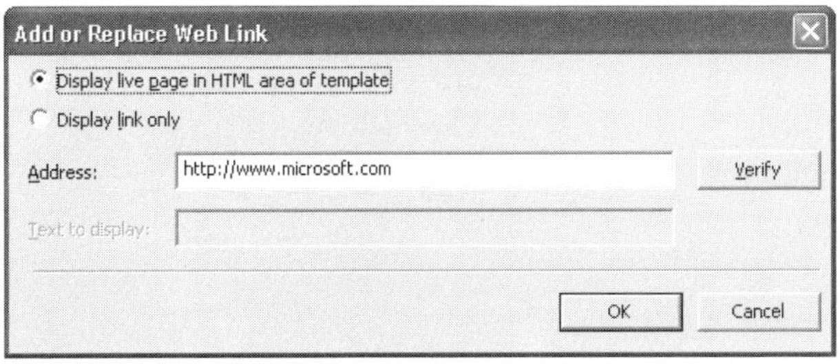

Figure 9.3 — The **Add or Replace Web Link** dialog box.

Whether you choose to display a live Web page or a link to the page, you must select a presentation template that displays HTML and add it to the timeline. If the template that is applied to the presentation does not display HTML, the Web link will not display in the presentation and the HTML content is not shown. Any Web links you add appear in the **HTML** folder for the current project.

You can easily replace an existing Web link. This lets you change the Web site that is displayed or the type of link that is used. For example, you might have a Web link where the entire Web page is displayed in your presentation. However, you may decide that you only want a link to the Web page to display in your presentation. You could select the existing Web link and use the **Display link only** option. If you have already added the Web link to the timeline, you will need to delete it from the timeline and then add it again for your changes to appear.

Adding a Web link lets you display live Web content rather than the static HTML page that appears if you choose to add an HTML file to your presentation. This lets you take full advantage of a live Web site without worrying about whether or not the information is current and updated. By displaying a live Web link, you can easily display live Web content in your presentation along with synchronized slides, audio, video, and other digital media files.

Adding Templates to the Timeline

The presentation template that is applied to the timeline determines the layout and appearance of the part of the presentation to which the template is applied. When editing a project, you will most likely want to add more than one template to the timeline based on the content you are using.

Figure 9.4 shows an example of a project that contains video, audio, slides, and HTML. At the beginning of the presentation, the video is displayed, along with the accompanying slides and HTML file. However, at about 1:05 into the presentation, the video is no longer displayed, and only the audio is played back. Therefore, at about 1:05 on the timeline, another presentation template, **Standard Audio – Resizable Slides and HTML**, was added. With this new template, the presentation only plays back the audio without displaying an empty monitor.

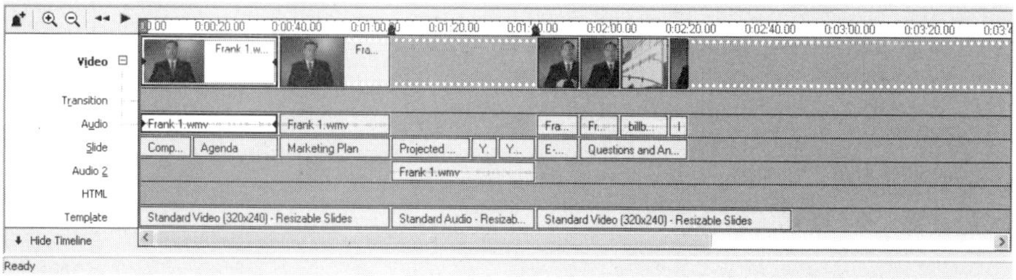

Figure 9.4 — Changing templates in a presentation.

In addition to adding one or more of the presentation templates that are installed with Producer, you can also create and add your own customized templates to further enhance the appearance of your final presentation. Creating customized presentation templates is discussed in chapter 12.

Removing Files from the Timeline

As you are editing your project, you may need to remove files from the timeline. To do this, you can simply select the file you want to remove from the timeline and then remove it by using the **Delete** command or by pressing the Del key. If you want to remove all of the contents on an individual track on the timeline, you can do so by clicking a file on that track, clicking the **Select All** command on the **Edit** menu, and then using the **Delete** command or pressing the Del key.

Immediately after a file is added to the timeline, you can remove it by using the **Undo** command. This command removes the last action. In this case, the last action is adding the file to the timeline.

There may be times when it is easier to simply start over from scratch. You can quickly remove all the files from the timeline by using the **Clear Timeline** command on the **Edit** menu. This lets you clear all of the files from all of the timeline tracks. When you do this, the files are removed from the timeline, but they still appear in the current project. This lets you start rearranging and editing your project from the beginning without needing to start a new project import the content for the current project again. Remember, you can delete files and edit the elements on the timeline as much as you like, and the original files are not affected.

A digital media file is removed from the timeline automatically, with the exception of a Web link, if you delete the file from the tree pane or contents pane in the **Media** tab as well. Furthermore, if you move or delete the original source file, then the digital media file is removed automatically from the timeline as well.

Editing Video and Audio

Up to this point, this chapter has discussed adding, removing, and positioning digital media on the timeline. However, when fine-tuning a presentation, you may spend the majority of your time focusing on editing the video and audio content. The edits you can make range from trimming the length of files to adding video transitions.

In Producer, you can edit video and audio you have imported or captured. By performing quick editing tasks, you can ensure that your audio and video plays back as you want it to in your published presentation. As you are editing audio and video, it is helpful to think about what role the video and audio plays in your presentation. By keeping this general thought in mind, it is easier to determine the edits you need to make to create your dynamic presentation.

Trimming Video and Audio

Video and audio you import or capture in Producer often contains footage that you do not want to appear in your final presentation. For example, when capturing video of a speaker giving a lecture, the video you capture might contain extra footage you captured during setup, such as instructing the presenter, testing the microphone, and making any other last-minute adjustments before the presenter begins to speak. In this situation, you could trim the extraneous video so that only the actual video and audio of the presenter discussing the topic appears in the final presentation.

When you trim video and audio in Producer, you only hide the unwanted parts of the video or audio file—the original content of the actual video or audio file you imported or captured remains intact. Therefore, you can experiment with trimming video frames, if you want, and then immediately add the frames back if you do not like the result.

In Producer, video and audio files (and clips) can only be trimmed after they have been added to the timeline. You can trim files in different ways, such as by using the **Set Start Trim Point** and **Set End Trim Point** commands on the **Clip** menu. You can also quickly trim audio and video files by moving the *trim handles* that appear when a video or audio file is added to the timeline. A double-sided arrow indicates that you can adjust the starting or ending points of the audio or video.

Figure 9.5 shows the trim handles for a selected video on the **Video** track of the timeline.

Figure 9.5 — Trim handles on a video file.

Trimming the beginning of an audio or video file sets the *trim in* point, whereas trimming the end of the file sets the *trim out* point. These points determine the start and end, respectively, of the audio or video when it is played back in your presentation. For audio and video, the playback time cannot be extended beyond the length of the original file.

When you are trimming audio and video files in Producer, you will also need to trim the playback duration for the accompanying slides you narrated or synchronized with the video and audio. This ensures that your slides are still synchronized with the audio and video after you trim them on the timeline.

Splitting Files and Clips

As mentioned earlier in this chapter, Producer uses clip detection to separate video files into smaller, more manageable clips. This allows you to create clips automatically in Producer. However, there may be times when you want to separate video files into clips yourself, or separate clips that are on the timeline for your current project into even smaller clips.

For example, let's say you have a long video file that was shot with an analog camera or Web camera, and you used the **Create Clips** command. Producer separates the video into clips based on background changes. If the presenter is in front of a stationary background, clips may not be created because there are not many significant changes from one frame to the next within the video. You can then manually split the clips based on how you intend to use the video in your project. The video you are splitting may already have video effects added to it. When video effects are added, the effects are applied to both clips when the video is split.

A common reason to create clips of video files is to insert another video clip in the middle of one large video file on the timeline. For example, if you have one video file that shows a speaker describing a new product, and you want to insert video that shows the product and then cuts back to the speaker, you could split the video file of the speaker in order to insert the video clip of the product. You would then split the video at the point where the speaker describes the product, add the video of the product, and then continue with the original video of the speaker.

In addition to splitting video files on the **Video** track, you can also split audio on the **Audio** and **Audio 2** tracks of the timeline. You can split audio on the **Audio 2** track the same way you split video on the **Video** track (or the accompanying audio for the video, which is displayed on the **Audio** track).

Combining Clips

Video or audio files that have been separated into clips can also be combined again. This is true whether clips were created through clip detection when the video was imported or by manually splitting the clips. Regardless of which method you used to create clips, you can select each contiguous clip that you want to combine again, and then use the **Combine** command to merge the video clips back into one large clip.

Clips can only be combined if they were contiguous segments of the original video file. For example, if you used clip detection on a video file named Speaker.wmv that was recorded and captured from an analog camera or Web camera, the clips would be named Speaker.wmv, Speaker.wmv (2), Speaker.wmv (3), Speaker.wmv (4), and so forth. In this case you could only combine the clips that are adjacent to one another in the contents pane, such as Speaker.wmv (2) and Speaker.wmv (3). This is true whether you are combing clips in the contents pane or on the timeline.

When determining whether you need to combine clips, think about how you want to work with the video and audio in your presentation. It may be easier to add one large clip to the timeline rather than adding several smaller contiguous clips to display the same video. However, working with the smaller video clips might be easier in other cases. Working with shorter clips enables you to synchronize the video more easily with shorter digital media files that also appear on the timeline, such as slides. If the video clips you combine contain video effects, the video effects that are applied to the first clip are kept for the combined clip.

Adding Video Transitions

In Producer, you have many choices of video transitions that you can add to your presentations. You can add video transitions between any two files or clips on the **Video** track of the timeline. The two files can be any combination of still images or videos. A video transition helps your presentation move smoothly from one video or still image to another. You can add video transitions to the timeline just as you would add any other digital media file.

The main purpose of video transitions is to add a different look to your presentation as video changes from one clip or file to the next. By default, a cut transition is inserted between clips or files. A cut is an abrupt transition that occurs in one frame. However, at times, you may want to add a longer video transition rather than leave a straight cut from one file to the next.

The transition choices appear in the **Video Transitions** folder on the **Media** tab. These transitions display an effect that plays back as the video or still image in the first file finishes playing and the next file begins to play. To add a video transition between two files or clips, they must be adjacent on the timeline, and the length of the video transition cannot exceed the combined time the two files display in your presentation. For example, you cannot add a five second transition at the end of a clip that is only three seconds long. The default duration of a video transition is determined by the time specified for the **Video transitions** option on the **Timeline** tab of the **Options** dialog box.

Although there are many different video transitions to choose from, you need to consider how the transition you use works with the design of your presentation. A basic video transition, such as a fade, may be the best choice when you want to maintain a professional look. You can add a basic fade by adding the **Fade** video transition between the two files (see Figure 9.6), or you can add a fade by dragging the second file over the end of the first file so they overlap. The amount of time the files overlap determines the time the video transition plays.

You can move the start trim handle of the transition on the **Transition** track to extend or decrease the amount of time the video transition displays between the two clips.

Because video transitions are often short, you may need to zoom in on the timeline so you can drag the start trim handle of the transition to change the playback duration.

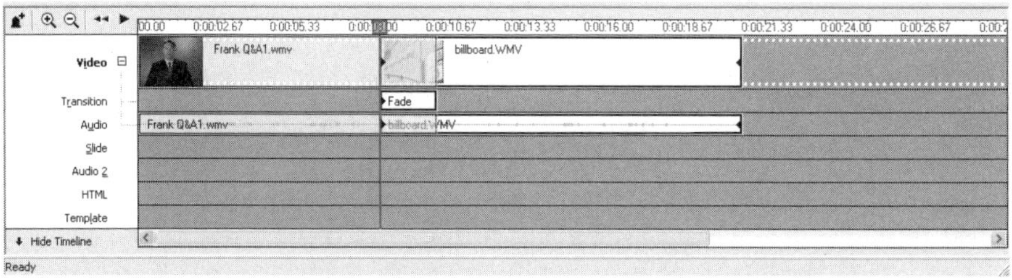

Figure 9.6 — A fade video transition between two video clips.

Video transitions can enhance the final outcome and appearance of your presentation. However, adding too many video transitions between video clips can distract from your presentation and its overall effectiveness.

Adding Video Effects

Video effects let you change the appearance of any video or still images that are displayed on the **Video** track of the timeline. The different video effects you can add to your presentation appear in the **Video Effects** folder on the **Media** tab. Whereas video transitions play between two files or clips on the **Video** track of the timeline, most video effects display for the entire duration of the clip or file to which the video effect is added.

You can add a variety of effects to video or still images on the timeline. Some of the basic video effects you can add are a *fade in* or *fade out*. A fade in effect is a gradual change from black to the image or video. Conversely, a fade out video effect changes gradually from the image or video to black.

You can choose to add one or more video effects to a single video clip or still image, depending on the effect you want for your presentation. When you add a video effect to a video or still image on the timeline, a small icon of a paint bucket appears in the timeline, indicating that a video effect has been added, as shown in Figure 9.7.

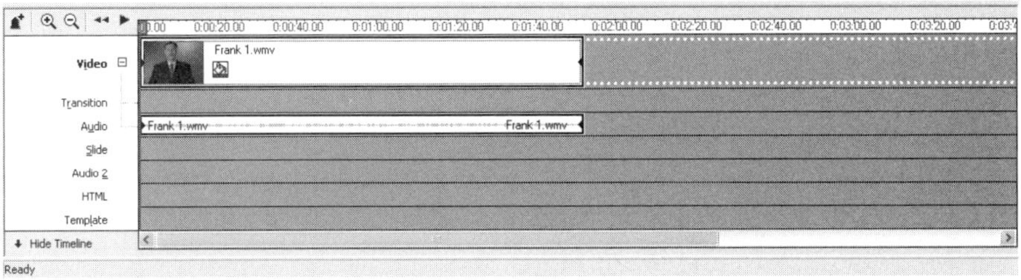

Figure 9.7 — A video with an added effect.

You can easily add new video effects or remove existing video effects by using the **Add or Remove Video Effects** dialog box. To quickly add a video effect, you can also drag the video effect from the contents pane to the video on the timeline to apply the effect.

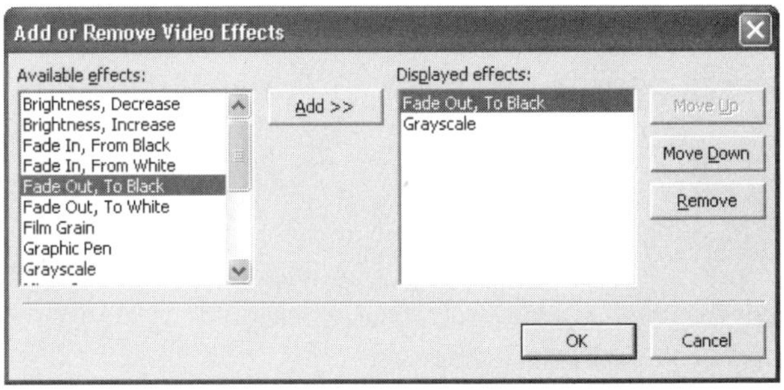

Figure 9.8 — The **Grayscale** and **Fade Out, To Black** video effects are added to the selected video.

Moving and Copying Files on the Timeline

Just as you can copy and paste files from the contents pane, you can copy, move, and paste files on the timeline—for example, you can copy or move files from one part of the timeline to another. For certain digital media files, such as still images and video clips, you can also copy or move the file from one track to another. You can also copy files so the files appear in two places.

When you copy a file or clip in the timeline, the properties of the file or clip are carried over to the copy. For example, if you trim a clip and add an effect, the copies have the same length and effect. If the selection contains effects or video transitions and you copy the selection to the same track on the timeline, any added effects or video transitions remain intact and are copied with the video and audio.

Producer lets you rearrange content on the **Slide**, **HTML**, or **Template** tracks in other ways besides moving or copying. You can also rearrange the order of files on these tracks by using the **Rearrange Items On** command on the **Tools** menu. This is equivalent of moving slides by using cut and paste or by dragging them from one part of the timeline to another.

For example, in the dialog box shown in Figure 9.9, you can rearrange and change the order that the slides appear on the timeline and in your final presentation.

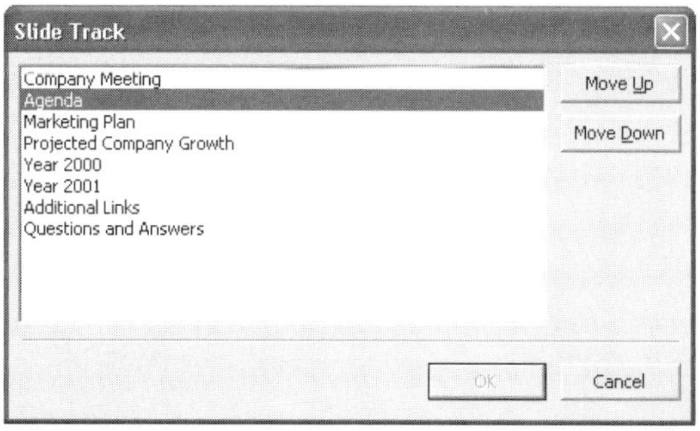

Figure 9.9 — The **Slide Track** dialog box used to rearrange and adjust the order of slides on the timeline.

When you rearrange items on the timeline, such as slides, HTML files, or presentation templates, you will need to rearrange the order of the video and audio that the slides, HTML files, or presentation templates are synchronized with. For example, if you narrated slides with video using the **Capture Wizard**, the resulting video and audio is separated into clips that have the same names as the slides they narrate. Therefore, if you rearrange the order of the slides on the **Slide** track, you will need to rearrange the order of the video clips so the video is still synchronized with the slides in your presentation.

Working with Audio

Up to this point, this chapter has mainly discussed editing the video within the presentation. However, your presentation can also contain only audio or segments where audio plays back in place of video. You can perform basic editing tasks on the audio—many that are similar to editing video—so your audio plays back as you want for your presentation. The following section describes audio editing features that you can use when editing audio in your presentation.

Using Audio Effects

Just as you can add effects to video files or clips, you can add basic effects to the audio in your presentation. The basic audio effects let you specify how you want the audio to be played back in your presentation, or whether you want it to be heard at all. You can add any of the audio effects to any audio file that appears on the **Audio** or **Audio 2** tracks of the timeline.

The basic audio effects you can add are fade in, fade out, or muting. By adding a fade in effect to a selected audio clip, the volume of the audio gradually transitions from silence to full volume as the file starts to play, rather than simply playing at the highest volume or level from the beginning. Conversely, when you add a fade out effect to an audio clip, the volume of the audio gradually changes to silence as the file reaches the end.

Another basic audio effect you can add is to mute the audio file or clip. This effect lets you silence any audio that you do not want to play back in your presentation. Muting audio is especially useful if you have a video file or clip on the **Video** track of the timeline with corresponding audio on the **Audio** track. If you only want the video to display in your presentation without the audio for a portion of the presentation, you could mute the clip on the **Audio** track. Muting audio can be especially useful if a video clip displays correctly, but the audio is distorted and unclear. It lets you hide these distortions, so you can still use the video in your presentation effectively.

You can add another audio effect by dragging one audio file or clip on top of another so that they overlap on the timeline. When two audio files overlap on the timeline, the audio content for both clips plays at the same time for the amount of time the two files or clips overlap. However, while a fade is automatically added when two video files or clips overlap on the timeline, no fade is added for overlapping audio files. The playback volume for each clip is automatically lowered by half during the time the two clips overlap in your presentation.

Normalizing Audio on the Timeline

The audio you import or capture will probably come from a variety of audio sources. Furthermore, the volume or level at which the audio was originally recorded could be different for each audio file in your project. Because of this, the audio files might play back at different volumes. This can be distracting because the volume for one audio file might be quite low, while the volume for the next audio file might be quite loud. These abrupt changes in the volume can distract from the overall quality of your presentation.

You can prevent this occurrence by *normalizing* the audio on the timeline, so all the audio plays at a uniform level. When you select **Normalize Timeline Audio**, Producer automatically analyzes the audio files on the timeline and then makes any necessary adjustments so that all audio files or clips on the timeline play back at the same level in the final presentation.

Adjusting Audio Levels

In Producer, your projects can contain many individual audio files. You can also have video with audio playing on the **Video** and **Audio** tracks of the timeline at the same time as an audio file plays on the **Audio 2** track. While having the ability to play multiple tracks of audio is very useful, it can also be confusing for your audience to hear different audio clips playing at the same time.

To make the audio play clearly to your audience, you can adjust the audio levels of two different sources: the sound on the **Audio** track (that plays with the video on the **Video** track) and the audio on the **Audio 2** track. You adjust the playback volume by using the **Audio Levels** slider, which you can access by clicking the **Audio Levels** command on the **Tools** menu. Once you set the slider, the audio level is applied for the entire presentation.

The **Audio Levels** control, shown in Figure 9.10, lets you adjust the volume so one audio source plays louder than the other, or so they both play at the same level. For example, in Figure 9.10, the audio from both sources would play at the same level because the slider is in the middle of the slider bar.

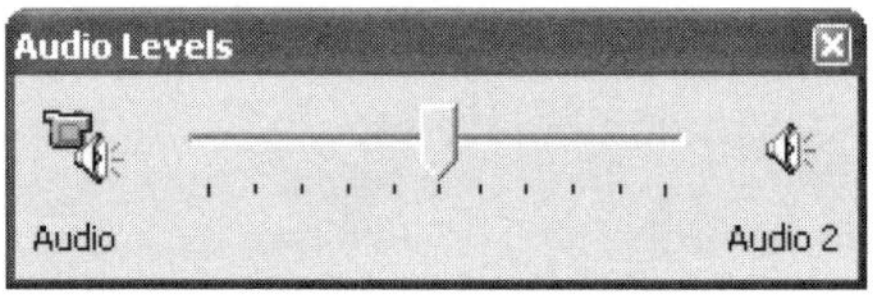

Figure 9.10 — Setting playback volume for the **Audio** and **Audio 2** tracks.

Determining which audio source should play back louder depends on the purpose of the audio in your presentation. For example, if your presentation had video with audio of a presenter describing slides on the **Slide** track, and you added background music to the **Audio 2** track, you could drag the slider in the **Audio Levels** dialog box towards the **Audio** side of the slider so the speaker's narration could be heard clearly over the music.

Editing the Table of Contents

The table of contents for your presentation is much like the table of contents in a book. Whereas a table of contents in a book shows the topics in the book and the page numbers on which each topic is discussed, the table of contents in a presentation provides a list of topics that are discussed in a presentation. Your audience can click an entry in the table of contents to play that part of the presentation. This can be especially helpful if you have a long presentation.

Table of contents entries are automatically added and attached to any slides that are added to the timeline for the current project. However, you can also click the **Table of Contents** tab and add new entries, edit existing entries, or delete existing entries by working in the **Table of contents** area. This lets you determine what topics and entries appear in the table of contents.

If you add a new table of contents entry, the entry you add corresponds to the current position of the playback indicator on the timeline. The item on the timeline that is currently selected determines what item the table of contents entry is associated with. In other words, it determines what will display or play back when your audience clicks the table of contents entry in your presentation. For example, if the entry is associated with a video file on the timeline, that particular part of the video will play when the entry is clicked.

If you later move the video to another part of the presentation, the table of contents entry moves with the video file. This is true for table of contents entries that are associated with items on the **Video**, **Audio 2**, **Slide**, **HTML**, or **Template** tracks. If a table of contents entry is associated with the **Timeline**, the items that display at that point on the timeline displays in your presentation if the entry is clicked. You can also change the association if you want the table of contents entry to be associated with a different element in your presentation.

In Figure 9.11, a table of contents entry would be associated with the selected video file if you chose to add a new table of contents entry.

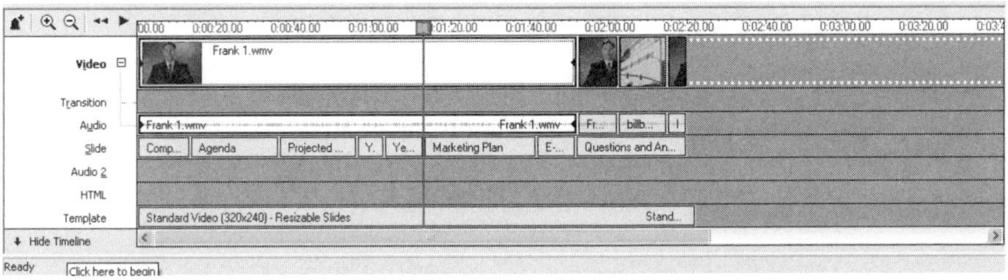

Figure 9.11 — Associating a table of contents entry with a selected video file.

In addition to editing overall entries in the table of contents, you can also choose to adjust the level at which the entry appears in the table of contents. Just as a chapter name in the table of contents of a book appears at a higher level than a section heading within the chapter, you may choose to have this type of hierarchy in the table of contents of your presentation. Figure 9.12 shows an example. You can do this by demoting a table of contents entry to a lower level or promoting an entry to a higher level.

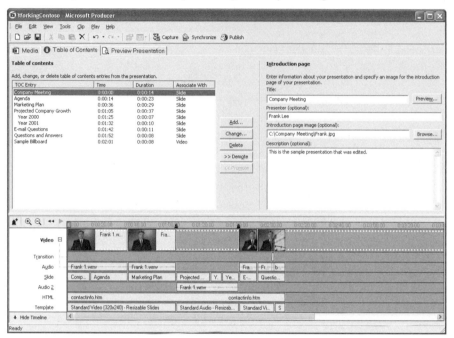

Figure 9.12 — Different entry levels in a table of contents.

Creating or Editing the Introduction Page

Part of editing your presentation is to make sure the introduction page of your presentation contains the correct information. If you used the **New Presentation Wizard** to create the initial presentation, the information you entered on the **Presentation Information** page appears in the **Introduction page** area of the **Table of Contents** tab.

The introduction page displays information about your presentation. This page appears while your presentation is loading in your audience's Web browsers. The page is optional; however, by providing information, you can tell your audience about your presentation and its purpose before they begin to watch it.

You can click **Preview** to see the introduction page for the current presentation. Previewing enables you to see the page as it will appear to your audience. After you preview, you can go back and make changes if necessary. For example, if you click **Preview** and see that the main background color is not the color you like, you could click **Presentation**

Scheme on the **Edit** menu, and then choose a different background color. This color then appears as the background of the introduction page, as well as in the presentation itself when one of the Standard presentation templates is applied to the presentation.

Previewing Presentations

As you edit your presentation, you can preview the presentation in the **Preview Presentation** tab. This tab allows you to see how the presentation will display after it is published and played back in a Web browser. You can then go back to the **Media** tab and make additional changes to the project, as necessary.

Previewing in the **Preview Presentation** tab is different from previewing in the **Media** tab. When you preview in the **Media** tab, only selected tracks play back in the monitor. This is useful for editing individual files and tracks. However, it does not enable you to see how all the elements work together.

To improve system performance when previewing a presentation in the **Preview Presentation** tab, hide the timeline by clicking the **Hide Timeline** button on the timeline.

Setting Security Zones for Previewing

In Producer, you can determine which Web content security zone you want Microsoft Internet Explorer to use for previewing presentations in Microsoft Producer. The security zone used for previewing presentations in Internet Explorer is determined by the **Choose which Microsoft Internet Explorer Web content security zone is used for previewing** option on the **Security** tab of the **Options** dialog box.

For example, in Figure 9.13, the Internet security zone settings in Internet Explorer are applied when previewing presentations in Producer.

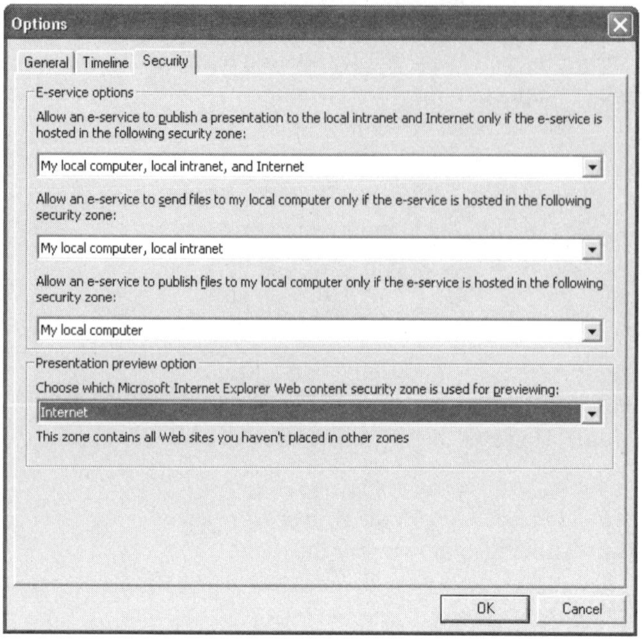

Figure 9.13 — The security zone used for previewing.

Whichever security zone setting you use, you should set the **Run ActiveX controls and plug-ins** option in Internet Explorer to **Enable** or **Prompt** in order to preview your presentation. This setting is necessary because Microsoft ActiveX controls are used when you preview your presentation.

You can see or change your security settings in Internet Explorer by doing the following:

1. Start Microsoft Internet Explorer.

2. On the **Tools** menu, click **Internet Options**.

3. In the **Internet Options** dialog box, click the **Security** tab. The security zone specified here is also used for previewing presentations in Microsoft Producer.

4. Click **Custom Level** and then choose the security setting you want to apply for the option **Run ActiveX controls and plug-ins**.

5. Click **OK** in the **Security Settings** dialog box, click **Yes** to confirm the change, and then click **OK** in the **Internet Options** dialog box.

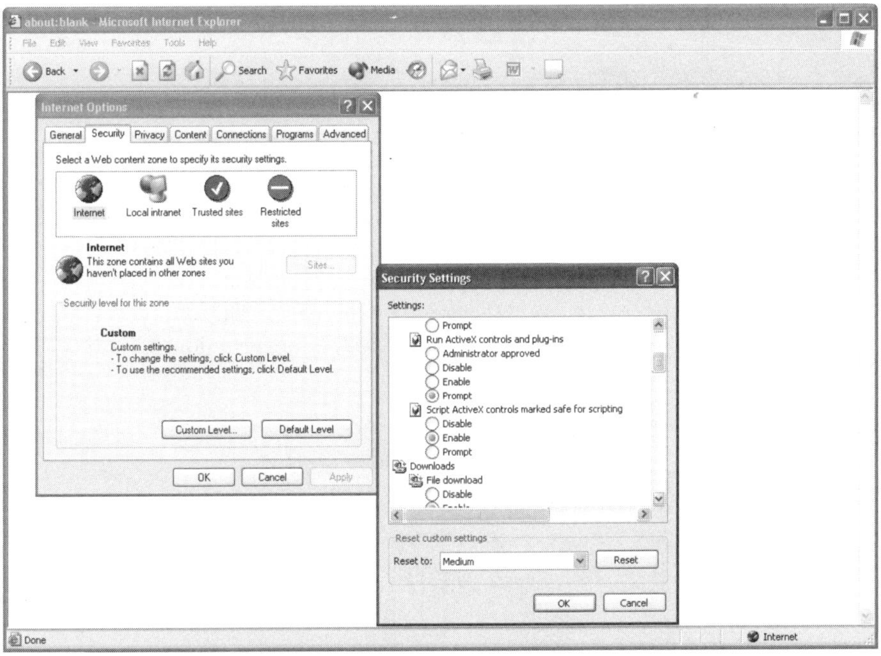

Figure 9.14 — The settings in Internet Explorer for the **Internet** security zone.

Using the security zone settings shown in Figure 9.14, you would be prompted each time you clicked the **Preview Presentation** tab to preview your presentation. The prompt shown in Figure 9.15 asks you whether you want to allow ActiveX controls and plug-ins to run. If you click **Yes**, you can preview the presentation. If you click **No**, a warning appears. You can click **OK** to preview the presentation, although it may not display correctly. If you selected **Enable** for the **Run ActiveX controls and plug-ins** security option in Internet Explorer, the required ActiveX control runs automatically so you can preview your presentation.

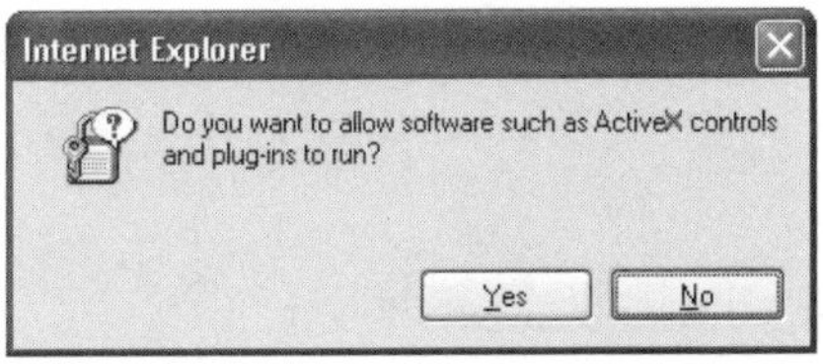

Figure 9.15 — Warning message for running ActiveX controls.

Editing a Project

The following procedures describe the processes for editing a project that has already been started. The procedures show you how you can use the different editing tools and features in Producer.

The order in which you perform the different editing steps will vary from one project to another. Although this section provides instructions for editing the sample presentation on the companion CD, the goal of this section is to enable you to edit your own presentation. You can choose to use your own content, or you can practice with the sample content provided on the CD. You can find both the unedited and edited sample presentations on the companion CD:

- The unedited presentation can be found at \Samples\Chapter9\UneditedSample.htm on the companion CD.

- The edited presentation, which you can create by following the steps in the procedures, can be found at \Samples\Chapter9\EditedSample.htm on the companion CD.

You can unpack the project archive StartingContoso.MSProducerZ from the folder \StepByStep\Chapter9 on the companion CD to your computer if you choose to follow the step-by-step procedures. For more information about packing and unpacking a Microsoft Producer project, see chapter 7.

Step-by-Step: Adding Files to the Timeline

The first step in editing a project is to add the files and clips you intend to use in your project to the timeline.

1. Select the file FrankQ&A1.wmv in the **Video** folder. On the **Clip** menu, click **Add To Timeline**. The video is added after the video file Frank1.wmv on the **Video** track.

2. To quickly add multiple files, press the Ctrl key, select each file you want to add, and then drag them to the timeline.

   For the sample project, select the **Video** folder, press the Ctrl key, and select Billboard.wmv and FrankQ&A2.wmv in the contents pane.

3. Drag the files to the **Video** track of the timeline.

   As you move the cursor over the two clips that are already in the timeline, a dark blue *insertion point* appears and changes position as you move the cursor back and forth. The insertion point indicates where the files will be inserted after you drop them. Move the cursor over the last clip (Frank Q&A1.wmv) until the insertion point is on the right edge of the clip, and then drop the files. The video track should appear as in Figure 9.16.

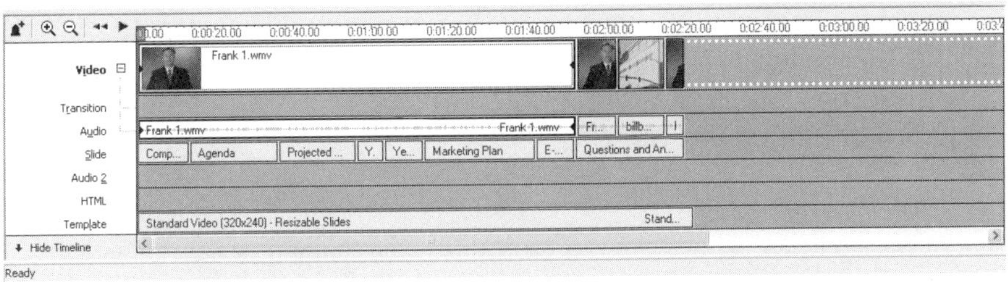

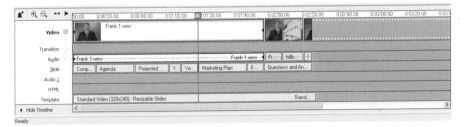

Figure 9.16 — The sample video track after adding three additional video files.

4. To preview the current presentation, click the **Preview Presentation** tab, and then click **Play**.

   Playback begins at the current position of the playback indicator on the timeline. To preview the presentation from the beginning, on the **Play** menu, click **Rewind**.

Step-by-Step: Splitting a Video Clip

For the sample project on the timeline, reorder the slides while making sure the slides and video files remain synchronized. To do that, split the video file so that you can move both the slide and the section of the video that corresponds to the slide to a different point in the presentation.

1. On the **Media** tab, drag the playback indicator on the timeline so it is positioned at the beginning of the Marketing Plan slide, as shown in Figure 9.17.

Figure 9.17 — The playback indicator position on the timeline for the sample presentation.

3. On the **Clip** menu, click **Split**. This splits the large Frank1.wmv file into two clips at the point where the Marketing Plan slide first appears.

3. Drag the playback indicator so it is positioned at the point where the Marketing Plan slide changes to the E-mail Questions slides. On the **Clip** menu, click **Split** again.

   The section of the video that plays with the Marketing Plan slide is now isolated.

4. Move the playback indicator on the timeline so it is positioned between the Agenda and Projected Company Growth slides. Select the Frank1.wmv clip where the indicator is positioned, and on the **Clip** menu, click **Split**.

This splits the large Frank1.wmv clip again. Later, you will move the Marketing Plan slide and corresponding video clip to this position.

Step-by-Step: Moving a Clip or File on the Timeline

Now, re-order the slides, and move the corresponding video clips.

1. To rearrange the order of the slides on the timeline, on the **Tools** menu, point to **Re-arrange Items On**, and then click **Slide Track**.

2. In the dialog box, you can change the position of a slide by clicking it, and then clicking **Move Up** or **Move Down**, depending on whether you want the slide to appear earlier or later in the presentation.

   For the sample, presentation, click **Move Up** or **Move Down** to arrange the slides in the order shown in Figure 9.18. Then click **OK**.

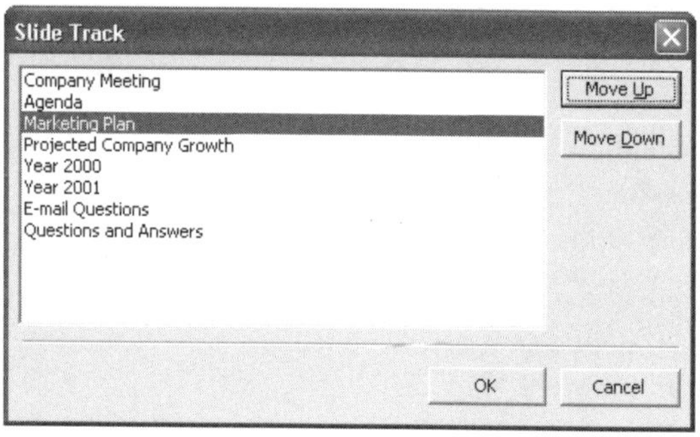

Figure 9.18 — The new order of the slides for the sample presentation.

When you click **OK**, the slides appear in the new order on the timeline.

3. On the **Video** track, select the Frank1.wmv clip that corresponded to the Marketing Plan slide before it was moved, and then drag the clip so the insertion point is at the beginning of the new position of the Marketing Plan slide. When you drop the clip, it inserts into the **Video** track at that point and moves all the clips after it to the right.

   Figure 9.19 shows the timeline for the current presentation.

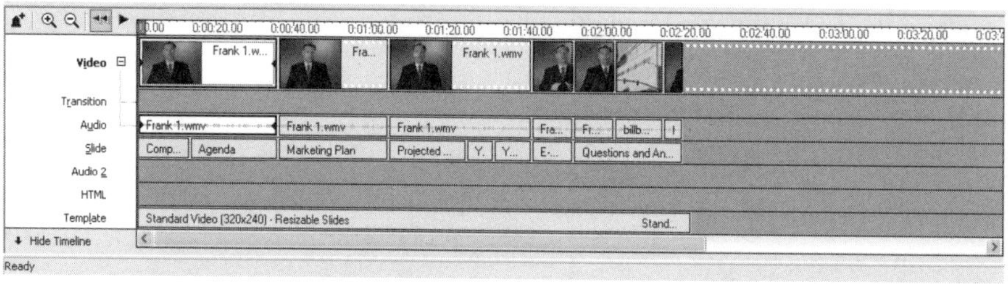

Figure 9.19 — Positions of the files on the timeline.

Step-by-Step: Playing only the Audio Portion of a Video Clip

There may be times when you want the audio portion of a video file to play without the video. In Producer, you do this by moving video clips to different tracks on the timeline.

1. Click the Frank1.wmv video clip that is synchronized with the slides Projected Company Growth, Year 2000, and Year 2001.

2. On the **Edit** menu, click **Cut**.

3. Move the playback indicator, either by dragging it on the timeline or by using the buttons under the monitor, so it is positioned after the Marketing Plan slide.

4. Click the **Audio 2** track to select the track, and then, on the **Edit** menu, click **Paste**. The video clip now appears on the **Audio 2** track. Only the audio portion of the video that describes these slides will play.

5. On the **File** menu, click **Save As**. In the **File name** box, type a name for your presentation, and then click **Save**. This saves the current project along with the content and arrangement of files on the timeline.

   Note that this step is not an integral part of editing the video file. However, it is a good practice to save your work often.

Step-by-Step: Adding Additional Presentation Templates

There is now a point in the sample presentation where audio plays without the accompanying video. If you play back the part of the presentation with the current template, the video monitor will be empty during this segment. However, if you apply an audio-only template to this part of the presentation, the empty monitor will not display. You can see this by viewing the edited presentation, EditedSample.htm, on the companion CD.

1. Click the timeline after the Marketing Plan slide, at the point where the audio-only section starts. The playback indicator moves to that part of the timeline.

2. On the **Tools** menu, click **Add Timeline Snap**.

   Timeline snaps are useful because they let you mark important parts of your presentation. When you move a digital media file to the part of the timeline that contains the timeline snap, the file will be inserted at that exact point automatically, so the elements in your presentation are synchronized and play back at the same time.

   When you add a timeline snap, it is placed at the current location of the playback indicator.

3. Click the **Presentation Templates** folder on the **Media** tab. In the contents pane, select the template named **Standard Audio – Resizable Slides**, and then drag it to the **Template** track of the timeline at the point of the timeline snap.

   This template has the same basic layout and appearance of the **Standard Video (320x240) – Resizable Slides** template that already appears on the timeline. The only difference is that the new template does not display video, so a monitor is not displayed during the segments of the presentation for which the new template is applied.

The default amount of time for which the added template displays is determined by the amount of time specified for the **Presentation templates** option on the **Timeline** tab of the **Options** dialog box. To open this dialog box, on the **Tools** menu, click **Options**, and then click the **Timeline** tab.

4. The added template may extend past the part of the timeline that displays on your computer screen. This can make editing difficult because you need to scroll across the timeline to see the entire template.

   To adjust the zoom level of the timeline so all the items on the timeline are displayed on your computer screen, on the **View** menu, click **Zoom To Fit**. All the content on the timeline will now display on your computer screen, so you do not have to scroll across the timeline to see your entire presentation.

   After you click **Zoom To Fit**, you may need to adjust the zoom level further so you can clearly see the files on the timeline. To do this, on the **View** menu, click **Zoom Timeline In** to increase the zoom level, or click **Zoom Timeline Out** to decrease the zoom level. When you zoom in on the timeline, the time interval displayed on the timeline becomes smaller. When you zoom out on the timeline, the time interval is larger.

5. In the **Media** tab, click **Play** on the timeline to begin playing your presentation. Click **Pause** when the Frank1.wmv video reaches the E-mail Questions slide. You can use the monitor buttons to move forward or backward frame-by-frame to find the exact point where the video that goes with the E-mail Questions slide starts.

   If you like, you can add a timeline snap as you did in step 2.

6. Select the new **Standard Audio – Resizable Slides** template on the timeline, and then drag the end point of the template so it lines up with the point at which the video begins to play. If you added a timeline snap, the template will automatically move to that point.

7. To resume video at that point, you can quickly copy the first presentation template on the timeline to the last portion of the presentation, by doing the following:

   - Click the **Standard Video (320x240) – Resizable Slides** template on the **Template** timeline track.

   - On the **Edit** menu, click **Copy**.

   - Move the playback indicator to the end of the **Standard Audio – Resizable Slides** template.

   - On the **Edit** menu, click **Paste**.

   Figure 9.20 shows the current state of the project.

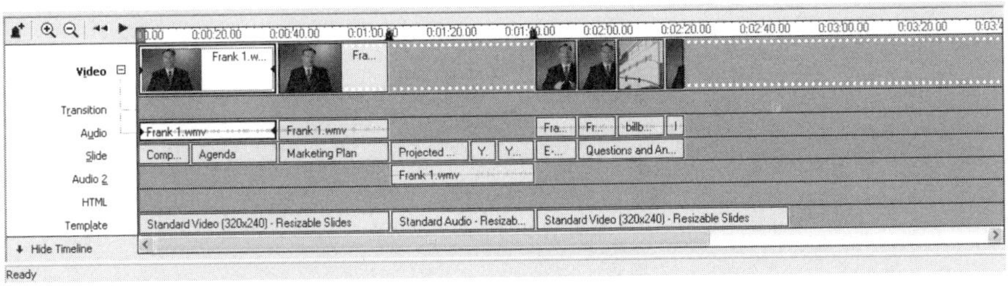

Figure 9.20 — The edited project to this point.

Step-by-Step: Trimming Video on the Timeline

The presentation you are creating might contain video footage that you do not want to display in your presentation. In this case, you could trim the video clip so the unwanted content is hidden and is not displayed in your presentation.

Trimming a file hides unwanted parts of the video (or audio) clip or file and prevents it from playing in your presentation. When you trim a file, the trimmed content still remains in the original file; it is not deleted or removed. Because the original file remains intact, you can always clear trim points so the entire video plays back.

This procedure is described in the following steps by trimming the video file named Billboard.wmv. In the presentation, the clip will be trimmed at the frame shown in Figure 9.21, so the clip ends after the phrase "Where we will be attending various trade shows."

Figure 9.21 — The frame at which the video clip is trimmed.

1. In the **Media** tab, select the video file Billboard.wmv on the timeline. Click the **Play** button on the monitor to begin playing the video file.

2. Click **Pause** after the phrase: "Where we will be attending various trade shows." Again, you can use the monitor buttons to move a frame backward or forward to reach the exact frame of the video.

3. On the **Clip** menu, click **Set End Trim Point**. This is the point at which the clip will end and the next clip will begin.

Step-by-Step: Adding a Web Link or HTML File

By adding a Web link or HTML file to your presentation, you can display HTML content. A live Web page or a link to the Web page is displayed in your presentation when you add a Web link. If you choose, you can add a static HTML page instead. Both Web links and static HTML files appear on the **HTML** track of the timeline.

For this sample presentation, a static HTML page is added. However, for your presentation, you might choose to add a link to a live Web site that relates to your presentation.

1. On the **Media** tab, select the **HTML** folder, and then select the HTML file named contactinfo.htm. Drag it to the **HTML** track on the timeline.

   The HTML file is added for the entire presentation. However, the file will not display unless the corresponding presentation template also displays HTML. The current templates on the timeline do not display HTML or Web links, so you need to add a template that does display HTML.

2. On the **Media** tab, select the **Presentation Templates** folder, and then click **Standard Video (320x240) – Resizable Slides and HTML** in the contents pane. Drag the template to the timeline so it begins to display when the Billboard.wmv file begins.

Step-by-Step: Deleting a File from the Timeline

For the sample presentation, there is a video named FrankQ&A2.wmv on the timeline. Since the sample presentation does not contain any additional questions and answers, delete this video file.

1. On the **Video** track, click the file FrankQ&A2.wmv.

2. On the **Edit** menu, click **Delete**. This removes the current selection from the timeline.

Step-by-Step: Adding Transitions and Effects

In the sample presentation, the video cuts from the presenter to the billboard. To soften the transition, you will add a video transition and an audio effect.

1. Select the video file Billboard.wmv on the timeline. When you add a video transition, it is placed before the selected video clip or still image on the **Video** track.

2. On the **Media** tab, click the **Video Transitions** folder, and then click **Fade**.

3. On the **Clip** menu, click **Add To Timeline**. The fade transition is added to the **Transition** track of the timeline. To see the **Transition** track, expand the **Video** track. When

you preview that section of the timeline, the video fades from the speaker to the billboard video.

As an alternative to adding a video transition, you could add a video effect. For example, you could click the billboard video and add a **Fade In** effect. This effect fades the billboard video in from black as the video starts playing. To add a fade-in video transition, on the **Clip** menu, point to **Video**, and then click **Fade In**.

Now add an audio effect to Billboard.wmv.

4. Click Billboard.wmv in the timeline. On the **Clip** menu, point to **Audio**, and then click **Fade In**. This effect fades the clip audio in as the video begins to play.

To make sure that the different elements in your presentation stop playing at the same time, do the following:

1. On the **Slide** track, click the last slide, Questions and Answers. Move the end trim handle of the selected slide so it ends when the last video file, Billboard.wmv, ends.

2. On the **HTML** track, click the file contactinfo.htm. Move the end trim handle of the HTML file so it ends when the last video file, Billboard.wmv, ends as well.

3. On the **Template** track, click the last template on the template track **Standard Video (320x240) – Resizable Slides and HTML**. Move the end trim handle of the template so it ends when the last video file, Billboard.wmv, ends.

This ensures that the individual files on the timeline stop playing at the same time in your presentation. It can be distracting to your audience if one element displays for a longer time than the others. However, you may choose to do this if you want an item, such as a Web link or slide, to display for a longer time so your audience can read any pertinent information, such as text on a Web site if you added a Web link.

Trimming templates and slides so they end at the same time as the video will reduce the amount of time it takes to publish the presentation when you publish the presentation. This is because blank video footage is created when a slide, presentation template, or HTML file, or Web link extends beyond audio or video that appears on the timeline.

Click the **Preview Presentation** tab, move the playback slider to the beginning, and then click **Play** to preview the timeline contents.

Step-by-Step: Editing the Introduction Page

The introduction page provides information about your presentation.

1. Click the **Table of Contents** tab.

   This tab lets you edit the introduction page information, as well as the table of contents. The information that appears for the unedited presentation was entered when the presentation was originally created using the **New Presentation Wizard**.

2. To change the information for the introduction page, do the following:

- In the **Title** box, type a new title for the presentation to replace the existing title.

- In the **Presenter (optional)** box, enter the presenter's name.

- In the **Introduction page image (optional)** area, click **Browse**. Locate the **Images** folder (which is in a subfolder of the location where you unpacked the original project archive), click **Frank.jpg**, and then click **Open**.

  For the introduction page image, any image that can display in a Web browser, such as a .jpg, .gif, or .png image file, can be used.

- In the **Description (optional)** box, type a description for the sample presentation.

3. Click **Preview** to see a preview of the introduction page as it will appear in a Web browser with the edited presentation information.

4. Close the preview window.

You also can see how the edits described in the following step-by-step procedures affect the introduction page if you play back both the unedited and edited presentations on the companion CD.

Step-by-Step: Editing the Table of Contents

The table of contents provides a way for your audience to see the topics discussed in your presentation. The individual entries in the table of contents are links that go to the corresponding parts of the presentation.

1. Click the **Table of Contents** tab.

   In the table of contents, entries are automatically added for each slide that is added to the timeline. The table of contents entries are reordered automatically when a slide is moved from one part of a presentation to another as we have done in this sample presentation. You can also add table of contents entries manually.

2. To add a table of contents entry, move the playback indicator to the beginning of the Billboard.wmv video. On the **Tools** menu, click **Add Table of Contents Entry**. In the **Name** box, type **Sample Billboard**.

3. Click **Video** from the **Associate with** box if it is not already selected, then click **OK**.

   The **Associate with** box lets you choose which digital media element in your presentation the entry is linked to. If you later move the element on the timeline, the associated table of contents entry moves as well. By default, a new table of contents entry is associated with the currently selected item on the timeline.

Another change you might want to make in the table of contents is to adjust the level at which an entry appears in the table of contents. Just like a table of contents in a book shows different levels to indicate chapters and sections within chapters, so can the table of contents in your presentation. To change the level of an entry, click the entry and then click **Demote** or **Promote**.

1. Click the entry Year 2000, and then click **Demote**. Do the same for Year 2001.

   These entries are indented, so they appear as entries below the main topic or entry, Projected Company Growth.

2. On the **File** menu, click **Save** to save the changes to the project.

CHAPTER 10

Microsoft PowerPoint Presentations in Producer

An important part of creating rich-media presentations in Producer includes incorporating existing Microsoft PowerPoint presentations into your Producer presentations. This lets you use your existing PowerPoint presentations in another way—to synchronize your PowerPoint slides with audio, video, HTML files, still images, and presentation templates in order to create one dynamic presentation. In other words, Microsoft Producer is a tool that helps you get even more out of your PowerPoint slides.

The previous chapters have discussed how to incorporate PowerPoint presentations into your Producer presentations. The goal of this chapter is take this one step further and provide specific information about working with your PowerPoint slides when using Microsoft Producer.

Using Slides in Your Presentations

Your PowerPoint slides can play different roles in your presentation, depending on the type of presentation you are creating. The following items will give you a few ideas of the ways Microsoft PowerPoint presentations can be used in the presentations you create in Producer.

- **Training presentations**. Whether the subject is technical or non-technical, your PowerPoint slides let you present existing training information alongside the audio and video that you add in Producer. This helps to accommodate the many different ways people learn. Some people learn best by hearing about the subject, while others learn best by reading the information in your slides.

- **Business-to-business communications**. Your PowerPoint slides can contain information about a product or service your company offers to other businesses. Your slides might contain background information about the product or service, images of the product, pricing information, technical specifications, and so on. The information contained in these slides, along with video or audio of a presenter discussing the slides, can enhance your marketing effort and reach a wider audience.

- **Internal corporate communications**. It is sometimes difficult (and expensive) to effectively communicate with all employees in a company. It may be very difficult to gather all company employees together at one time in one location. Therefore, you can create a Producer presentation for an online company meeting. In this type of presentation, your PowerPoint slides can include graphs and charts to show sales and revenue figures. These slides help to give a visual representation of the information that presenters are discussing in the online meeting.

Using PowerPoint to Edit Slides in Producer

As you are working with imported slides in Producer, you may need to edit them for use in your presentation. The types of changes you may need to make can range from correcting a small typing mistake to adding a whole new slide. You might also need to redesign slides to work with the other elements in your presentation.

If you discover that you need to make changes while you are working with the slides in Producer, you can edit your slides by opening them in PowerPoint. You can make any necessary changes, and then save your revised slides. When you go back to Producer, the edited PowerPoint presentation is automatically re-imported into Producer with the changes you made.

You can also open and edit a selected slide by using the **Edit Slide** command on the **Edit** menu in Producer, which is available only when a PowerPoint presentation or individual slide is selected.

Producer lets you open and edit your slides, whether they are saved and imported as a PowerPoint presentation with a .ppt file name extension or saved as a Web page with an .htm file name extension in PowerPoint. PowerPoint presentations are stored in the **Slides** folder on the **Media** tab in Producer. Producer retains information about the slides so you can edit them in PowerPoint regardless of whether they were saved as a PowerPoint presentation or a Web page.

Producer does not enable you to directly edit a PowerPoint Show with a .pps file name extension. If you want to edit a PowerPoint Show in PowerPoint after it has been imported into Producer, do the following:

1. Delete the show from the Producer project.

2. Change the file's .pps file name extension to a .ppt file name extension.

3. Import the PowerPoint presentation again.

You can then edit the presentation in Producer using PowerPoint.

Note that performing these steps removes all timing and synchronization between the slides and other elements on the timeline. When the slides are imported again, Producer will use either the PowerPoint timings (if they have been specified) or the default timing for PowerPoint slides.

When to Edit Slides

It's best to edit your slides before adding them to the timeline. If you edit the slides after they have been added to the timeline, the types of edits you make determine whether the slides are updated on the timeline automatically.

For example, if you added your slides to the timeline in Producer, and then decided that you wanted to change the slide design, you could choose the slide and then click **Edit Slide** on the **Edit** menu. After you applied the new design for the overall presentation, saved your changes in PowerPoint, and then went back to Producer, the slides would be re-imported automatically. The revised slides would appear in both the contents pane of the **Media** tab and on the timeline.

Other changes are not updated on slides that have already been added to the **Slide** track of the timeline. For example, if the slides have associated slide timings when they are imported into Producer and you change any slide timings in PowerPoint, the slides in the contents pane will contain the new slide timings. However, any slides that have been placed on the timeline will not have the new slide timings and will display in your presentation for the amount of time specified by the original slide timings. If you want the slides to display with the new slide timings, you would have to delete the slides from the timeline, and then add the revised slides to the timeline so the new timings would be applied to your presentation.

If you import slides that do not have any slide timings, and then add the slides to the timeline, the slides display for the default amount of time specified by the **Microsoft PowerPoint slide** option on the **Timeline** tab of the **Options** dialog box. If you later add timings, the slides in the contents pane of the **Media** tab will have the new slide timings. The slides on the timeline, however, will not have the timings.

As a general rule, editing your slides before they appear on the timeline can help you work more effectively in Producer. This prevents you from redoing work you have already done, such as synchronizing slides with audio or video you have already incorporated into your presentation.

Inserting Images in Slides

Many of your PowerPoint slides will contain images. When working with slides that you are going to use in Producer presentations, make sure you insert the image in the slide. To insert an image in Microsoft PowerPoint, on the **Insert** menu, point to **Picture**, click **From File**, and then choose the image you want to insert. The dialog box shown in Figure 10.1 appears.

In the dialog box shown in Figure 10.1, make sure you select **Insert** to embed the image in the actual PowerPoint slide. If you click **Link to File** rather than **Insert**, the image will not display in your Producer presentation because the link will be broken. However, if you click **Insert** and embed the image into the slide, the image will be correctly displayed in your final Producer presentation.

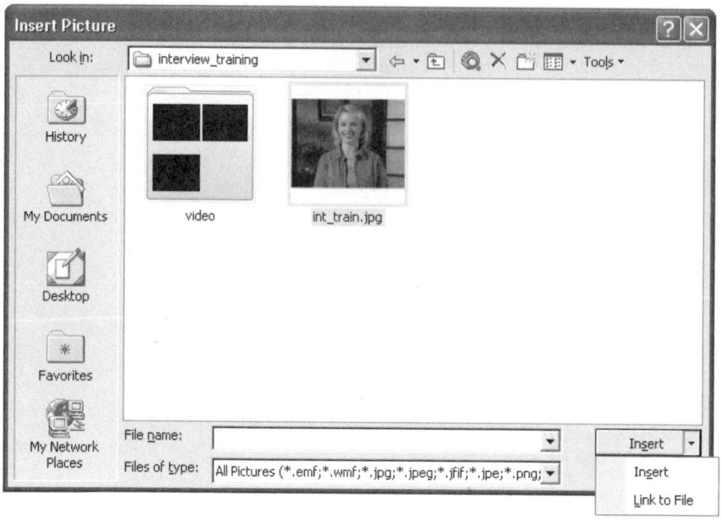

Figure 10.1 — Inserting an image in Microsoft PowerPoint 2002.

Editing Imported Slides in PowerPoint

The following procedure describes the step-by-step process for editing slides that have already been imported into Producer. A sample presentation was created using the following step-by-step instructions. You can watch this presentation by opening the file \Samples\Chapter 10\EditedInterview.htm on the companion CD.

You can follow the steps below to edit your own PowerPoint slides and Producer project, or you can edit the sample project archive that is included on the companion CD.

Step-by-Step: Opening the Sample Project Archive

The following steps explain how to open the sample Microsoft Producer project archive found on the companion CD. You can unpack this project archive to your own computer to begin editing the sample project—this is another use for packing a Microsoft Producer project, which is discussed in chapter 7.

1. Insert the companion CD in the CD-ROM drive of your computer.

2. In Producer, on the **File** menu, click **Open**.

3. In the **Open Project** dialog box, select your CD-ROM drive, and then select the Microsoft Producer project archive named Start_int_train.MSProducerZ. Click **Open**.

The project archive is located in the \StepByStep\Chapter10\ folder on the companion CD.

4. In the **Browse For Folder** dialog box, select a folder where you want the unpacked project to be stored. Click **OK** to unpack the project archive to the selected location.

   This project archive contains the digital media files that have already been imported into the current project, as well as a project file you can use.

Step-by-Step: Editing Imported Slides in PowerPoint

This procedure describes the steps required for editing slides in PowerPoint that have already been imported into a Producer presentation.

1. On the **View** menu, click **Preview Presentation Tab**. Click **Play** to begin playing the presentation so you can see how the slides are displayed.

   To increase system performance and to see more of the presentation elements, you can hide the timeline. To hide the timeline, click the **Hide Timeline** button below the timeline. After previewing your presentation, click the **Show Timeline** button to display the timeline again.

2. On the **View** menu, click **Media Tab**. This is the tab you can use to edit slides that have been imported into the current project.

3. In the tree pane, in the **Slides** folder, select the PowerPoint presentation you want to edit.

   If you are editing the sample project, choose the PowerPoint presentation Int_train.ppt in the **Slides** folder.

4. On the **Edit** menu, click **Edit Slide**. Microsoft PowerPoint automatically starts and the presentation you selected to edit opens.

   You can also select the PowerPoint slides you want to edit on the contents pane or the timeline. When you click the **Edit Slide** command with a slide that is selected in the contents pane or on the timeline, Microsoft PowerPoint automatically opens, and the slide you chose to edit is selected. You can then edit your slides using Microsoft PowerPoint.

5. If you are editing the slides from your own presentation, make the necessary edits in PowerPoint. However, if you are editing the Microsoft PowerPoint presentation from the sample project, do the following steps:

   - On the **View** menu, point to **Master**, and then click **Slide Master**. The slide master stores information about the colors, fonts, font sizes, and the positioning of elements in your slides.

   - On the **Format** menu, click **Slide Design**. This lets you change the slide design template that is used for your PowerPoint presentation.

- In the **Slide Design** task pane, choose a new design for the PowerPoint presentation. In the final sample presentation, the design named Digital Dots.pot is used.

- On the **Slide Master View** toolbar, click **Close Master View** to see the changes that are applied to all the slides.

- You will notice that the first slide, Train the Interviewer, displays incorrectly. This is because this slide is based on the Title Master slide rather than the Slide Master itself. To correct the title slide, on the **View** menu, point to **Master**, and then click **Slide Master**. Select the Title Master slide, shown in Figure 10.2. The Title Master slide is displayed.

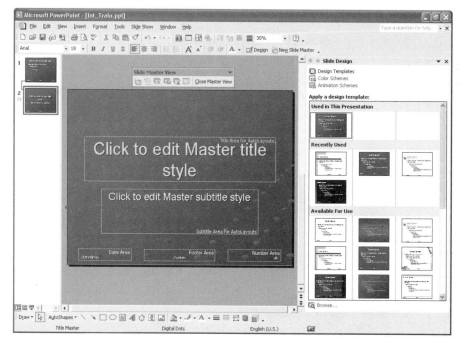

Figure 10.2 — The selected Title Master for the Digital Dots.pot slide design.

Click **Title Area for AutoLayouts**, and move the box near the top of the slide. You can drag the box with your mouse or press the Up Arrow on the keyboard to move the box up.

- On the **Slide Master View** toolbar, click **Close Master View** to see the change for the title slide.

6. On the **File** menu, click **Save** to save the changes to the PowerPoint presentation. Your changes will appear in the PowerPoint presentation that is already imported into Producer.

7. Do one of the following to go back to Producer:

- Hold down the Alt key and press Tab until the Producer icon is selected, and then release the Alt key.

- Click the **Microsoft Producer** button on the taskbar.

The updated PowerPoint presentation is re-imported automatically, and the changes you made to your slides appear in the PowerPoint slides in Producer. The changes are made to the slides in the contents pane and on the timeline.

As noted earlier in the chapter, if you make changes to the slide timings in PowerPoint, the updated slide timings will appear for the slides in the contents pane. However, the timings for slides on the timeline will not be updated.

Using the Microsoft Producer PowerPoint Add-in

The Microsoft Producer PowerPoint add-in program is a feature that is added into Microsoft PowerPoint 2002 when you install Producer. The add-in can help you quickly synchronize recorded video and audio (or audio only) with a slide show or presentation. To use the Microsoft Producer add-in program to record timings during a live presentation, in Microsoft PowerPoint, on the **View** menu, click **Show Slides And Record Timings**. The presentation automatically goes into the **Slide Show** view, where slides are displayed full screen and timing begins (see Figure 10.3).

For example, you can use a video camera to record video and audio of a speaker giving a presentation with a PowerPoint slide show. After the presentation, you can capture the video and audio to your computer by using Producer, and then add the PowerPoint presentation to the timeline.

If the speaker used the Microsoft Producer PowerPoint add-in program when giving the presentation, slide timings are recorded with the presentation in PowerPoint. When you add the presentation to the timeline, the slide timings are applied, making it easy to synchronize the slides with the video track. All you have to do is align the first slide with the beginning of the video and the rest of the slides shift to synchronize with the video.

When the presenter advances to the next slide or animation, PowerPoint automatically records the slide timing. The presenter does not need to do anything different from the normal process of displaying a slide show. After the presentation is completed and the slide show ends, the presenter only needs to save the PowerPoint presentation, and the new slide timings will be saved with the PowerPoint slides.

When you record the video and audio of the presentation, the camera should be focused on the presenter rather than on the slides. This lets the online audience see the presenter, including all of the gestures he or she makes while discussing the topic at hand. You can easily add the slides to the **Slide** track, just as you would in any other presentation created in Producer.

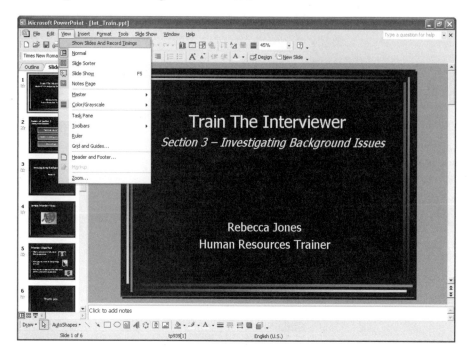

Figure 10.3 — Starting the Microsoft Producer PowerPoint add-in program.

Working with Slide Timings

One advantage of the Microsoft Producer PowerPoint add-in program is that the presenter can change to any slide at any time, and the slide timings are recorded to reflect those changes. For example, if a presenter is giving a live presentation and he or she is speaking about the fifth slide, but someone in the audience asks a question about the third slide, the presenter can go back in the slide show to display the third slide. When the presenter does this, PowerPoint records slide timings for both the first and second times the third slide was shown. When you add the entire presentation to the **Slide** track of the timeline, the third slide is added twice on the **Slide** track, in the same sequence and timing as the live presentation.

Slide animations are only shown the first time the slide is displayed during the slide show. Therefore, when you add the slides to the timeline in Producer, any slide animations are only shown the first time the slide appears on the timeline. The second time the slide with animations is displayed, the entire slide is displayed without playing back the slide animations. If you want the animations to appear the second time the slide is shown, you need to delete the second instance of the slide on the timeline and then add the original slide from the contents pane to the timeline again.

If you use the **Rehearse Timings** feature in PowerPoint to record slide timings and you go back and forth during the presentation, PowerPoint only records the last time the slide appears for the slide timing. If you use this feature and the presenter goes back and forth in the slideshow when giving the live presentation, the slide that was shown multiple times would only be added once to the timeline with timings for the last time the slide was shown in the presentation. Therefore, if you use **Rehearse Timings**, you will need to rearrange your slides on the timeline in Producer if you want to synchronize the slides with the audio and video recorded during the live presentation.

When working with slides that you have timed with the add-in program and then imported into Producer, avoid editing the slides. Because the slide timings are recorded and then synchronized with the captured audio and video, any changes you make to the slides can disrupt the timing so that the slides are no longer synchronized with the video and audio. For example, if you have a PowerPoint presentation timed with the add-in program and the video and audio, but you decide to add a new bulleted item in your slide, the timing for the entire presentation could be disrupted. In this situation, you may have to resynchronize your slides with the video and audio.

Understanding Add-in Security Issues

The Microsoft Producer PowerPoint add-in program is automatically installed with Microsoft Producer. Therefore, if you can run Producer, the PowerPoint add-in program is already installed on your computer. However, to see the **Show Slides And Record Timings** command on the **View** menu of PowerPoint, which is the command to start and use the add-in program, the security settings in Microsoft PowerPoint must be set to allow the add-in program to run. If you do not see this command on the **View** menu, adjust your security settings to use the add-in.

The security settings in Microsoft PowerPoint appear in the **Security** dialog box. You need to find the right balance when making security level choices, so you can work comfortably with PowerPoint while maintaining adequate security. For example, if your PowerPoint security settings were set as shown in Figure 10.4, you could use the add-in program as well as any other add-ins and installed templates in Microsoft PowerPoint.

You could increase your security level by making the security settings for macros more restrictive, allowing you to choose on an individual basis which add-in programs (which contain macros) you want to allow in PowerPoint. You can change these settings in the **Security** dialog box on the **Security Level** tab, which you can find by clicking the **Macro Security** button on the **Security** tab of the **Options** dialog box. Figure 10.5 shows the **Security** dialog box in relation to the **Options** dialog box.

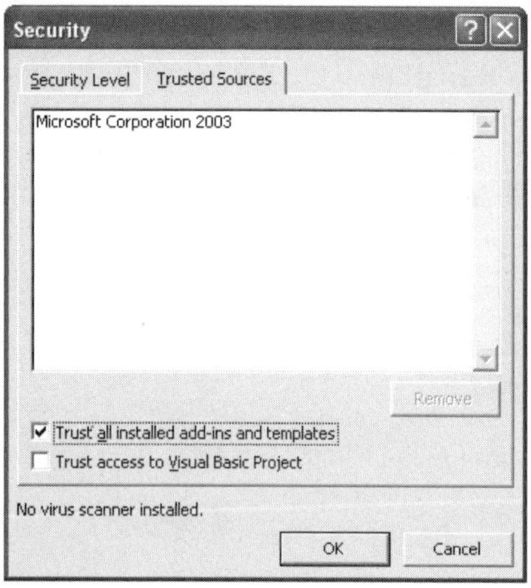

Figure 10.4 — Security settings to trust all installed add-ins and templates.

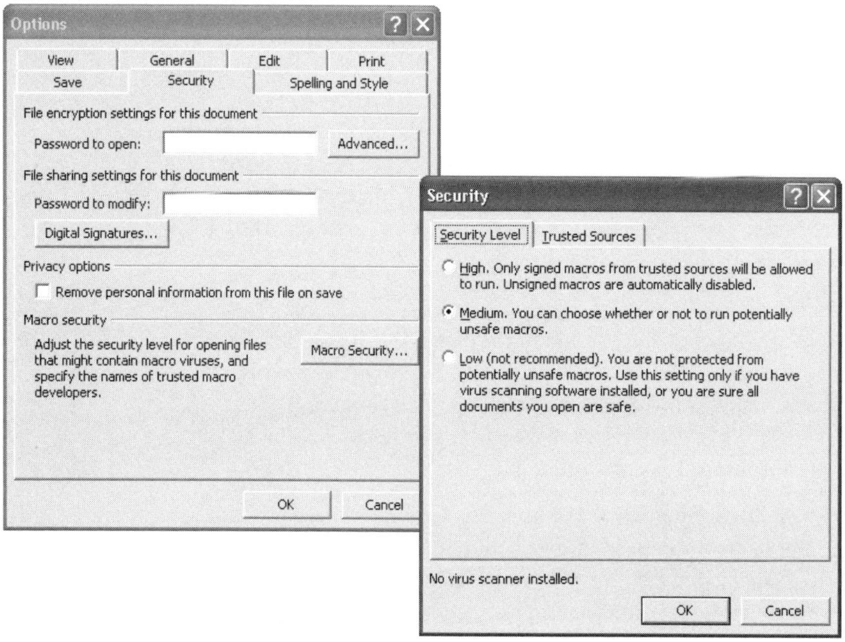

Figure 10.5 — The **Security** dialog box.

If the **Trust all installed add-ins and templates** check box is not selected, Microsoft Corporation is not listed as a trusted source, and the security settings shown in Figure 10.5 are applied, then a warning dialog box will appear each time you want to use the PowerPoint add-in. This warning will ask whether you want to enable the add-in program (see Figure 10.6). If this occurs, click **Enable Macros** to use the Microsoft Producer PowerPoint add-in program.

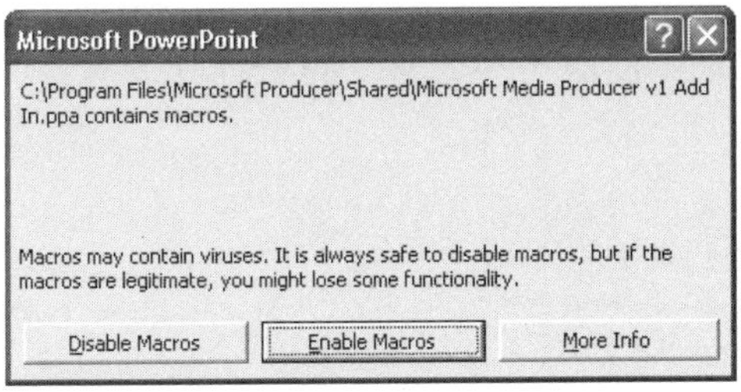

Figure 10.6 — Warning message for the Microsoft Producer PowerPoint add-in program.

Using Slide Animations and Transitions

You can add animations and transitions to your Microsoft PowerPoint presentations. Animations let you add movement to particular parts of a slide, such as text. A slide transition determines how the slides will change from the current slide to the next slide in your presentation.

Not all animations and transitions that you can use in PowerPoint will appear in your Producer presentations. Therefore, when creating slides that you plan to use in Producer presentations, it is a good idea to periodically preview your slides as a Web page (on the **File** menu in PowerPoint, click **Web Page Preview**). If the slide displays correctly in this preview, it should display correctly in your final Producer presentation.

Whether or not slide animations and slide transitions are shown in Microsoft Producer is determined when the PowerPoint presentation is imported into the current project. If the **Disable slide transitions on import** or the **Disable slide animations on import** settings are selected, slide transitions and slide animations are not displayed in your presentation. Though animations and transitions can add visual interest to your slide show, you can improve the playback quality of a Producer presentation by limiting their use.

In PowerPoint, you add two main types of animations: time-based animations and on-click animations. The type of animation that is applied to the slide in PowerPoint determines how the slide is displayed in your Producer presentation.

Using Time-based Animations

Time-based animations are slide effects such as custom slide animations, which occur with or after a specific event in the slide. These types of time-based animations are displayed in the **Custom Animation** task pane in PowerPoint with either a small icon of a clock next to the applied animation or no icon at all as shown in Figure 10.7. These animations have start values of **With Previous** or **After Previous**. Animations that start **With Previous** do not have an icon, whereas animations that start **After Previous** feature the small clock icon.

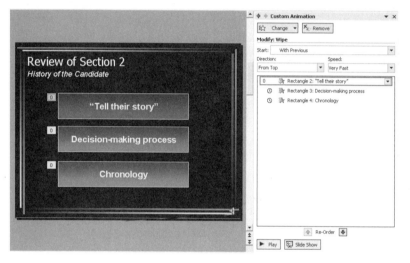

Figure 10.7 — A PowerPoint slide with time-based animations.

When slides that have time-based animations are used in a Producer presentation, the effects are not controlled by Producer. The time-based animations occur according to the settings applied in PowerPoint, including the speed at which they play and the direction from which they appear, such as **From Top**, **From Bottom**, and so forth.

You can see how these effects are displayed when you add the slides to the timeline and then preview the presentation in the **Preview Presentation** tab. When you are synchronizing these types of slides with video or audio, either through the slide narration options in the **Capture Wizard** or the **Synchronize Slides** dialog box, the animations occur automatically. You will be able to see the animations and synchronize the narration or other digital media with them appropriately.

Using On-click Animations

On-click animations are slide effects, such as custom slide animations, that occur after a mouse click. Figure 10.8 shows an example of a slide with an on-click animation. These types of animations are displayed in the **Custom Animation** task pane with a small icon of a mouse. These animations have the start value of **On Click**.

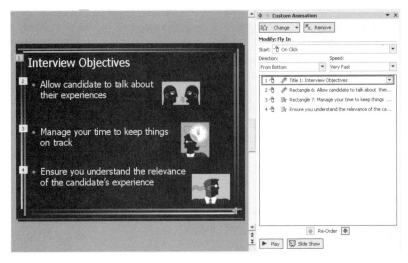

Figure 10.8 — A PowerPoint slide with on-click animations.

You can set the timing for slides with on-click slides animations in several ways:

- Using the **Rehearse Timings** command on the **Slide Show** menu in PowerPoint.

- Using the **Record Narration** command on the **Slide Show** menu in PowerPoint.

- Using the Microsoft Producer PowerPoint add-in program.

- Using the **Narrate slides with video and audio** or **Narrate slides with audio** capturing options in the **Capture Wizard** in Producer.

- Using the **Synchronize Slides** dialog box in Producer.

On-click animations let you control when the slide animation or slide transition appears. Therefore, when you set the slide timings in PowerPoint or Producer, the timings of the slide, animations, and transitions are determined by when the presenter clicks the mouse to go to the next slide event.

When a slide with an on-click animation is added to the **Slide** track of the timeline, the slide is displayed with small stars, as shown in Figure 10.9. Each star indicates an individual on-click effect and when it appears in the slide.

If the slide timings for on-click animations are not set in PowerPoint, or if the effects are not synchronized with audio or video in Producer, the animations are evenly spaced during the duration of the slide when it is added to the **Slide** track. Furthermore, if a slide is trimmed, the slide animations move so they are still evenly spaced during the duration of the slide on the timeline. However, the timings of these slide animations are not changed if you increase the amount of time the slide displays in your presentation.

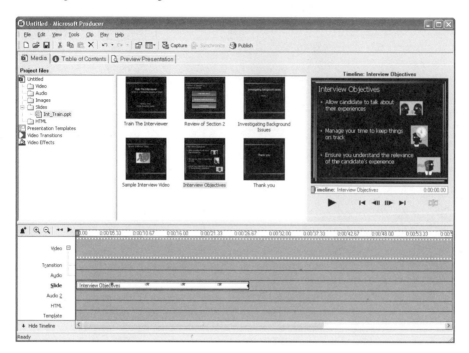

Figure 10.9 — A slide that contains four on-click slide effects.

After you add slide timings to your PowerPoint slides and import them into your Producer project, you should limit the number of changes you make to your slides so that you do not need to resynchronize your slides. For example, if you add slide timings and then later delete a slide on the timeline that is already synchronized with audio and video, you would need to resynchronize your slides with the video and audio so that the changes you made are reflected in your final presentation.

Viewing Slide Animations in Producer

As mentioned earlier in this book, you can preview your Producer presentations using either the **Media** tab or the **Preview Presentation** tab. The preview format of your presentation and what is displayed in the preview is determined by the tab in which you are previewing. Previewing in the **Media** tab lets you see individual digital media files in your presentation, whereas previewing in the **Preview Presentation** tab lets you see a preview of your entire presentation as it will appear when published. When previewing slides in Producer, the type of preview is also determined by the tab in which you are previewing the slides. Previewing a slide in the **Media** tab only displays a static image of the slide—any added slide effects are not displayed, regardless of whether you are previewing the slide from the **Slides** folder or from the timeline.

When you play a presentation from the beginning in the **Preview Presentation** tab, slides are displayed dynamically, with slide effects and transitions. If you select an individual slide and play it back from the beginning in the **Preview Presentation** tab, any slide transitions and animations are also displayed. Slide animations and transitions are not displayed if you start the slide preview when the playback indicator is not positioned at the beginning of the slide.

Moving forward or backward in an individual slide is also possible. In this situation, if you skip past a slide effect, the resulting text or object of the effect is still shown in the slide and the next slide effect will still be displayed.

Video and Audio in PowerPoint Slides

Your PowerPoint slides may already contain audio and video content. For example, audio and video might be embedded in the slide, or a narration might already be added to the slide through the **Record Narration** feature in PowerPoint. If you are creating PowerPoint slides that you plan to use in a Producer presentation, you should add the audio and video in Producer rather than in PowerPoint.

When you import slides that contain video and audio, you can choose to have the audio and video separated from the slides (as discussed in chapter 7). You can do this by selecting the **Separate video and audio from slides on import** check box in the **Options** dialog box. This lets you add the video and audio separately in your presentation, so you can edit it or add it to other parts of your presentation. The separated audio and video are imported and added to the **Audio** or **Video** folders in the project, respectively, with the name of the PowerPoint presentation added to the file name. If this check box is not selected, the video and audio remain in the slide.

Other than WAV audio files, any audio and video you insert in your PowerPoint slides are inserted as links in your slides. If you choose not to separate the video and audio from your slides, the links are maintained in your PowerPoint slides. However, if you publish your presentation, these links will not be updated. Therefore, if the audio or video you inserted in your PowerPoint slide is only located on your local machine, it will not be displayed or played back during the presentation. If you choose to add video and audio to your slides using PowerPoint, make sure the audio and video files are linked and inserted from a location that your audience has access to, such as a Web site or shared network location.

The easiest way to use audio and video in your PowerPoint slides is to have the audio and video separated on import and then to add it to the correct location on the timeline, so it plays with the appropriate slide. This ensures that your audio and video will be played back correctly in your final published Producer presentation.

If you choose not to have the audio and video separated from the slides, they will play as specified in PowerPoint. If you inserted a video or audio file and specified that you wanted it to play automatically in your slides, it will play automatically in your Producer presentation when the slide displays.

When working with video and audio in your slides, be aware of possible issues that can arise. For example, if you inserted an audio or video file in your PowerPoint slide, and the audio or video plays for one minute, but the slide only displays in your presentation for 20 seconds, the audio or video will be cut off after 20 seconds. Therefore, if slide timings were not already added when you imported the slides, you would need to lengthen the duration that the slide appears on the timeline in order to play back the entire digital media file.

CHAPTER 11

Publishing Your Presentation

Up to this point, your focus has been on creating the presentation. You've arranged your digital media on the timeline, and refined the look and feel of your presentation. Now you probably can't wait to show it to someone else. You might have already had a colleague or two look over your shoulder and watch your masterpiece in the **Preview Presentation** tab. But how can you show your work to people outside of your office?

To get your presentation to its intended audience, you use some means of distribution. In Microsoft Producer this is called *publishing*. Publishing your presentation means making it available to your audience, and it involves roughly four steps:

- Choosing the distribution medium

- Packaging the contents of your presentation for the selected distribution medium

- Creating the final product

- Delivering the presentation to your audience

Microsoft Producer includes a feature called the **Publish Wizard**, which makes it easy to package your finished presentation and make it available for viewing from a CD, a shared network location, a corporate intranet, or the Internet. The **Publish Wizard** guides you through a series of steps in which you provide information about how and where you would like to publish your presentation, automatically creates all the files necessary for viewing it, and copies each file to the appropriate destination.

When the publishing process is complete, other people can view your presentation as a Web page by using Internet Explorer 5.0 (or later). The Web page that the viewer sees contains all the elements you included in your presentation, and the finished product looks just like what you saw in the **Preview Presentation** tab when you were creating the presentation. Your audience is not required to have Microsoft Producer or Microsoft PowerPoint installed to play a published presentation.

Understanding the Publishing Process

Before you jump into publishing your presentation, it is helpful to understand some of the concepts you'll encounter during the publishing process. This includes learning about the files published by Producer, information about servers, publishing profiles, and e-service providers.

Files Published by Microsoft Producer

When Microsoft Producer publishes your presentation, it works with data files. There are three basic types of files that Producer deals with in the publishing process:

- **Files that you supply.** These are files that contain content that you've created, such as HTML pages or PowerPoint slides.

- **Files that Producer creates from files that you supply.** These are Windows Media files that Microsoft Producer encodes by combining the audio and video clips that you placed on the timeline.

- **Files that Producer creates from scratch.** These are files that Microsoft Producer generates dynamically based on the requirements of your presentation.

Once Microsoft Producer assembles all the files necessary to create your presentation, it copies them to one or more destinations. Where it copies your files depends upon the information you supply in the **Publish Wizard**. In most cases, Producer copies all the files to the same destination folder; in certain cases, Producer copies the digital media files to a separate destination folder. The list of files that Producer publishes varies depending upon the presentation. You will have an opportunity to view a list of files to be published when you use the **Publish Wizard**.

Microsoft Producer Help contains detailed information about the file name extension and purpose of each file type used by Producer.

One very effective way to deliver your presentation to an audience is over a computer network, such as the Internet or a corporate intranet. Producer makes it easy to do this by handling many of the details for you. In order to make your presentation available for delivery over a network, you publish your content to a computer called a server.

Understanding Servers

While it is beyond the scope of this book to instruct you in the art and science of server administration, there are some things you should know about the servers that host your Microsoft Producer presentations.

What Is a Server, and Why Do You Need One?

A *server* is a computer, connected to a network or the Internet, that stores data that can be accessed by other computers on demand. A computer (or the software) that accesses data stored on a server is called a *client*. A Web server is a particular kind of server that is specifically designed to deliver content using the standards and protocols of the World Wide Web. The browser software that retrieves and displays a Web page is the Web server's client.

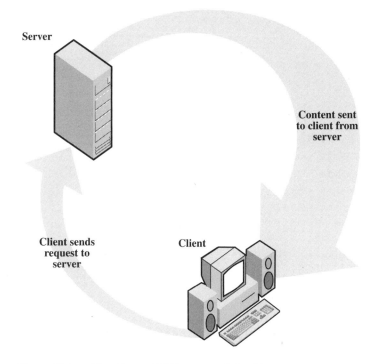

Server

Content sent to client from server

Client sends request to server

Client

Figure 11.1 — The client and Web server relationship.

The terms client and server refer to the relationship between the computers on the network. There is no reason a particular computer can't act as a Web server one moment and as a client the next. In fact, a computer can act as both client and server simultaneously.

When you publish your Producer presentation using the **My Network Places** or **Web server** options (which will be explained later in this chapter), Producer copies the presentation files to the server computer. When someone wants to view the presentation, he or she must use Internet Explorer as the client software. The server delivers the data that comprises your presentation when the client requests it.

What Kind of Server Do You Need?

Microsoft Producer can publish presentations to Web servers that support the Web-based Distributed Authoring and Versioning (WebDAV) protocol, such as Microsoft Internet Information Server (IIS). WebDAV is a set of extensions to the HTTP protocol that are controlled by the Internet Engineering Task Force (IETF) WebDAV Working Group. In order for Producer to publish your presentation directly to a WebDAV server, the server location must be configured to allow your computer to read files from it and copy files to it. This is called *read and write access*. You can find out more about WebDAV at the Web site *http://www.webdav.org*.

What Is the Difference Between Downloading and Streaming?

To view your presentation from a network, digital media is delivered over the network to client computers. When a server delivers a digital media file to a client computer, it can transfer the content in one of two ways:

- The content can be copied to a new file created on the client. This process is called *downloading*. When enough of the file is copied to the client to reasonably assure smooth playback, the player can begin playing the content.

- The content can display immediately as it is delivered to the client. This process is called *streaming*. In practice, Windows Media Player creates a temporary storage area, called a *buffer*, to hold a portion of the streaming content. When enough data has accumulated in the buffer, the player begins to play the stream. This allows the player to play back the content smoothly.

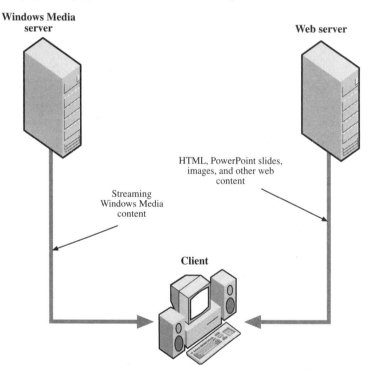

Figure 11.2 — The client, Web server, and Windows Media server relationship.

What Is a Windows Media Server?

A Windows Media server is a computer on which Windows Media Services has been installed. Windows Media Services is software that is specifically designed to deliver Windows Media content across a network or the Internet. Windows Media Services is included with each installation of Microsoft Windows 2000 Server and newer Windows server operating systems.

You have a choice of using a Windows Media server or a Web server to deliver the Windows Media files that are part of your presentation. If you choose to use a Windows Media server, it takes on the job of streaming the digital media files, while the Web server continues to perform the rest of the functions required to play back the presentation. There are several things to consider when deciding whether to use a Windows Media server to deliver your Microsoft Producer Windows Media files:

- There are important differences between the way a Windows Media server delivers digital media and the way a Web server does the job. A Web server attempts to deliver the greatest amount of content in the shortest possible time. This works great for Web pages, but is not the preferred method for streaming digital audio and video.

   A Windows Media server attempts to deliver data in real time, as it is needed. It can use feedback from the client to determine network conditions and adjust the timing of data delivery to make the most efficient use of the network bandwidth. If you expect that viewers will attempt to connect to your presentation on a busy network, a Windows Media server can make better use of the network resources than a Web server can.

- If a Web server delivers your presentation to a client computer that has only Windows Media Player 6.4 installed, the viewer will have to wait for any Windows Media files to finish downloading to the local hard drive before watching the presentation. Depending on the length of your presentation, this can be very time-consuming. If your Windows Media files are streamed from a Windows Media server, the content will begin to play after a short buffering delay. In this case, the Windows Media server provides a far better user experience.

- Windows Media servers can use a special communication protocol—the User Datagram Protocol (UDP)—to greatly improve streaming performance. UDP allows for fast, high-priority data transmission, and uses a more intelligent data-rate management system than protocols used by Web servers. This means that content delivered from a Web server is more likely to be interrupted by periods of silence than content streamed from a Windows Media server.

- Windows Media servers can deliver better audio and video quality than Web servers. The constant communication between Windows Media Player and the Windows Media server allows the server to continually fine-tune the delivery of the streaming content. For example, if the network suddenly becomes congested, the Windows Media server might lower the video frame rate in order to allow the audio quality to remain high.

In fact, the only reason not to use a Windows Media server to stream your presentation on an intranet or the Internet is that you don't have access to the Windows Media Services software. If your infrastructure simply doesn't allow you to use a Windows Media server, then a Web server will do the job.

How Do I Publish to a Windows Media Server?

Publishing using a Windows Media server requires that you supply more information in the **Publish Wizard** than publishing to just a Web server.

Windows Media Services uses the concept of *publishing points*. Basically, a publishing point is a name that you assign to the location of your content on the server. The client uses this name to access the content, rather than the physical location.

For detailed information about Windows Media Services, configuring your Windows Media server, and using publishing points, see Windows Media Services Help. For a complete overview of Windows Media and streaming technologies, see the book *Inside Windows Media* (Que, 1999).

Selecting a Publishing Profile

When Microsoft Producer creates the files for your published presentation, it encodes the content you have placed on the timeline into output files. During this process, Producer examines each item on the **Video**, **Audio**, and **Audio 2** tracks to determine its type (audio, video, or screen capture). Producer then appropriately combines and compresses the content into one or more Windows Media files. There are two main advantages to this process. First, combining content makes playback easier since several items of content can be streamed from the same file. Second, Windows Media files occupy much less space than uncompressed audio and video content on a hard drive.

A *profile* is a related group of settings that tell Producer which *codec* to use to create a Windows Media file for your published presentation. (A codec is the software that determines how to compress or decompress a Windows Media file.) When you use the **Publish Wizard** to publish your presentation, you choose one or more publishing profiles from a list. Producer only includes in this list profiles that are compatible with the content on the timeline. The name of each profile in the list describes the intended use of the profile. Typically this will include two pieces of information:

- The type of connection for which the profile is intended, such as local playback (playback from the viewer's computer) or target audience playback (playback from a network server or the Internet).

- The *bit rate* at which the resulting Windows Media file will play.

Bit rate refers to the speed at which the Windows Media content transfers between the source (which could be a server computer, a CD, or a local hard drive) and the player, in this case a Windows Media Player ActiveX control embedded in a Web page created by Producer. Bit rate is measured in kilobits per second (Kbps). The bit rate value relates directly to the playback quality: the lower the bit rate, the lower the perceived quality; the higher the bit rate, the better the perceived quality.

A typical profile name in Producer might look like this: **For target audience playback at 300 Kbps.**

The **Publish Wizard** displays a **Published Size** value for each profile, as well as the total size required for all selected profiles, so you can estimate how much hard drive storage space your presentation requires.

You'll need to decide which profiles to choose, depending on several factors. The following sections cover questions you should ask yourself when selecting profiles. Once your presentation is published, test the playback using the appropriate connection and computer hardware and see what happens. You can always go back and try publishing with different profiles until you get the results you want.

How Will My Audience View the Presentation?

You'll need to know some details about how viewers are connected to the network or the Internet, or whether viewers will be downloading the presentation to their local computers. The important term here is *bandwidth*, the capacity of the user's computer and network connection to transfer data. If viewers are receiving your presentation through a dial-up connection to the Internet, the bandwidth of the connection will typically be low, perhaps up to 56 Kbps. On the other hand, if viewers have a CD that contains your presentation, the available bandwidth is restricted only by the internal transfer rate of the CD-ROM drive, which is typically very high—much higher, in fact, than the highest profile bit rate available in Producer.

You'll want to try to match the profile bit rate to the anticipated bit rate at which your audience will connect to the presentation. If you can't make a direct match, you should use the next lower profile bit rate. Forcing viewers to stream content at a higher bit rate than their connection bandwidth allows will result in a poor playback experience.

What Playback Quality Does the Presentation Require?

Remember that the lower the bit rate, the lower the perceived quality during playback. You may want to set a minimum connection speed requirement for viewers to help keep the quality of your presentation high.

How Much Storage Space Is Available on the Server?

As the bit rate and playback quality of a Windows Media file increase, so does the amount of hard disk space needed to store the file. You may have storage constraints that dictate which and how many profiles you select.

How Does My Video or Screen Capture Fit into the Presentation Template?

You can choose from a wide variety of interesting presentation templates in Producer, or even create your own. You'll notice when choosing a template that many are designed to display at a particular video image size, for example 640x480 pixels.

When you choose to apply a profile in the **Publish Wizard** to a presentation that contains video or screen captures, the associated bit rate and codec are designed to display at a particular image size for optimal viewing. However, when the viewer plays back the presentation, the image size will change to match the size specified by the template. This means that a low bit rate video, for instance, may not look very good if the image expands beyond its intended viewing size. Conversely, shrinking the size of a very high bit rate video display might be a waste of bandwidth and storage space since the increased quality of the image might not be obvious.

How Many Different Profiles Should I Use?

You don't have to publish using only one profile. How many you choose will depend on how you answered the previous questions. If your audience might connect to your presentation in more than one manner—both dial-up and corporate network, for instance—then you may want to use two profiles.

On the other hand, each profile adds additional information to the published presentation, which takes up additional hard disk space. If you want to publish using five different profiles for a variety of bandwidth compatibility options, you might find you don't have sufficient hard drive space available on the server. Also, keep in mind that each additional profile adds to the amount of time it takes to publish your presentation. You should start out by publishing with only as many profiles as you require to get the job done.

Publishing with E-services

In Microsoft Producer, an *e-service* is a publishing solution that customizes and simplifies the publishing process. Producer exposes an object model to programmers, which they can use to change the way the **Publish Wizard** works.

When you choose to publish with an e-service, you'll be presented in the **Publish Wizard** with a custom user interface that was designed by the e-service author. This may look and operate very differently from the default **Publish Wizard**. Typically, an e-service will be designed to allow you to choose publishing options (such as profiles or server addresses) that are compatible with the hosting services offered by the e-service provider. This may hide some of the details of the publishing process from you, making the publishing process much simpler and friendlier.

You can use e-services from several sources, such as:

- A third-party company that charges a fee for hosting your presentations on its Web server.

- Your company's own internal e-services, if available.

- An e-service you design.

The Microsoft Producer for PowerPoint 2002 Software Development Kit (SDK) is included with each installation of Microsoft Producer. The SDK contains details about how to create Producer e-services, including an object model reference, a programming guide, and sample code. The Producer SDK can be viewed by double-clicking the file named ProdSDK.chm, which is located in the subfolder named Shared where you installed Producer on your hard disk. Chapter 14 discusses how to create a basic e-service.

Adding an E-service to the Publish Wizard

To use an e-service, you must first add the e-service to the **Publish Wizard**. There are several ways to do this; you should follow the directions given by the e-service provider.

Typically, you will navigate through a series of Web pages that display when you click **Learn More** on the first page of the **Publish Wizard**, or run a file with a .reg file name extension, called a registry file. In either case, the e-service details are added to the registry on your computer, and the e-service becomes accessible during your next Producer session. You may have to close Producer, start a new session, and click **OK** in a dialog box to grant permission to use the new e-service.

Once an e-service has been added successfully, the e-service name will appear as an option in the **Web server** list on the first page of the **Publish Wizard**. When you select the e-service in the list and click **Next**, the e-service's custom interface appears. Each e-service is different, so take the time to familiarize yourself with the individual details.

Configuring Security Settings for E-services

Producer allows you to change the default security settings for e-service publishing. Producer determines whether you can publish your presentations to an e-service provider based on the settings on the **Security** tab in the **Options** dialog box. (To display the **Options** dialog box, click **Options** on the **Tools** menu.) The e-service options for publishing map directly to the security settings for Internet Explorer.

You can use these settings to prevent an e-service provider from sending or publishing files to your local computer, or publishing files to the local intranet or Internet, if the e-service is not hosted in the specified security zone. For example, to prevent an Internet-based e-service from publishing files to your local computer, in the drop-down list labeled **Allow an e-service to publish files to my local computer only if the e-service is hosted in the following security zone** select **My local computer, local intranet**. For more information about security settings in Producer, see the Microsoft Producer Help.

Publishing by using the **Web server** option in the **Publish Wizard** is discussed later in this chapter.

Using the Publish Wizard

When you click **Publish** on the Producer toolbar, or choose **Publish Presentation** from the **File** menu, the **Publish Wizard** is displayed. The first page of the wizard allows you to select one of three choices that represent three types of publishing destinations.

- **My Computer.** Select this option if you want to publish your presentation to a folder on your local computer or to a recordable or rewritable CD drive. If you publish to your hard drive, you'll be able to watch the presentation on your computer in Internet Explorer. If the folder you publish to is shared on a network, other users with permission to access the shared folder will be able to see your presentation as well. If you publish to a CD, your presentation becomes portable and can be viewed on any computer that meets the system requirements for presentation playback and also has the appropriate CD drive for the recorded media.

- **My Network Places.** Select this option if you want to publish your presentation to a network location, such as a shared folder on a corporate network server. Using this option is identical to publishing using the **My Computer** option, except clicking **Browse** on the **Publishing Destination** page opens a file dialog box that allows you to browse only network locations.

- **Web server.** Select this option if you want to publish your presentation to a remote server, such as an Internet site. You should also use this choice if you want your Windows Media files to be streamed from Windows Media server, if you want to publish to a Web server you have used previously, or if you want to publish your presentation using an e-service.

Publishing to My Computer

The easiest way to get a feel for the **Publish Wizard** is to use it to publish your presentation to your hard drive on the same computer you use to run Producer. The following steps will guide you through the process:

1. Start Producer and open your presentation.

2. Click **Publish** on the toolbar. The **Publish Wizard** appears as shown in Figure 11.3. Click **My Computer.**

   Click **Next** to proceed to the **Publishing Destination** page, shown in Figure 11.4.

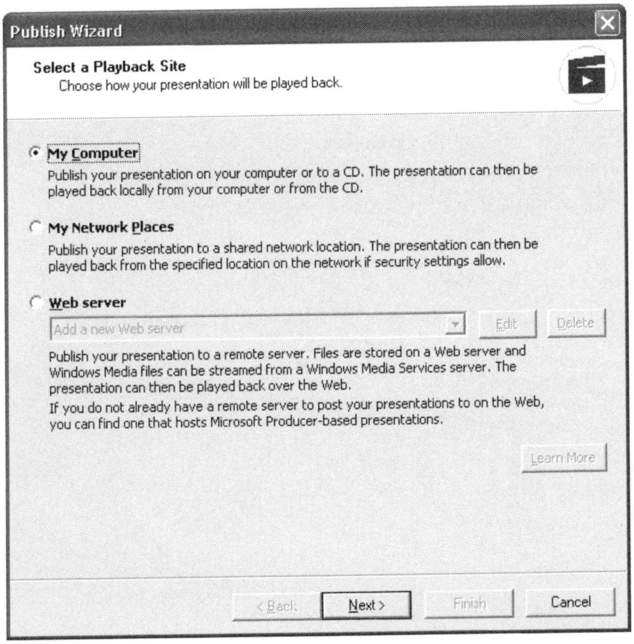

Figure 11.3 — The first page of the **Publish Wizard**.

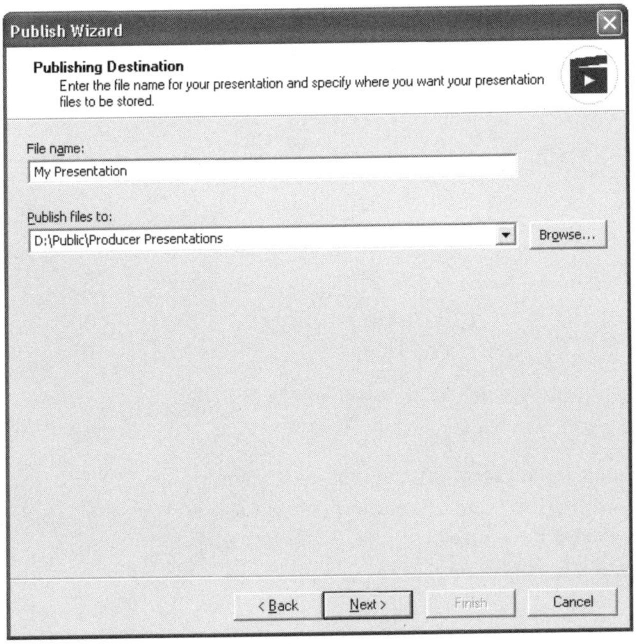

Figure 11.4 — The **Publishing Destination** page.

3. Type a name for your presentation in the **File name** box. The wizard provides the project name by default.

4. In the **Publish files to** box, enter the location of a folder to which Producer can publish your presentation. Alternatively, click **Browse** and use the **Browse For Folder** dialog box to select a folder. Over time, as you use different folder locations, Producer will add the paths to the drop-down list so you can easily reuse file paths in the future.

Click **Next** to proceed to the **Presentation Information** page, shown in Figure 11.5. If a presentation with the same name exists in the publishing folder, Producer will ask you for permission to overwrite it.

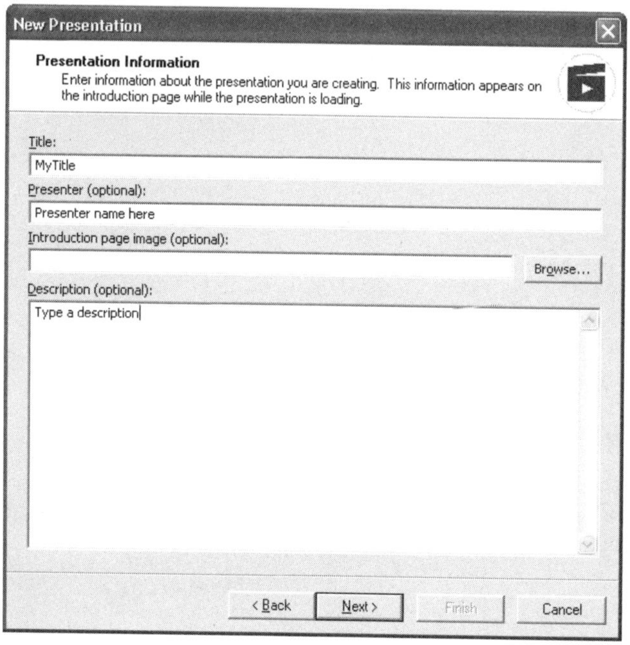

Figure 11.5 — The **Presentation Information** page.

5. In the **Title** box, type a title for your presentation. The title will appear on the introduction page and the title bar of the presentation playback window.

You can also provide the name of the presenter, a path to an image, and a description. All this information will be added to the introduction page when the presentation is published and will be visible to the viewer. If you have already entered the information for your project in the **Table of Contents** tab, it will appear on this page, and you can skip this step.

Click **Next** to proceed to the **Playback Quality** page, shown in Figure 11.6.

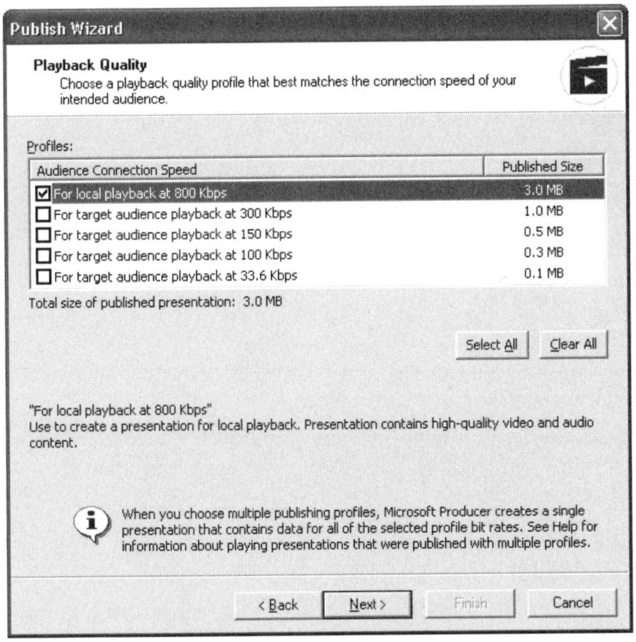

Figure 11.6 — The **Playback Quality** page.

6. Select at least one playback quality profile. The **Publish Wizard** will offer you only profiles that are appropriate for the type of content in your presentation. Since you're publishing to your local computer, make sure only one local playback profile is selected for now.

Click **Next** to proceed to the **Publish Your Presentation** page, shown in Figure 11.7.

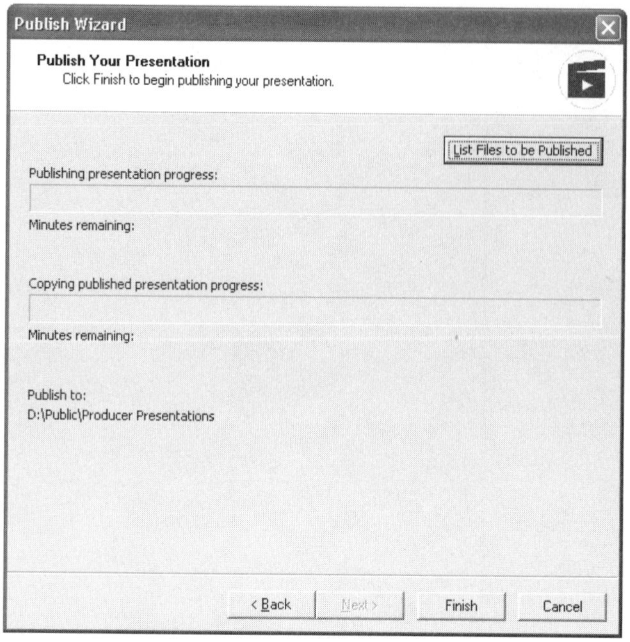

Figure 11.7 — The **Publish Your Presentation** page.

7. If you're the curious type, click **List Files to be Published**. A separate window opens that displays the name of each file that Producer creates and copies to the publishing destination folder. It will look something like Figure 11.8, though the file names will be different. Click **OK** when you are ready to continue.

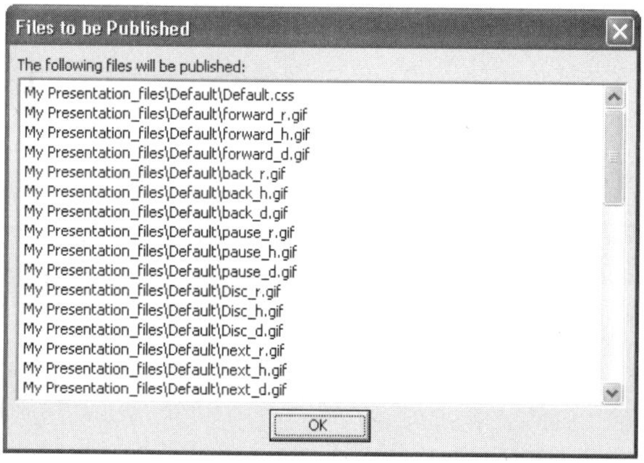

Figure 11.8 — The listing of files to be published in your presentation.

8. Read the **Publish to** path, which is displayed near the bottom of the **Publish Your Presentation** page, and verify that it is correct. If you want to make any changes, now is the time to click **Back**.

9. Click **Finish**. You'll see a dialog box like the one shown in Figure 11.9. The two progress bars near the top and middle of the page display the current condition of the publishing process, and the **Publish Wizard** also displays the estimated time remaining until completion.

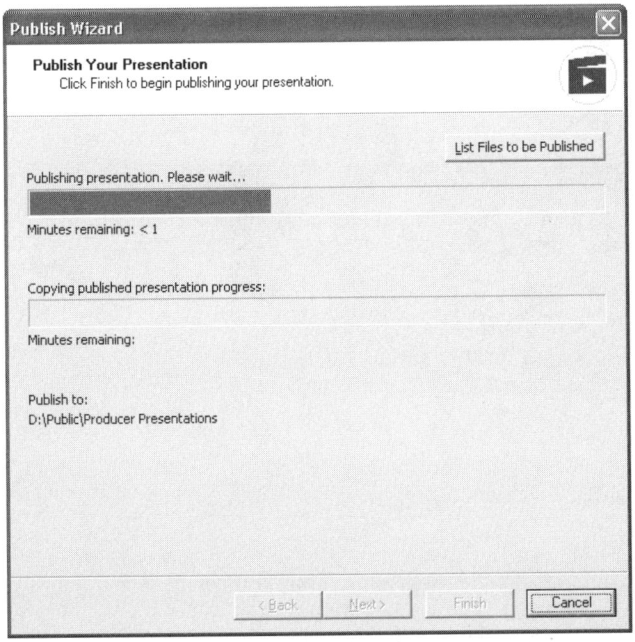

Publish Wizard

Publish Your Presentation
Click Finish to begin publishing your presentation.

List Files to be Published

Publishing presentation. Please wait...

Minutes remaining: < 1

Copying published presentation progress:

Minutes remaining:

Publish to:
D:\Public\Producer Presentations

< Back   Next >   Finish   Cancel

Figure 11.9 — Progress is reported as Producer publishes your presentation.

When the publishing process is complete, the **Publish Wizard** allows you to preview your presentation. Click **Yes** in the window that asks, "Would you like to view your published presentation?" The introduction page for your presentation opens in a separate Internet Explorer window, like that shown in Figure 11.10. Click **Play** to view your published presentation.

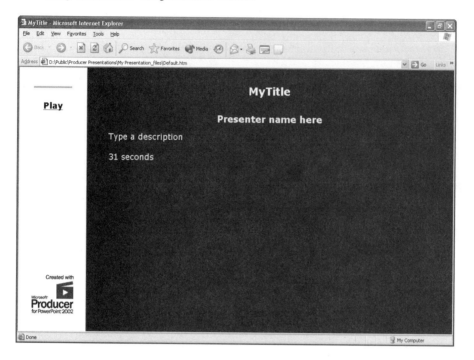

Figure 11.10 — The presentation's introduction page displayed in Internet Explorer.

When you've finished watching your masterpiece, close the Internet Explorer window. Click **Close** to exit the **Publish Wizard**.

Congratulations! You've published your first Microsoft Producer presentation. You can view the presentation again at any time. Simply use Windows Explorer to browse to the folder you specified in the **Publish files to** box in the **Publish Wizard**, and then locate the HTML file that has the name you provided in the **File name** box. Double-click the file to open it, and your introduction page will appear in the browser window.

Publishing to a CD

Publishing your Producer presentation to a recordable CD has several advantages. First, the presentation can be viewed on a computer that isn't connected to a network or the Internet. As long as the computer meets the minimum system requirements for playback and has a CD drive capable of reading the CD, the presentation will play.

Second, you can publish multiple presentations on the same CD. This is useful if, for instance, you have a series of lectures you'd like to offer as a package. You can also hand out your CDs at a trade show, sell them through the mail or at a retail store, or provide them as classroom materials.

If you are using the Microsoft Windows XP operating system and have a recordable or rewritable CD drive, the **Publish Wizard** makes publishing to a CD easy. You can follow these steps to make a Microsoft Producer presentation CD:

1. Start Producer and open your presentation.

2. Click **Publish** on the toolbar. The **Publish Wizard** appears. If it isn't already selected, click **My Computer**.

   Click **Next** to proceed to the **Publishing Destination** page.

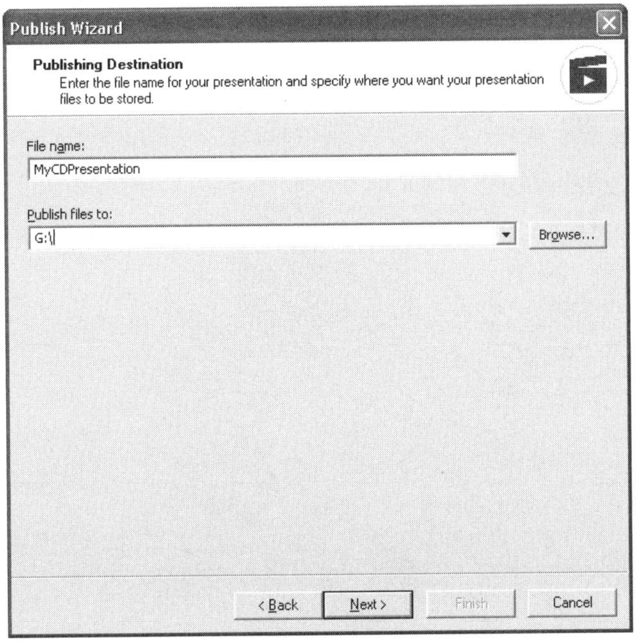

Figure 11.11 — Specifying the location of a recordable CD drive.

3. Type a name for your presentation in the **File name** box. The wizard provides the project name by default.

4. In the **Publish files to** box, type the drive letter that corresponds to your recordable CD drive, such as G:\, as shown in Figure 11.11. Alternatively, click **Browse** and use the **Browse For Folder** dialog box to select the drive.

   Click **Next** to proceed to the **Presentation Information** page.

5. In the **Title** box, type a title for your presentation.

   Optionally, provide the name of the presenter, a path to an image, and a description. All these will be added to the introduction page when the presentation is published and will be visible to the viewer.

Click **Next** to proceed to the **Playback Quality** page.

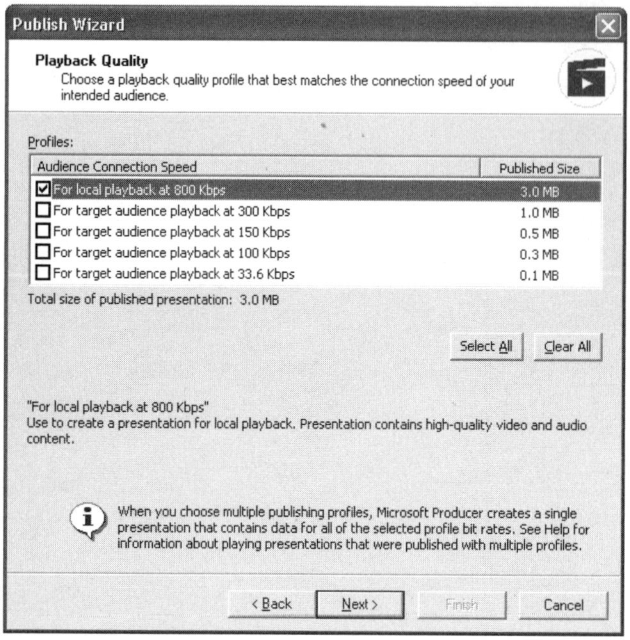

Figure 11.12 — Selecting a local playback profile.

6. Select at least one playback quality profile, as shown in Figure 11.12. The **Publish Wizard** will offer you only profiles that are appropriate for the type of content in your presentation. For now, since you're publishing to a CD, select a local playback profile to get the best quality.

   Click **Next** to proceed to the **Publish Your Presentation** page.

7. Click **List Files to be Published** if you want to see the file name of each file that Producer creates and copies to the publishing destination folder. Click **OK** to continue.

8. Read the **Publish to** path, which is displayed near the bottom of the **Publish Your Presentation** page, and verify that it displays the drive letter specifier of your recordable CD drive.

9. Click **Finish**. The two progress bars near the top and middle of the page display the current condition of the publishing process, and the **Publish Wizard** also displays the estimated time remaining until completion.

10. When the publishing process is complete, the Windows XP **CD Writing Wizard** appears automatically, as shown in Figure 11.13. Type the name you want to give to the CD. The wizard offers the current date as the default name.

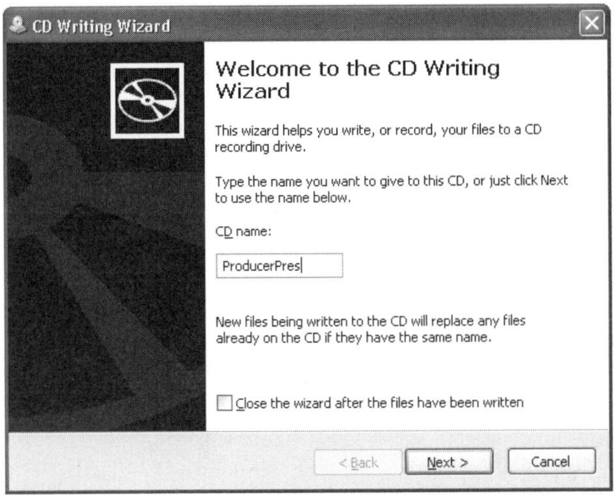

Figure 11.13 — Creating a presentation CD in Windows XP.

11. Insert a recordable CD in the drive you specified in the **Publish Wizard**. Click **Next** to write the files to the CD. The operation progress will be shown in a dialog box like the one in Figure 11.14.

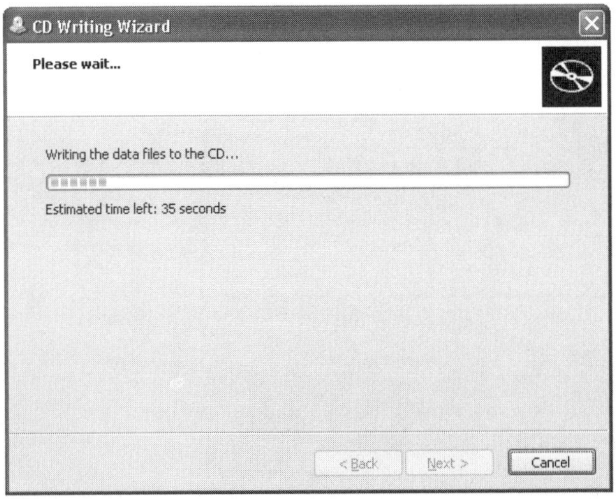

Figure 11.14 — Writing files to the CD.

12. When the CD writing completes, click **Finish** to exit the **CD Writing Wizard**. Click **Close** to exit the **Publish Wizard**.

You can repeat this process as many times as you like using the same recordable CD, as long as there is sufficient space on the disc to contain your next presentation. If you choose to do this, you should be certain to give each presentation a unique title in the **Title** box in the **Publish Wizard**.

When the viewer places a CD containing one presentation into a CD drive, the presentation automatically displays the introduction page. When the viewer places a CD containing more than one presentation into a CD drive, Windows automatically opens a Web page titled **Select a Presentation**, which acts as a main menu for the Producer content on the disc. Here, the viewer will see a list of all the presentations available on the CD. Each title appears as a link, which the viewer can click to open the introduction page for that presentation in a separate Internet Explorer window.

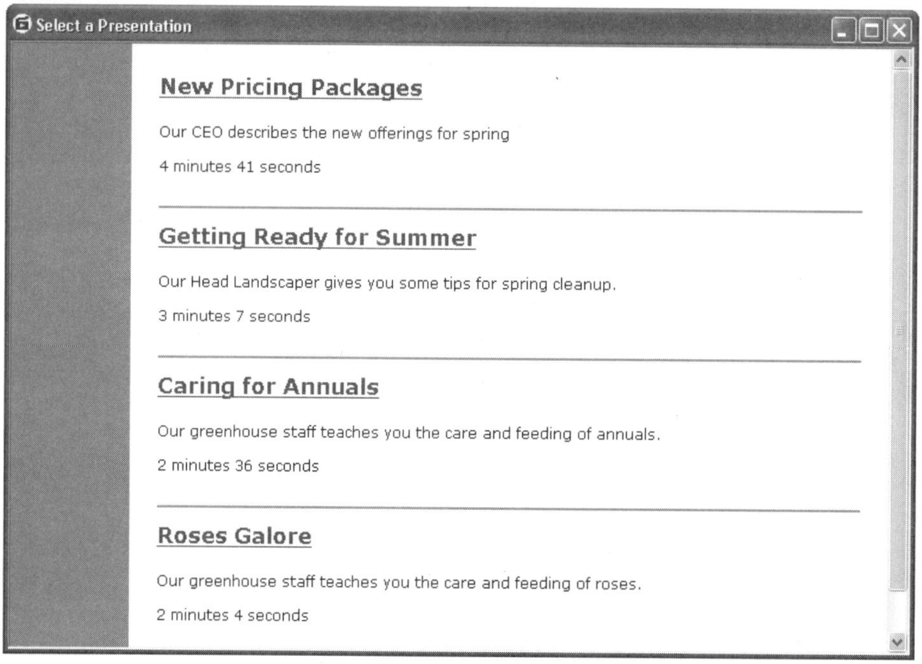

Figure 11.15 — The **Select a Presentation** page.

It's worth noting that the Windows CD AutoPlay feature can be disabled by the user, and the details of how to enable or disable this feature vary depending on the version of the operating system. When Producer creates a CD, it includes in the root directory a file named autorun.inf, which is a text file that Windows reads to determine what to do when a CD is inserted into the drive. The autorun.inf file that Producer includes on a CD points Windows to the file named scan.hta, which is the HTML application file that displays the **Select a Presentation** Web page. This means that the Producer presentation CD can be run manually by double clicking the scan.hta file in Windows Explorer, or by clicking **Run** on the **Start** menu and typing the path and file name—for example, E:\scan.hta. You might want to tell users of your CD about this alternate way to start your

Producer presentations, just in case the AutoPlay feature is not enabled on the user's computer.

Creating a Presentation CD Without Using the Publish Wizard

It is possible to copy your presentations to a CD manually. You might want to do this if you are using an operating system other than Windows XP, or if you want to change the published files before creating the CD. The following steps describe the process:

1. Create one temporary folder on your local computer to contain all the presentations you'd like to copy to the CD.

2. Publish each presentation to the temporary folder using the **My Computer** option.

3. Use your favorite CD writing software to copy all the files and subfolders from your temporary folder to the CD. Be certain not to copy the temporary folder itself, otherwise AutoPlay will not work and viewers will have to open the folder manually to view the presentations.

Publishing to My Network Places

Publishing to a folder on your corporate network is a great way to make your presentation available to a large audience. This is especially useful for corporate training seminars, meetings, and any other presentation that should reach a specific audience. The following steps will guide you through using the **Publish Wizard** to publish your presentation to a network folder:

1. Start Producer and open your presentation.

2. Click **Publish** on the toolbar. The **Publish Wizard** appears. If it isn't already selected, click **My Network Places** as shown in Figure 11.16. Click **Next** to proceed to the **Publishing Destination** page.

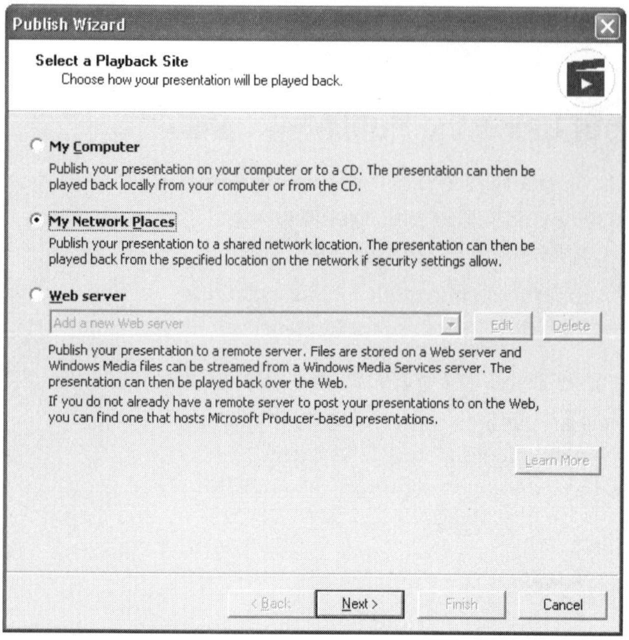

Figure 11.16 — Using the **My Network Places** option.

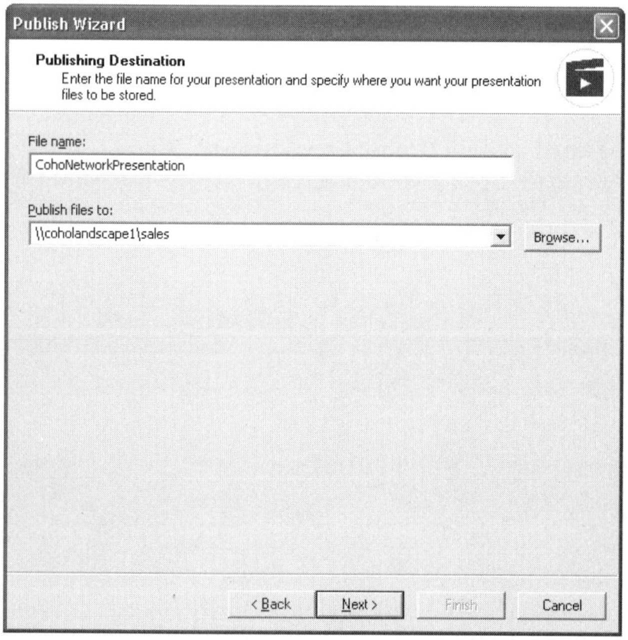

Figure 11.17 — Publishing files to a network location.

3. Type a name for your presentation in the **File name** box. The wizard provides the project name by default.

4. In the **Publish files to** box, type a path to a shared network folder to which Producer can publish your presentation. An example is shown in Figure 11.17. Alternatively, click **Browse** and use the **Browse For Folder** dialog box to select a folder.

5. Click **Next** to proceed to the **Presentation Information** page. The **Publish Wizard** will prompt you for permission to overwrite a presentation with the same name, if one exists. If the **Publish Wizard** cannot find the network path you specified, a warning message displays and you cannot proceed.

6. In the **Title** box, type a title for your presentation.

   Optionally, provide the name of the presenter, a path to an image, and a description. All these will be added to the introduction page when the presentation is published and will be visible to the viewer.

   Click **Next** to proceed to the **Playback Quality** page.

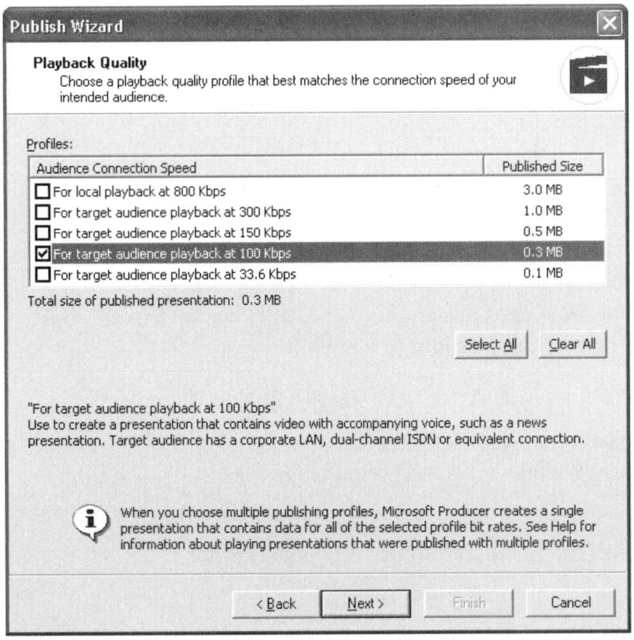

Figure 11.18 — Selecting a profile for network playback.

7. Select at least one playback quality profile. The **Publish Wizard** will offer you only profiles that are appropriate for the type of content in your presentation. Since you're publishing to a network, click a profile that uses a medium bit rate, such as **For target audience playback at 100Kbps**. Figure 11.18 shows an example.

Click **Next** to proceed to the **Publish Your Presentation** page.

8. If you want, click **List Files to be Published**. A separate window opens that displays the file name of each file that Producer creates and copies to the publishing destination folder. Click **OK** to continue.

9. Read the **Publish to** path, which is displayed near the bottom of the **Publish Your Presentation** page, and verify that it is correct.

10. Click **Finish**. The two progress bars near the top and middle of the page display the current condition of the publishing process, and the **Publish Wizard** also displays the estimated time remaining until completion.

11. When the publishing process is complete, the **Publish Wizard** allows you to preview your presentation. Click **Yes** in the window that asks, "Would you like to view your published presentation?" Be sure to pay attention to the speed at which the presentation loads and plays from this point on, since you might want to make changes based on the performance you observe.

12. The introduction page for your presentation will open in a separate Internet Explorer window.

    Click **Play** to view your published presentation. When you've finished watching your masterpiece, close the Internet Explorer window.

13. Click **Close** to exit the **Publish Wizard**.

As you can see, the process in the **Publish Wizard** to publish your presentation to a network location is exactly like publishing to **My Computer**. If you select the **My Network Places** option on the first page of the wizard, all the subsequent pages will look just like what you've seen before when publishing to your local hard drive. There are, however, a number of considerations you should be aware of when publishing to a network:

*   The network folder to which you publish must have sharing or Web sharing enabled.

*   You must have read and write access permissions for the shared folder in order to publish. You may need to contact your network administrator to request these permissions.

*   The viewer must have read access permission for the shared folder that contains the presentation files.

*   If you've never worked with network file paths, you'll have to learn to use the Universal Naming Convention (UNC). This means that the path you'll provide in the **Publish files to** box in the **Publish Wizard** will take the form of *\\YourServerName\YourSharedFolderName\YourPath*. If you're working with a remote server, you may need your network administrator to provide you with the correct path to your publishing folder. Of course, you can also click **Browse** on the **Publishing Destination** page of the **Publish Wizard** and use the **Browse For Folder** dialog box to browse to the correct folder.

- All your presentation files will be copied to the shared folder, which means that any-one with read access permission will be able to examine or copy the individual files, and anyone with write access permission will be able to alter or delete them.

- When people play your presentation from a shared network folder, any associated files are downloaded to a folder on their computers. This includes Windows Media files, which can be quite large depending on the length of your presentation and the playback quality profile you selected when you published the presentation. If the presentation is large, you may want to tell your audience about the possibility of a delay when you send them the link to the presentation.

The Web page that plays your presentation will begin playback when a sufficient portion of the Windows Media files has been downloaded. On a congested or slower network this might result in a noticeable delay to the viewer, so you should carefully test your presentation after you publish it. If necessary, use lower bit rate playback quality profiles. You might also want to consider setting up a Windows Media server so your Windows Media content can be streamed instead of downloaded.

Publishing to a Web Server

The **Web server** option offers the maximum flexibility and control over the Microsoft Producer publishing process. This option allows you to publish your presentation Web files and Windows Media files to separate locations, which is important if you want to publish to a Windows Media server. You will also use the Web server option if you choose to use an e-service for your publishing needs.

You can specify a discussion server address to enable viewers of your presentation to ask questions or provide comments. You can also provide user name and password informa-tion for logging into a secure server.

You can choose the **Web server** option in the **Publish Wizard** to accomplish any of the following tasks:

- Adding a new Web server

- Using an existing Web server

- Editing a Web server

- Deleting a Web server

- Learning more about publishing

The following sections describe these options .

Adding a New Web Server

You can provide the details about the server to which you want to publish, and give a friendly name to that server. The friendly name is added to the **Web server** drop-down list in the **Publish Wizard**, and the publishing details are saved. When you want to publish to the server in the future, you don't have to type all the information into the **Publish Wizard** again.

The following steps will guide you through the process of adding a new Web server in the Producer **Publish Wizard**:

1. Start Producer and open your presentation.

2. Click **Publish** on the toolbar. The **Publish Wizard** appears. If it isn't already selected, click **Web server**.

3. In the **Web server** drop-down list, choose **Add a new Web server**. Click **Next** to proceed to the **Internet or Intranet Host Settings** page, which is shown in Figure 11.19.

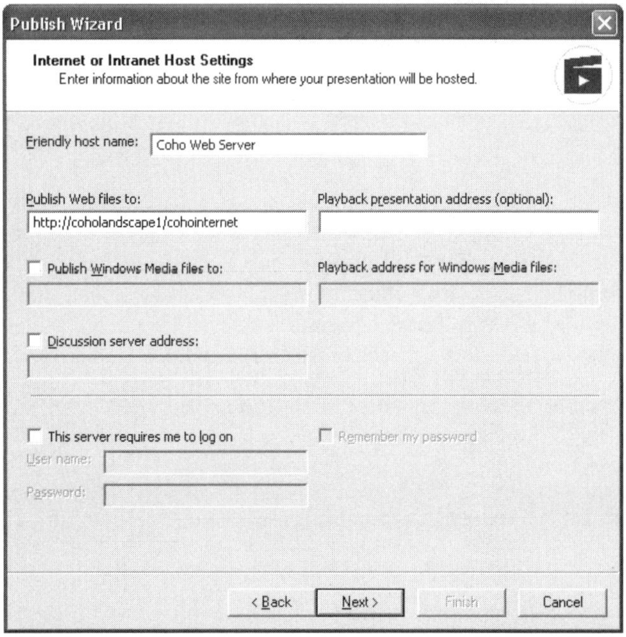

Figure 11.19 — The **Internet or Intranet Host Settings** page.

4. In the **Friendly host name** box, type the name you want to give this Web server. Make it something descriptive so you can remember the purpose of this server. Also, make sure you use a unique name for each Web server. For example, you might call this server Marketing Department Meetings, or something equally descriptive.

5. In the **Publish Web files to** box, type the URL or UNC address of the server to which you want to publish your presentation Web files, for example:

http://yourserver/yourpath

Optionally, type a URL in the **Playback presentation address (optional)** box, if the URL used to view the presentation differs from the one you typed in the **Publish Web files to** box. The presentation address is the address that Producer will use if you choose to preview the presentation at the end of the publishing process, and is only relevant for that purpose. For example, you might publish your files to a network location using a UNC address, but the folder to which you publish your files might be the home directory for a Web site. In this case, you'd type the URL of the Web site in the **Playback presentation address (optional)** box.

6. If you are publishing to a Windows Media server, click the **Publish Windows Media files to** check box. Type the URL of the path to which you'd like the **Publish Wizard** to copy your Windows Media files. For example, if the location of the streaming server has the alias MarketingDept, you would type http://WMServer/MarketingDept.

   In the **Playback address for Windows Media files** box, type the URL of the publishing point from which your Windows Media files will be streamed. Windows Media servers require the mms protocol. For example, the URL of the MarketingDept publishing point would probably be something like mms://WMServer/MarketingDept.

7. If you want to provide a Web discussion server by using Microsoft Office Server Extensions or SharePoint Portal Server, click the **Discussion server address** check box and type the URL of the discussion server.

8. If the server to which you are publishing requires you to log on, click the check box labeled **This server requires me to log on**. Enter the appropriate logon information in the **User name** and **Password** boxes. Click the check box labeled **Remember my password** if you would like Producer to save this information for this Web server.

   Click **Next** to proceed to the **Web Publishing Destination** page, which is shown in Figure 11.20.

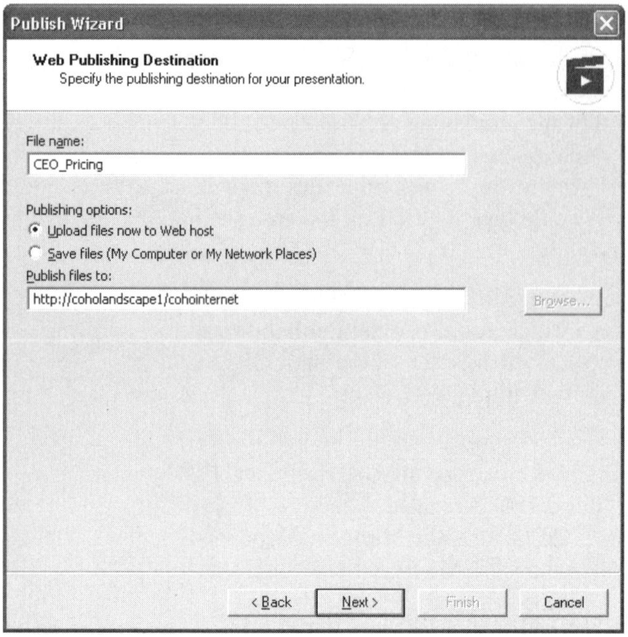

Figure 11.20 — The **Web Publishing Destination** page.

9. Type a name for your presentation in the **File name** box. The wizard provides the project name by default.

10. If it isn't already selected, click **Upload files now to Web host**. Verify that the correct path is displayed in the **Publish files to** box.

    Click **Next** to proceed to the **Presentation Information** page.

11. In the **Title** box, type a title for your presentation.

    Optionally, provide the name of the presenter, a path to an image, and a description. All these will be added to the introduction page when the presentation is published and will be visible to the viewer.

    Click **Next** to proceed to the **Playback Quality** page.

12. Select at least one playback quality profile. The **Publish Wizard** will offer you only profiles that are appropriate for the type of content in your presentation. Since you're publishing for the Web, make sure one profile is checked that uses a low bit rate, such as **For target audience playback at 33.6Kbps**.

    Click **Next** to proceed to the **Publish Your Presentation** page.

13. If you're the curious type, click **List Files to be Published**. A separate window opens that displays the file name of each file that Producer creates and/or copies to the publishing destination folder. Click **OK** when your curiosity has been satisfied.

14. Read the **Publish to** path, which is displayed near the bottom of the **Publish Your Presentation** page, and verify that it is correct. If you want to make any changes, now is the time to click **Back**.

15. Click **Finish**. The two progress bars near the top and middle of the page display the current condition of the publishing process, and the **Publish Wizard** also displays the estimated time remaining until completion.

16. When the publishing process is complete, the **Publish Wizard** allows you to preview your presentation. Click **Yes** in the window that asks, "Would you like to view your published presentation?" Be sure to pay attention to the speed at which the presentation loads and plays from this point forward, since you might want to make changes based on the performance you observe.

The introduction page for your presentation will open in a separate Internet Explorer window.

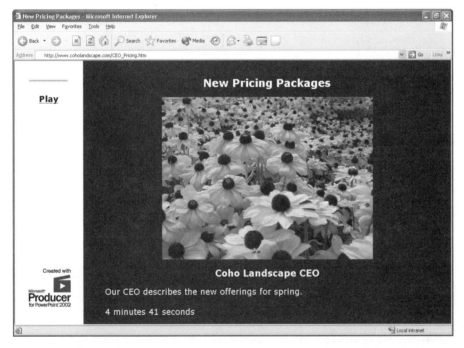

Figure 11.21 — The presentation's introduction page displayed in Internet Explorer.

Click **Play** to view your published presentation. When you have finished watching, close the Internet Explorer window. Then click **Close** to exit the **Publish Wizard**.

Using an Existing Web Server

Once you've added a Web server to the **Publish Wizard**, publishing to that server again is easy. Producer remembers all the values you provided during your last publishing session. To use an existing Web server:

1. Start Producer and open your presentation.

2. Click **Publish** on the toolbar. The **Publish Wizard** appears. If it isn't already selected, click **Web server**.

3. In the **Web server** drop-down list, choose the Web server you want to use, as shown in Figure 11.22.

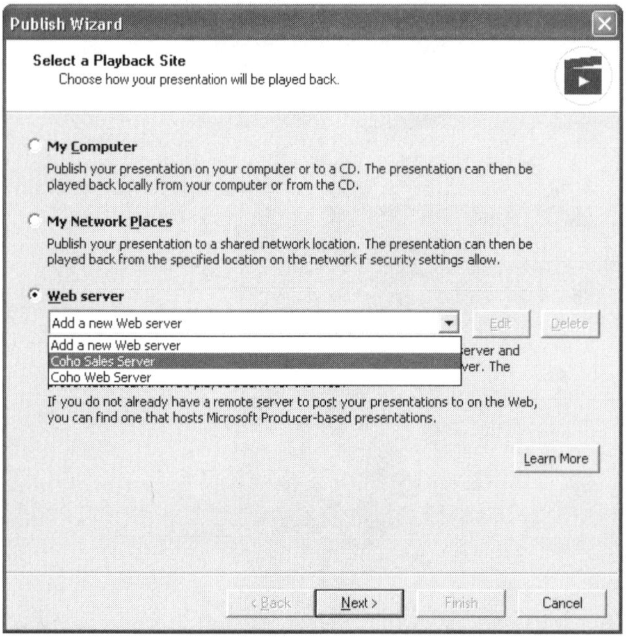

Figure 11.22 — Selecting a Web server for publishing.

Editing a Web Server

You can change the values associated with your Web server anytime. Here's how:

1. Start Producer and open your presentation.

2. Click **Publish** on the toolbar. The **Publish Wizard** appears. If it isn't already selected, click **Web server**.

3. In the **Web server** drop-down list, choose the Web server you want to edit.

4. Click **Edit** to proceed to the **Internet or Intranet Host Settings** page.

5. Change any values you'd like. Remember that the **Friendly host name** must be unique. Click **Next** to save the changes and proceed to the **Web Publishing Destination** page.

From there, you can proceed to publish normally, or click **Cancel** to close the **Publish Wizard**. Your changes will be saved for your next publishing session.

Deleting a Web Server

You can easily remove a Web server from the drop-down list in the **Publish Wizard** and delete all the details from memory. The following steps will guide you:

1. Start Producer and open your presentation.

2. Click **Publish** on the toolbar. The **Publish Wizard** appears. If it isn't already selected, click **Web server**.

3. In the **Web server** drop-down list, choose the Web server you want to delete.

4. Click **Delete**.

6. Click **Yes** when prompted to confirm that you wish to delete the Web server.

Learning More About Publishing

You can view a Web page that provides details about utilizing e-services and adding e-services to the **Web server** list in the **Publish Wizard**. To do this, click **Web server** (if the option is not already selected) and then click **Learn More**. Producer displays a Web page, in a separate window, that contains information about e-services that you can use to publish your presentation.

The Web page that displays by default is a page on the Microsoft Web site that contains links to third-party hosting providers. These are companies that, for a fee, provide you with storage space on their servers for your Producer presentations. It is also possible that the URL of this Web page may have been changed by your corporation to display information about publishing using your company's preferred locations.

To add an e-service as a Web server that you can use in the **Publish Wizard**, follow the instructions given by the e-service provider.

Understanding Presentation Playback

When Producer copies the files for your presentation, it creates a shortcut HTML page that redirects Internet Explorer to the introduction page using the name you specified in the **File name** box in the **Publish Wizard**. For instance, if you specified the file name MyPresentation, Producer names the new shortcut MyPresentation.htm. You should supply the address of the shortcut to your viewers so they can see your presentation in Internet Explorer. You can either supply the URL or path of the presentation Web page, which they can paste or type into the Internet Explorer Address Bar, or you can supply an HTML link on another Web page or in e-mail. The form the address takes is as follows:

http://*server_name*/*webpath*/*presentation_name*.htm

Similarly, if you published to a network location using **My Network Places**, you would send them the UNC path, for example:

*server_name**path**presentation_name.htm*

On the Internet, *server_name* might be an Internet domain name, such as www.microsoft.com. On an intranet, it would simply be the name of a server on the corporate domain.

When the viewer opens the introduction page in Internet Explorer, he or she sees the title, description, and image you specified in the **Publish Wizard**, as well as the total time for the presentation and a link labeled **Play**. Clicking the link starts the presentation playback using the appropriate template.

It is not uncommon that several seconds might elapse before the **Play** link is available for a user to click. This occurs because the browser and embedded Player must download sufficient content so that playback can proceed smoothly. If the network connection is slow, some additional time might elapse, during which the user might see the message "Loading, please wait…" in place of the **Play** link.

If the network connection is slow and the data being received cannot keep up with playback of the presentation, the embedded Player may pause occasionally to buffer content. During buffering, playback pauses until sufficient data is downloaded to continue.

This buffering mechanism is called *pre-caching*; under certain circumstances, the user experience could be improved by disabling it. To do this, the user must click the Internet Explorer **Stop** button, which disables pre-caching of content files in the presentation until the Web page is refreshed or reloaded. Clicking the **Stop** button pauses presentation playback as well, and the user must click **Play** to continue viewing the presentation. Once pre-caching is disabled, the presentation will continue playing whether all the necessary content files have been downloaded or not.

Specifying a Profile for Presentation Playback

When you publish your presentation to a Web server and distribute it with multiple pro-files over a network, you can send your audience a separate playback address for each one. This is how you match the various profiles to your audience. If, for example, you offer two bit rates, such as 300-Kbps and 33.6-Kbps, viewers can choose which address (and therefore profile) best fits their connection speed. You can do this whether the viewer types the address into the Internet Explorer Address Bar or you create HTML links to your presentation. To understand how to create the addresses, it helps to know how the **Publish Wizard** works when it encodes multiple profiles. When going through the **Publish Wizard**:

1. Producer generates a list of valid profiles and displays them in the **Publish Wizard** as check box items.

2. You click the check boxes to select the profiles you want to use for publishing.

3. Behind the scenes, Producer assigns an index number to each profile you select, start-ing with the highest bit rate profile and counting up from zero. For example, if you only select one profile, it has the index number 0 by default. If you select three pro-files, they have index numbers 0, 1, and 2, with 0 corresponding to the highest bit rate profile you selected, and 2 corresponding to the lowest.

After you complete the **Publish Wizard**, Producer automatically creates separate Win-dows Media files for each profile you select, and copies each file to the appropriate desti-nation folder. Producer also creates and copies a Windows Media metafile (with a .asx file name extension) for each profile. This metafile is called a *playlist*. The playlist acts as a shortcut to the Windows Media files.

Producer names each playlist by prefixing the word "Media" with an index number that corresponds to the profile you selected, such as 0Media.asx, 1Media.asx, 2Media.asx, and so forth. Each playlist is a shortcut to the Windows Media file that was encoded us-ing the profile that corresponds to the index number in the playlist file name.

If you publish a presentation using an e-service, the index numbers may not be assigned to each profile in the order mentioned previously. E-service authors have control over how profiles are numbered, so you may need to inquire about this information from the e-service provider.

To create a playback address for each profile, append a # character as a separator charac-ter to the playback address, and then append the text "profile=*index number*" (without the quotation marks), where *index number* corresponds to the index of the profile used to encode the digital media. For example, to play a presentation using the second-highest bit rate you selected in the **Publish Wizard**, you would use the following address format:

http://*server_name*/*webpath*/*presentation_name*.htm#profile=1

This address tells the Producer presentation to play using the Windows Media file that the playlist file named 1Media.asx points to.

Using Other Playback Parameters

There are other parameters you can add to your playback address to change the playback behavior of a Producer presentation. You can use multiple parameters in the playback address—simply separate the parameters using a & character.

Autostart

This parameter tells the Producer presentation to start playing immediately, bypassing the introduction page. If the parameter value is 0, the introduction page displays and the viewer must click **Play** to see the presentation. If the parameter value is 1, the presentation plays automatically. For example:

http://*server_name*/*webpath*/*presentation_name*.htm#autostart=1

The default value is 0.

Time

This parameter allows you to specify a starting time, in seconds. For example, to start playback from two minutes into your presentation, the address would be:

http://*server_name*/*webpath*/*presentation_name*.htm#time=120

By default, the presentation plays from the start.

Event

This parameter allows you to start playback from a specific event within your presentation. An event occurs for slide changes, internal slide changes (such as animations), template changes, and HTML changes. Each event occurs sequentially, and the first event has the number 0, which is the start of the presentation.

For example, if the second event in your presentation is an animation that occurs in the first PowerPoint slide that displays, you might use an address like the following to start the presentation playback at the animation event:

http://*server_name*/*webpath*/*presentation_name*.htm#event=2

Using the event parameter can be a bit tricky, so you'll have to experiment a bit to find the correct parameter number to get the result you desire. Also, if you use both the **Time** and **Event** parameter in the same playback address, the **Event** parameter takes precedence. For example:

http://*server_name*/*webpath*/*presentation_name*.htm#time=60&event=2

In the preceding example, the Producer presentation will start playback at the second event, not at one minute.

Using parameters in your playback address can give you a great deal of flexibility in how your presentation is displayed.

Part IV
Advanced Producer Topics

Chapter 12: Customizing Producer Templates

Chapter 13: Customizing Your Presentations

Chapter 14: Creating Custom Publishing Solutions

Customizing Producer Templates

Up to this point, the templates that have been discussed have been default presentation templates that are installed with Microsoft Producer. You may decide to take another step in creating presentations by creating your own Producer templates. By customizing templates, you can enhance your presentations by adding your company's branding or some personal touch.

You can take the idea of customizing your Producer presentations a step further by creating and incorporating your own PowerPoint templates as well. When you combine custom PowerPoint templates with custom Producer templates, you can create a really unique look for your presentations.

The goal of this chapter is to help you create new Producer templates. In doing so, you will be able to create dynamic presentations that are customized for your company or organization and are based on your company's needs.

Template Basics

Microsoft Producer presentation templates are Cascading Style Sheet (CSS) files. Using CSS allows you to write programming code that determines how your presentation displays when your audience watches it in Microsoft Internet Explorer.

This chapter is in no way an attempt to describe everything about CSS. This chapter is provided solely to help you edit CSS properties and values as they relate to presentation templates for Producer. The goal is to help you understand how you can edit the CSS code in Producer templates to create your own customized Producer presentations.

CSS Selectors and Properties

A presentation template contains numerous CSS selectors, properties, and values for those properties. In Microsoft Producer, a selector begins with the # character or a period (depending on its type) and declares a specific property. You can change the values associated with these properties in the CSS template.

Understanding how specific selectors relate to the appearance of your presentation template is very important. Figure 12.1 shows an image of a published presentation where the labels, which are associated with specific selectors, are shown to indicate what part or element of the presentation is determined by each selector.

#MediaPlayerDiv   **#MediaPlayer**   **#MediaPlayerControlsDiv**

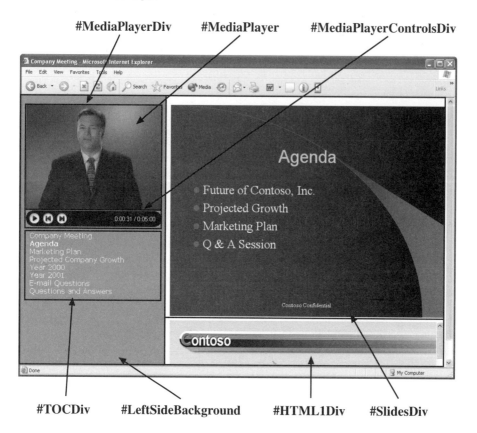

#TOCDiv   **#LeftSideBackground**   **#HTML1Div**   **#SlidesDiv**

Figure 12.1 — A presentation, with the corresponding selectors defined in a presentation template.

The following code sample shows the **#WMTemplate** selector. This selector contains two properties, **WMName** and **WMDesc.** The value for each property follows the semicolon after the property name, and is enclosed in quotation marks.

```
#WMTemplate
{WMName: "Custom Standard Video (320x240) -
Resizable Slides and HTML";
WMDesc: "Customized medium video display (320x240) template with
resizable slide and HTML areas. This template has background images.";
}
```

All of the CSS selectors that are discussed in this chapter are documented in Microsoft Producer Help. For basic information about these selectors and their editable properties, see the Help file.

Template Naming and Styles

The easiest way to create your own Producer template is to make a copy of one of the default template folders and then edit the code in the CSS file. Before choosing a presentation template to copy and then customize, it's helpful to have a basic understanding of the naming conventions and presentation template styles. This helps you identify a presentation template you want to customize.

Five main template styles are installed with Microsoft Producer. Each style offers a variety of layouts that are designed to suit different types of presentations. You can choose to customize any of these templates. The following list provides a quick summary of the template styles:

- **Default**. The Default template style contains solid background colors. The video display is located in the top-left area of the template; the slides display is located in the top-center area. The colors and fonts that appear in these templates are determined by the settings specified in the **Presentation Scheme** dialog box as shown in Figure 12.2. To open the **Presentation Scheme** dialog box, on the **Edit** menu, click **Presentation Scheme**.

- **Clouds**. The Clouds template style contains one large background image. The style of the text and colors is specified in the presentation template. Slides and HTML are displayed at a fixed size.

- **Globe**. The Globe template style contains one large background image and a header image. The style of the text and colors is specified in the presentation template.

- **Organizational**. The Organizational template style contains a large background image. The style of the text and colors is specified in the presentation template. Slides and HTML are resizable.

- **Standard**. The Standard template style contains solid background colors. The colors and fonts that appear in these templates are determined by the settings specified in the **Presentation Scheme** dialog box.

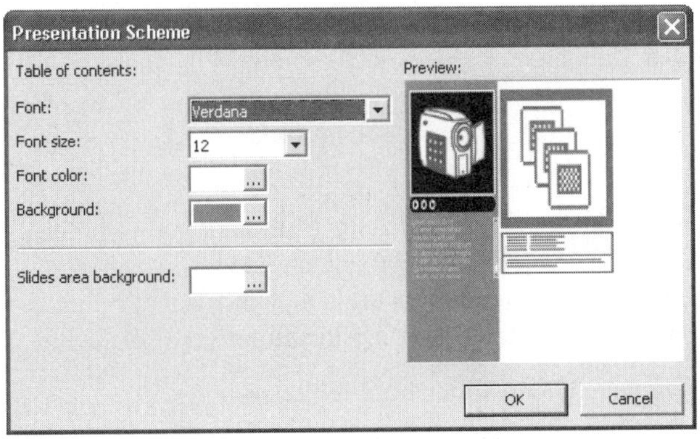

Figure 12.2 — Specifying the colors and fonts used for a Standard template.

In addition to the template style, information about which elements are displayed (and how they are displayed) in the specific presentation template is conveyed in the presentation template name and description. The following elements change from one template to another:

- **Video**. These templates display video (or still images) that appear on the **Video** track, along with any added video transitions or video effects. In presentation templates that display video, the display size, in pixels, is included in the template name.

- **Audio**. These templates play back audio that appears on the **Audio 2** track of the timeline. These templates do not display video.

- **Slides**. These templates display Microsoft PowerPoint slides (or still images) that appear on the **Slide** track on the timeline. The slides are either a fixed size or resizable. Resizable slides change size automatically if the Web browser window size is changed when the presentation is played back. Fixed-size slides remain one size, even if the Web browser window is resized.

- **HTML**. These templates display HTML files or Web links that appear on the **HTML** track on the timeline. HTML and Web content is either a fixed size or resizable. A resizable HTML area changes size automatically if the viewer changes the Web browser window size when the presentation is played back. However, a fixed HTML area remains one size, even if the Web browser window is resized.

Choosing a Presentation Template

To customize your own Producer template, choose a presentation template folder and then copy that folder in the Templates folder.

When you are working on a presentation in Microsoft Producer, the presentation templates you can choose from appear in the **Presentation Templates** folder, as shown in Figure 12.3. The previews in this folder can help you to decide which template best suits your needs as a starting point for creating your own custom template. Whether you are viewing the presentation templates as large icons, thumbnails, or in the details view in Microsoft Producer, you can pause the mouse pointer on the template to see the template name, a description of the template, and the location in which that template is stored on your computer.

For example, the selected presentation template name shown in Figure 12.3 is **Standard Video (320x240) – Resizable Slides and HTML**. If you wanted to copy this template for customization, you could make a copy of the source folder that contains the template file named video slides html toc resize.css, which you can find in the following location:

C:\Program Files\Microsoft Producer\1033\Templates\video slides html toc resize

Using the **Presentation Templates** folder, you can quickly find the source location for any Producer template you want to copy and then customize.

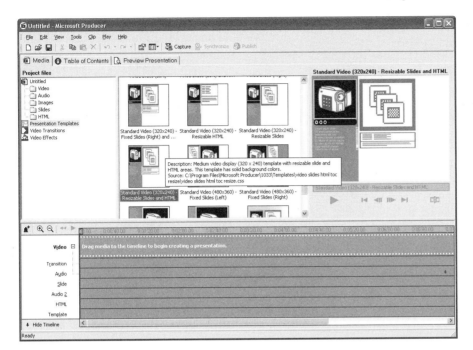

Figure 12.3 — Selecting a presentation template.

Getting Started

The presentation templates that are installed by default with Microsoft Producer are installed in the following location on your computer:

<Drive>:\Program Files\Microsoft Producer*<LanguageID* >\Templates

<Drive> is the hard disk that Microsoft Producer is installed on, and *<LanguageID>* is a folder whose name is a number that varies by language. This folder is where the Templates folder can be found. You can locate and open this folder through My Computer or in Windows Explorer.

In the Templates folder, there are some additional subfolders. In each subfolder, a Microsoft Producer presentation template file with a .css file name extension appears. In the same subfolder, you will also notice that there are several image files with either .jpg or .gif file name extensions. These images are associated with the presentation template in that subfolder.

When you are determining which presentation template folder to copy, choose one of the presentation templates that displays all of the different digital media files you want to use in your custom template, such as video, slides, and HTML content, as well as a table of contents. Such a template will already contain many of the properties you need. If you later decide that you do not want a particular element to display, it is often easier to remove that element from the template than to add an element that is not already part of the template.

Step-by-Step: Copying a Presentation Folder

The following step-by-step procedure describes the beginning of the customization process: copying a templates folder and then editing the template name and description. After you make a copy of the template folder, which contains the presentation template as well as the images associated with that template, you can then open the CSS file in Notepad to begin customizing the template.

In the following steps, the template named **Standard Video (320x240) – Resizable Slides and HTML** is used. The procedures in this chapter describe customizing this template. You should copy this template folder if you want to follow the procedures in this chapter. However, you can choose any presentation template folder that you wish to copy and then customize the template and images contained in that folder.

1. In the Microsoft Producer **Media** tab, click the **Presentation Templates** folder, and momentarily pause your mouse on the different presentation templates in the contents pane. The description, source location, and name for that template are displayed.

2. For this procedure, look at the presentation template name **Standard Video (320x240) – Resizable Slides and HTML**. This is the presentation template you will customize. Note the location and name for the template.

3. When you copy a presentation folder and customize a presentation template, you need to restart Microsoft Producer for the new template to display in Microsoft Producer. On the **File** menu, click **Exit** to close Microsoft Producer.

4. Using Windows Explorer, locate the folder that contains the presentation template and images for the template you want to customize. For this procedure, the folder is at the following location (as noted in step 2):

   <Drive>:**\Program Files\Microsoft Producer***<LanguageID>***\Templates\video slides html toc resize**

5. Click the folder to select it. From the **Edit** menu, click **Copy**.

6. Click the folder named Templates to select it. From the **Edit** menu, click **Paste** to paste a copy of the presentation template folder into the Templates folder. A copy of the template folder named "Copy of video slides html toc resize" appears in the right pane of Windows Explorer.

   The folder for your custom template must be in the **\Program Files\Microsoft Producer***<LanguageID>***\Templates** folder if you want the template to be displayed as an option in the Producer **Media** tab and the **New Presentation Wizard**.

7. Click the new folder to select it. From the **File** menu, click **Rename**. Type a new name for the folder, so can you quickly find it later. For this example, name the folder customizedsampletemplate.

8. Open the customizedsampletemplate folder and click the CSS file named video slides html toc resize.css. From the **File** menu, click **Rename**. Give the CSS file a new name that you will remember. For this example, use the name customizedsampletemplate.css.

Naming a Presentation Template

Changing the name and description of your template is often the first edit you should make when customizing a presentation template. This new name and description appears in Producer when you pause your mouse pointer on the template in the **Presentation Templates** folder of the **Media** tab or when you are selecting a presentation template in the **New Presentation Wizard**.

If you do not change the name and description of the template, the old name and description for the template will appear in Producer. This can be confusing when you are ready to add your own customized template to the timeline because you might have more than one template that displays the same name.

Step-by-Step: Editing the Presentation Name and Description

The following procedure describes the step-by-step process for editing the template name and description in the CSS file.

1. Using a plain text editor, such as Microsoft Notepad, open the CSS file you want to modify.

2. Near the top of the template is the selector **#WMTemplate**, which contains the properties and values you need to edit. Do the following:

   - For the **WMName** property, replace the current value "Standard Video (320x240) - Resizable Slides and HTML" with a new template name. Make sure that the quotation marks appear at the beginning and end of the new value.

     If you are following along in the procedure, type the following for a new name: "Custom Standard Video (320x240) - Resizable Slides and HTML". This value is the name that appears for the template in Producer.

   - For the **WMDesc** property, replace the current value "Medium video display (320 x 240) template with resizable slide and HTML areas. This template has solid background colors" with a new value for the template description.

     If you are following along in the procedure, type the following for a new description: "Customized medium video display (320 x 240) template with resizable slide and HTML areas. This template has background images." This value is the description for the template that appears when you pause the mouse on the template in Producer.

3. Save the changes to the presentation template file. Close your text editor.

4. Start Microsoft Producer. In the **Media** tab, select the **Presentation Templates** folder, and then locate the template named **Custom Standard Video (320x240) - Resizable Slides and HTML**. You should see something like Figure 12.4.

Notice that the name you entered now appears in Producer. If you pause the mouse pointer on the template or view templates in the **Details** view, you can see the description for the template as well.

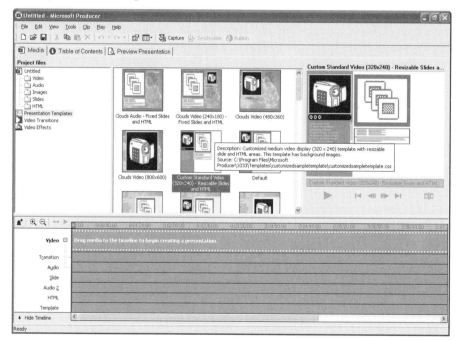

Figure 12.4 — The customized template in Microsoft Producer.

Customizing a Presentation Template

Customizing Microsoft Producer templates lets you determine the appearance and layout of a presentation when a template you customize is applied to a presentation.

Incorrectly editing a Producer presentation template file and then including it in a presentation may cause your presentation to play back or display incorrectly. In other words, be careful when editing presentation templates.

The steps in this chapter that show you how to customize a template include changing values that can be *safely* modified. It is strongly recommended that you stick to editing *only* these values. This chapter provides information and guidelines about which values in certain selectors can be safely changed. Additionally, Microsoft Producer Help provides a listing of the selector properties that can be safely edited, as well as the syntax for adding the CSS code with the possible values.

A sample presentation was created using the following step-by-step instructions for creating the customized presentation template that displays video. You can watch this presentation by opening the file \Samples\Chapter12\ContosoSampleTemplate.htm on the companion CD.

Customizing Background Images

Customizing your presentation template can begin with editing the background image. The image needs to be Web-safe—that is, it can be viewed in a Web browser, such as PNG, JPG, or GIF image files. A majority of popular graphics editing programs today, including Microsoft Paint, let you save images in one or both of these Web formats.

The first step in adding a background image is to determine its size. In doing so, you should think about the resolution settings for the computer monitors your audience will be using to watch your presentation. For example, if a majority of users in your company or organization have monitors set to display 1024x768 pixels, you would then want to use images that will accommodate this screen resolution.

The goal is to have the image fill the window of the Web browser while minimizing the amount of scrolling your audience would need to do when watching your presentation. Remember, even though your audience may have their screen resolution set to something like 1024x768, this entire area is not available for you to display your image because of the other items that appear in the Web browser window: a menu bar, toolbars, address bar, horizontal and vertical scroll bars, and possibly a status bar.

A quick way to estimate the correct size for the image is to take a screen shot of the Web browser window (with the screen set to your best estimate of your audience's screen resolution and with the window maximized).

Step-by-Step: Estimating Background Image Size

The following procedure describes the process for capturing an image of your computer screen to determine the appropriate size for a background image.

1. Start Microsoft Internet Explorer, maximize the browser window, and then open a Web page.

2. Press the Print Screen key to capture an image of the screen with the current Web content displayed in the browser window.

3. Open a graphics editing program, such as Microsoft Paint.

4. On the **Edit** menu, click **Paste** to insert the screen shot.

5. Select the area of the Web browser window where the actual Web content is displayed and note the dimensions in the bottom right-hand corner for the selected area. These dimensions provide an estimate for the image size. For example, in Figure 12.5, the estimated image size based on a 1024x768 screen resolution is 990x590 pixels.

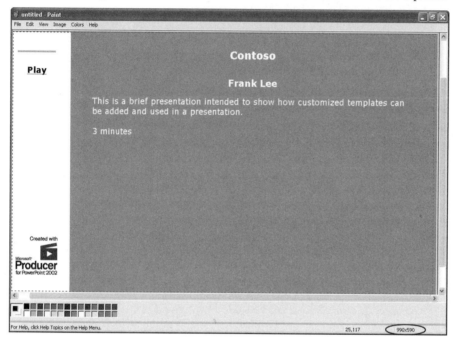

Figure 12.5 — Finding the image area in Paint.

6. Close the graphics editing program. You do not need to save your changes.

Adding Images to Your Template

You can incorporate your own images into the presentation template. In Producer, you add images using a **MiscDiv** selector. You can have up to nine selectors of this type which you can use to incorporate miscellaneous Web content, such as a background image. These divs are numbered, starting with 1, and are named **#Misc1Div**, **#Misc2Div**, and so forth, up to **#Misc9Div**.

You can use the **MiscDiv** selectors to determine how the Web content in layered. If you had nine **MiscDiv** selectors, **#Misc9Div** would appear on the top, or closest to the viewer, and **#Misc1Div** would appear on the bottom. In the Standard templates, no **MiscDivs** exist by default.

In Producer, any images included in the presentation template are stored in the same folder as the presentation template CSS file.

Step-by-Step: Adding a Background Image

The following procedure shows you how to add CSS code to incorporate a large background image into an existing standard template. This procedure uses the sample presentation template folder that you copied earlier, customizedsampletemplate, and the sample template CSS file named customizedsampletemplate.css.

Before you begin, do the following:

- Make sure you have the renamed the *copy* of the original video slides html toc resize.css file in the customizedsampletemplate folder in the following location on your computer:

    <Drive>:**\Program Files\Microsoft Producer**<*LanguageID*>**\Templates**.

- If you want to follow the step-by-step procedures, copy the image examplebkg.jpg from the \StepByStep\Chapter12\TemplateImages folder on the companion CD to the customizedsampletemplate folder on your computer. This is the sample background image that will be inserted in the customized template.

- Close Microsoft Producer.

1. Using Notepad, on the **File** menu, click **Open**. Browse to the folder named customizedsampletemplate. Click the file named customizedsampletemplate.css to select it, and then click **Open**.

    To see all files in the current folder, including the CSS file you want to open, make sure the **Files of type** box is set to display **All Files**.

2. In the CSS template file, add the following CSS code to the end of the text document exactly as it appears.

```
#Misc1Div
{POSITION: absolute;
TOP: 0px;
LEFT: 0px;
HEIGHT: 580px;
WIDTH: 970px;
BACKGROUND-IMAGE: URL(examplebkg.jpg);
BACKGROUND-REPEAT: no-repeat;
DISPLAY: none;
WMPrerollDisplay: none;
}
```

In this code example, the background image named examplebkg.jpg is inserted in the **#Misc1Div** section. The height and width of the entire **#Misc1Div** area is set to the same size as the background image itself, where the size is based on the available space for Web content to be displayed in a Web browser window based on a screen resolution of 1024x768. The background does not repeat because it contains one large background image.

3. Because this background image needs to cover the entire Web page, you also must edit the **#LeftSideBackground** selector in the CSS file. Change the text so it appears exactly as follows.

```
#LeftSideBackground
{POSITION: absolute;
TOP: 0px;
LEFT: 0px;
WIDTH: 100%;
HEIGHT: 100%;
BACKGROUND-COLOR: transparent;
}
```

4. On the **File** menu, click **Save** to save the changes to the file in Notepad.

5. Start Microsoft Producer. On the **File** menu, click **Open**. On the companion CD, open the project archive \StepByStep\Chapter12\ContosoSample.MSProducerZ.

6. In the **Browse For Folder** dialog box, choose a location for the unpacked project file and the associated project files, and then click **OK**.

7. Click the **Presentation Templates** folder for the current project. Choose the customized template named **Custom Standard Video (320x240) - Resizable Slides and HTML** and add it to the timeline.

8. On the **View** menu, click **Preview Presentation Tab**, and then play back your presentation. When you preview the presentation, you will be able to see how the presentation displays with the customized presentation template.

In this code example, the area associated with the **#LeftSideBackground** selector now covers the entire page because you set the values for the **WIDTH** and **HEIGHT** properties to 100 percent. Also, you set the value for the **BACKGROUND-COLOR** property to transparent, which prevents a solid-colored rectangle from covering the new background image. One large background image will now be visible for the entire page of the presentation, including the areas of the page where video, the table of contents, slides, and HTML are displayed. This probably isn't the final result you would like, but you'll have the opportunity in upcoming procedures to refine the look of the template.

When you are going to make further edits to the template, delete the template from the timeline, save your project, close Producer, and then edit the CSS file in Notepad. You can then restart Producer and then add the customized template to the timeline again, so the changes you make are shown when you preview your presentation. You'll need to do this each time you make changes to a template. Failing to remove the template from the timeline may yield unexpected results.

Step-by-Step: Adding a Logo or Header Image

The following procedure describes the step-by-step process for adding a header image. This image could be a logo that identifies your company or organization. The procedure shows the CSS code you can add to a standard template so the header image is displayed on a large background image, such as the one you added in the previous step-by-step procedures.

These procedures use the sample presentation template folder that was copied earlier, CustomizedSampleTemplate, and the sample template CSS file named customizedsampletemplate.css.

If you want to follow the step-by-step procedures, copy the image exampleheader.jpg from the \StepByStep\Chapter12\TemplateImages folder from the companion CD to the folder CustomizedSampleTemplate folder on your computer. This is the sample header image that will be inserted in the customized template.

1. Using Notepad, open the custom presentation template named customizedsampletemplate.

2. Add the following CSS code at the end of the text document exactly as it appears.

```
#Misc2Div
{POSITION: absolute;
TOP: 0px;
LEFT: 0px;
HEIGHT: 65px;
WIDTH: 970px;
BACKGROUND-IMAGE: URL(exampleheader.jpg);
BACKGROUND-REPEAT: no-repeat;
DISPLAY: none;
WMPrerollDisplay: none;
}
```

In the previous code, the header image named exampleheader.jpg is inserted in the **#Misc2Div** selector. The area defined by the selector is positioned at the top-left corner of the template, and the height and width of the entire **#Misc2Div** area is set to the same size as the header image itself. The **BACKGROUND-REPEAT** property is set to "no-repeat" to prevent the image from displaying in a tiled fashion. This header image appears on top of the background image specified in the **#Misc1Div** because the div is named with a higher number.

If you do not know the size of the image you are working with, you can open the image in Paint. On the **Image** menu, click **Attributes** to see the width and height values of the image.

3. On the **File** menu, click **Save** to save the changes to the presentation template file in Notepad.

4. Start Microsoft Producer. On the **File** menu, click **Open**, and open the Microsoft Producer project you saved in the earlier exercise.

If you did not do the earlier exercise, you can open the project archive named \StepByStep\Chapter12\ContosoSample.MSProducerZ from the companion CD, and then work with the resulting project.

5. Click the **Presentation Templates** folder for the current project. Choose the customized template named **Custom Standard Video (320x240) - Resizable Slides and HTML** and add it to the timeline.

If you see two custom templates with the same name, make sure you add the one from the Templates folder, not the one saved in the temporary folder.

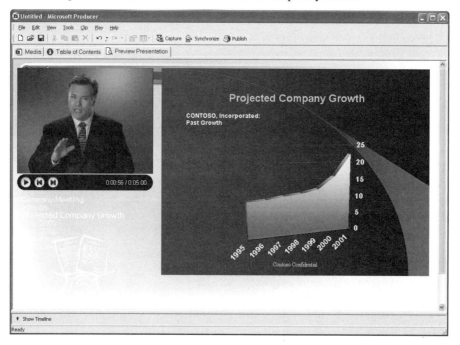

Figure 12.6 — The customized presentation template.

6. On the **View** menu, click **Preview Presentation Tab**, and then play your presentation. When you preview the presentation, you will be able to see what it looks like with the customized template.

As you preview your presentation in Producer, you will notice that the video area and the slides display incorrectly and cover the header image (see Figure 12.6). You'll make the adjustments to remedy this in the upcoming step-by-step procedures for customizing the display of the media player and slides in your presentation.

Customizing the Media Player

Any video in your presentation is displayed in a media player that has both controls and a video display area. The media player controls let viewers control the playback of your presentation when they watch it in Internet Explorer. If your presentation only contains audio, the media player controls appear, but the video display does not.

If your presentation template has an area set to display video, but only audio is added to the timeline for the part of the presentation where the template is applied, audio visualizations—a feature of Windows Media Player—appear in the video display while the audio plays.

You can customize the position and appearance of the media player by editing CSS code. The media player size and position are defined by the **#MediaPlayer** and **#MediaPlayerDiv** selectors. The values associated with the properties contained in these selectors determine where the controls for the media player display.

Step-by-Step: Displaying Video with Audio

The following procedure describes the step-by-step process for customizing the media player. The procedure shows the CSS code you can add to a standard template so video is displayed in your presentation.

In the previous series of step-by-step procedures, a background image and header image were added to the template. However, the media player incorrectly displayed over the header image, as shown in Figure 12.6. The goal for this step-by-step procedure is to change the media player position so the presentation template displays correctly.

If you want to follow the step-by-step procedures, copy the image \StepByStep\Chapter12\TemplateImages\smallmediaframe.gif from the companion CD to the customizedsampletemplate folder on your computer. This is the sample image that will be inserted into the customized template to frame the video display area.

1. Using Notepad, open the copy of the template named customizedsampletemplate.css that you saved in the folder customizedsampletemplate.

2. Change the text in the **#MediaPlayerDiv** selector to match following code. Copy the code exactly as it appears.

```
#MediaPlayerDiv
{POSITION: absolute;
TOP: 69px;
LEFT: 52px;
HEIGHT: 305px;
WIDTH: 345px;
BACKGROUND-IMAGE: URL(smallmediaframe.gif);
BACKGROUND-REPEAT: no-repeat;
}
```

In the template, the area that displays the media player is defined in the selector **#MediaPlayerDiv**, and is located 69 pixels from the top of the template. This number was selected to allow space for the header image you inserted using **#Misc2Div**. A few extra pixels are added to allow some empty space between the header image and the media player. The **LEFT** value is set to 52 pixels to align the media player with the header image. The height and width of the area is set to allow sufficient space to contain the entire media player, including the controls.

Just as you can add a background image for the entire Web page, you can add an image to frame the video display. In the previous example, the image named smallmediaframe.gif is used to customize the appearance of the media player. The value for the **BACKGROUND-REPEAT** property is set to "no-repeat", so the media player graphic only appears once without displaying in a tiled fashion.

3. Change the values of the **#MediaPlayer** selector properties as shown below. If properties do not exist, add them. Copy the code exactly as it appears here. The **#MediaPlayer** selector determines the size and position of the video display area.

```
#MediaPlayer
{POSITION: relative;
TOP: 11px;
LEFT: 11px;
HEIGHT: 240px;
WIDTH: 320px;
}
```

The video display size is 320 pixels wide by 240 pixels high. This value is already set in the sample template. However, if you used a large frame graphic for the video display, you could change these values to change the width and the height of your video. The placement of the area defined by the **#MediaPlayer** selector is relative to the one specified in **#MediaPlayerDiv**, which contains the image that frames the video. The **TOP** and **LEFT** values are set to 11 pixels because the image that is used contains a border around it which is 11 pixels wide on each side. These values cause the media player to appear centered in the background image.

If you are unsure where you need to position the video frame in an image, you can determine the appropriate values for the **LEFT** and **TOP** properties using Microsoft Paint. Open the image in Paint, and then point to the spot where the border of the image ends and the area for the video to display begins. Paint displays the pixel coordinates for the location you point to in the lower-right portion of the window as shown in Figure 12.7.

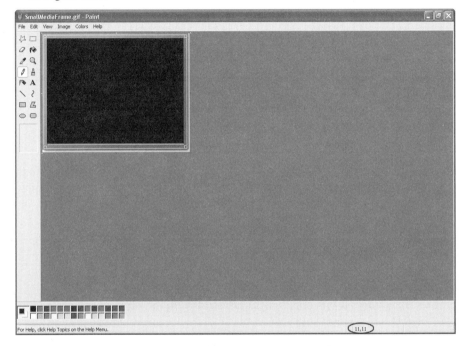

Figure 12.7 — Finding appropriate **Left** and **Top** coordinates.

The values for the **HEIGHT** and **WIDTH** properties determine the size of the video display area in the template. This size should match the display size of the digital video on the timeline. If the display size in the presentation template does not match the display size of the video content, your video may not display correctly in your presentation.

For example, if you captured the video using the **Medium video display (320x240) for delivery at 150 Kbps capture** profile, and the presentation template is set to display video at 640x480, your video image will be stretched to fit the video display area. This may adversely affect the quality of the image.

Also, when choosing the size of the video, make sure to retain the 4:3 width-to-height aspect ratio. If you do not, the video will appear distorted and unclear. For video to play back correctly, the values for the **HEIGHT** and **WIDTH** properties of the **#MediaPlayer** selector must be set to a number that is divisible by 4.

4. Add text in the **#MediaPlayerControlsDiv** selector to match the following example.

```
#MediaPlayerControlsDiv
{POSITION: absolute;
WIDTH: 320px;
TOP: 30px;
LEFT: 15px;
}
```

The entire div for the media player controls is set to display at 320 pixels wide. If you like, you can change this value to widen the controls. When resizing **#MediaPlayerControlsDiv**, the value for **WIDTH** needs to be set to at least 300 pixels so that all the controls display properly in your published presentation.

5. Save the changes to the presentation template file.

6. Start Microsoft Producer. On the **File** menu, click **Open**, and open the project you saved in the earlier exercise.

   If you did not do the earlier exercise, you can open the project archive named \StepByStep\Chapter12\ContosoSample.MSProducerZ from the companion CD, and then unpack and work with the resulting project.

7. Click the **Presentation Templates** folder for the current project. Choose the customized template named **Custom Standard Video (320x240) - Resizable Slides and HTML** and add it to the timeline.

8. On the **View** menu, click **Preview Presentation Tab**, and then play your presentation. When you preview the presentation, you will be able to see the changes made to the template.

As you preview your presentation, you will notice that the layout of the template is getting better, but things still aren't quite perfect. As you continue through the step-by-step procedures that follow, you'll fine-tune the appearance of the template even more.

Step-by-Step: Playing Audio without Video

The previous procedures discussed working with video and audio. However, if your presentation contains audio only, you might want to customize your template so the media player appears without the video display. The following step-by-step procedure details how you customize a video template to play audio-only presentations. The procedure shows the CSS code you can add to a standard template so the media player is not displayed in your presentation.

If you want to follow the step-by-step procedures, copy the customizedsampletemplate folder in Windows Explorer, and then rename the folder customizedsampletemplate-audio. This lets you continue customizing the video template so only audio plays.

1. Open your customized presentation template in Notepad.

   If you want to follow the specific procedures in this section, open the copy of the template named customizedsampletemplate.css in the folder customizedsample-templateaudio.

2. Change the values for the **WMName** and **WMDesc** properties in the **#WMTemplate** selector as shown below. The value for the **WMName** property determines the name for the presentation template, while the value for the **WMDesc** property determines the description that appears in Microsoft Producer.

```
#WMTemplate
{WMName: "Custom Standard Audio - Resizable Slides and HTML";
WMDesc: "Customized standard audio template with resizable slide
and HTML areas. This template has background images.";
}
```

3. Edit the **#MediaPlayer** selector as shown below. The **#MediaPlayer** selector determines the display size and position of video in your presentation.

```
#MediaPlayer
{POSITION: relative;
HEIGHT: 0px;
WIDTH: 0px;
}
```

   The preceding code hides the video display area by setting the **WIDTH** and **HEIGHT** values to 0 pixels.

4. Change **#MediaPlayerDiv** selector to hide the container area for the video display. This will also hide any background frame image. Enter the code as it appears here.

```
#MediaPlayerDiv
{POSITION: absolute;
HEIGHT: 0px;
WIDTH: 0px;
TOP: 0px;
LEFT: 0px;
}
```

5. Change the **#MediaPlayerControlsDiv** selector to reposition the transport controls. This will eliminate the empty space left behind by the missing video display.

```
#MediaPlayerControlsDiv
{POSITION: absolute;
WIDTH: 320px;
TOP: 69px;
LEFT: 52px;
}
```

6. Save the changes to the presentation template file. Start Microsoft Producer. On the **File** menu, click **Open**, and open the project you saved in the earlier exercise.

   If you did not do the earlier exercise, you can open the project archive named \StepByStep\Chapter12\ContosoSample.MSProducerZ from the companion CD, and then unpack and work with the resulting project.

7. Click the **Presentation Templates** folder for the current project. Choose the customized template named **Custom Standard Audio - Resizable Slides and HTML** and add it to the timeline.

8. On the **View** menu, click **Preview Presentation Tab**, and then play your presentation.

As you play back the presentation, you'll notice that the audio for the presentation is played back normally. The main difference is that the video does not appear because the values for the **HEIGHT** and **WIDTH** properties of the **#MediaPlayer** style were set to 0 pixels in the customized audio template.

You will also notice that the slides still cover the header image. This is because the value for the **TOP** property in the **#SlidesDiv** selector still needs to be adjusted to accommodate the header image. This is explained in the step-by-step procedures for customizing the display of slides in your presentation.

The entries for the table of contents now display incorrectly as well and need to be adjusted. This is because the value for the **TOP** property in the **#TOCDiv** selector still needs to accommodate the new position of the media player. This is explained in the step-by-step procedures for customizing the display of the table of contents.

The upcoming step-by-step procedures let you continue editing the customized sample template that displays video, which was the subject of earlier exercises. If you wanted to continue editing the sample customized audio template, you could follow the upcoming step-by-step procedures and then edit the style for **#SlidesDiv** and **#TOCDiv**.

Working with Slides

Customizing a presentation template also involves determining whether slides are displayed and, if so, how and where they display in the final presentation.

As mentioned previously, slides can be displayed as a fixed size or they can be resizable. If the template has slides that are a fixed size, the size of the slides in your presentation will remain the same when the viewer resizes the browser window. However, slides that are resizable will scale to fill the available space when the browser window is resized.

Step-by-Step: Customizing Slide Display

The following procedure describes the step-by-step process for customizing how slides display in your presentation. The procedure shows the CSS code you can add to a standard template so slides are displayed.

In a previous step-by-step procedure, a background image and header image were added to the template. However, the slides were positioned incorrectly over the header image. The goal for this step-by-step procedure is to change the slide position so the presentation displays correctly.

1. If the template you want to further customize has been added to the timeline in Producer, delete the template from the timeline, save your project, and close Microsoft Producer.

2. Using Notepad, open your custom presentation template file.

   If you want to follow the specific procedures in this section, open a copy of the template named customizedsampletemplate.css in the folder customizedsampletemplate. This is the template that displays video in a framed video display.

3. Change the **#SlidesDiv** selector to match following example. The values for the properties in the **#SlidesDiv** selector determine how slides display in your presentation.

```
#SlidesDiv
{POSITION: absolute;
TOP: 69px;
LEFT: 420px;
HEIGHT: 315px;
WIDTH: 420px;
WMAlignProportional: 19;   /* Do  not  edit. */
}
```

   The area that contains slides, defined by the **#SlidesDiv** selector, begins 69 pixels from the top. This number is based on the height and position of the header image inserted using the **#Misc2Div** selector. A few extra pixels are included so that empty space appears between the header image and the slides. This value is set so the top of the media player and the top of the slides area are aligned.

Notice that the area defined by the **#SlidesDiv** selector is set to display 420 pixels from the left edge of the browser window. This value is based on the **WIDTH** properties in the **#TOCDiv** and **#MediaPlayerDiv** selectors, so the slides do not obscure the media player or table of contents in your presentation.

The value for the **WIDTH** property determines the width at which slides display in your presentation. For templates that contain resizable slides, the width of slides is based on the width of the Web browser window. The value for the **HEIGHT** of the slides is based on the **WIDTH**. The ratio of the width to the height in the **#SlidesDiv** selector should be 4:3. If you resize the slides and the aspect ratio is not maintained, your presentation may not display correctly.

When editing the **#SlidesDiv** selector, do not change the values for properties that begin with "WM", such as **WMAlignProportional**. The display of resizable slides is determined by code in Producer that uses the values for these properties. Changing these values can cause your presentation to display incorrectly. If you change your slides from resizable to a fixed size by removing the custom WM properties and the corresponding values, remove the custom WM properties from the **#HTML1Div** style as well.

To customize this presentation template so slides are not displayed, type the following CSS code for the **#SlidesDiv** selector. This code would appear instead of the sample CSS code shown previously.

```
#SlidesDiv
{VISIBILTY: hidden;
TOP: 0px;
LEFT: 0px;
HEIGHT: 0px;
WIDTH: 0px;
}
```

4. Save the changes to the presentation template file.

5. Start Microsoft Producer. On the **File** menu, click **Open**, and open the project you saved in the earlier exercise.

   If you did not do the earlier exercise, you can open the project archive named \StepByStep\Chapter12\ContosoSample.MSProducerZ from the companion CD, and then unpack and work with the resulting project.

6. Click the **Presentation Templates** folder for the current project. Choose the customized template named **Custom Standard Video (320x240) - Resizable Slides and HTML** and add it to the timeline.

7. On the **View** menu, click **Preview Presentation Tab**, and then play your presentation.

As you preview your presentation in Producer, you will notice that the table of contents and Web content display incorrectly. This is because the values for the **TOP** properties of **#HTML1Div** and **#TOCDiv** need to be adjusted. This is explained in the upcoming step-by-step procedures for customizing the display of HTML content and the table of contents in your presentation.

Customizing HTML Display

Customizing presentation templates also means you can customize how (or if) HTML-based Web content displays in your presentation with the customized template. The type of Web content you can display can be a link that displays a live Web page, a link to a Web page, or a static HTML file. The settings for HTML display are determined by the **#HTML1Div** selector.

Like slides, HTML content can be displayed as fixed-size or resizable. The size of fixed-size HTML content within your presentation will remain the same if the viewer resizes the browser window. However, HTML content that is resizable will scale to fill the available space when the viewer resizes the browser window.

Step-by-Step: Customizing the Display of Web Content

The following procedure describes the step-by-step process for customizing how HTML content displays in your presentation. The procedure shows the CSS code you can add to a standard template so Web links are displayed.

In the previous procedures, a background image and header image were added to the template and the position of the slides was adjusted. The goal for this step-by-step procedure is to change the Web content's position so the presentation displays correctly.

1. If the template you want to customize is currently on the timeline in Producer, delete the presentation template from the timeline and then save your project. Close Microsoft Producer.

2. Using Notepad, open your custom presentation template file for editing.

   If you want to follow the specific procedures in this section, open the copy you created of the template named customizedsampletemplate.css in the folder customizedsampletemplate.

3. Change the values in the **#HTML1Div** selector to match the following example. These values determine how HTML files or Web links display in your presentation.

```
#HTML1Div
{VISIBILITY: visible;
POSITION: absolute;
TOP: 380px;
LEFT: 420px;
```

```
HEIGHT: 180px;
WIDTH: 420px;
WMBodyHeight: 0;  /* Do  not  edit. */
WMAlignSpacing: 10;  /* Do  not  edit. */
}
```

In the preceding code, the value associated with the **LEFT** property positions the HTML to display to the right of the table of contents. The **#HTML1Div** area is aligned on the left-hand side with the **#SlidesDiv** area.

Producer automatically provides scroll bars if the entire contents of the HTML file or Web page cannot be displayed in the window. If a template contains both slides and HTML content and the slides are resizable, the HTML is resizable as well. Likewise, if fixed-size slides appear in the template, any HTML or Web content will also be fixed-size.

An HTML area that is resizable contains custom properties such as **WMBodyHeight** and **WMAlignSpacing**. When editing the **#HTML1Div** selector, do not edit the values for the properties that begin with WM, such as **WMBodyHeight** or **WMAlignSpacing**. The display of a resizable HTML area is determined by code in Producer that uses the values for these properties. Changing the value for these properties can cause your presentation to display incorrectly.

4. Save the changes to the presentation template file.

6. Start Microsoft Producer. On the **File** menu, click **Open**, and open the project you saved in the earlier exercise.

    If you did not do the earlier exercise, you can open the project archive \StepByStep\Chapter12\ContosoSample.MSProducerZ from the companion CD, and then unpack and work with the resulting project.

6. Click the **Presentation Templates** folder for the current project. Choose the customized template named **Custom Standard Video (320x240) - Resizable Slides and HTML** and add it to the timeline.

7. On the **View** menu, click **Preview Presentation Tab**, and then play your presentation.

As you preview your presentation in Producer, you will notice that the table of contents displays incorrectly. The entries in the table of contents still obscure the video transport controls, and the text for entries is difficult to read because it does not contrast with the background image. The upcoming step-by-step procedure explains how to fix this and customize the table of contents in your presentation.

Customizing the Table of Contents

The table of contents displays links that the viewer can click to jump to a corresponding part of the presentation. The table of contents in Producer functions much like the table of contents for a book—it provides a structure for your presentation so the viewer can quickly find the information he or she wants.

You can customize the table of contents for a presentation. First, you must determine where the table of contents appears in relation to other parts of your presentation, such as video, audio, slides, or Web content. This positioning is determined by the **#TOCDiv** selector. In addition to positioning the table of contents, you can also customize how the entries in the table of contents display when an entry is playing or not playing; this is determined by the values for the **.TOCEntryNormal** and **.TOCEntryNowPlaying** selectors. You can change the font, font size, color, and formatting for entries in the table of contents by changing the values for the properties in these selectors.

Step-by-Step: Customizing Table of Contents Display

The following procedure describes the step-by-step process for customizing the table of contents and entries in the table of contents. The procedure shows the CSS code you can add to a standard template so the appearance, positioning, and entries in the table of contents are customized.

1. Using Notepad, open the copy of the customized presentation template.

    If you want to follow the procedures in this section, open the copy of the template named customizedsampletemplate.css in the folder customizedsampletemplate.

2. Edit the values for the properties of the **#TOCDiv** selector as shown below. **#TOCDiv** determines the display size and positioning of the table of contents.

```
#TOCDiv
{POSITION: absolute;
TOP: 380px;
LEFT: 52px;
HEIGHT: 140px;
WIDTH: 320px;
WMAlignBottom: 19;   /* Do not edit. */
}
```

The table of contents is set to display 380 pixels from the top. This value is based on the positioning and size of the media player in the **#MediaPlayerDiv** section. For example, **#MediaPlayerDiv** starts 69 pixels from the top, and the div is 305 pixels high (305 + 69 = 374 pixels). A few extra pixels are included so some empty space appears between the bottom of the media player controls and the top of the table of contents.

The width of the table of contents is set to 320 pixels, which matches the width of the video display. The value for the height in the table of contents is 140 pixels. Producer provides a scrollbar so that presentations with many table of contents entries will still display properly.

Similar to the slides and HTML displayed in this template, the table of contents is resizable. In this case, the height is set according to the size of the browser window. Do not edit the value for the **WMAlignBottom** property. Changing the value for this property can cause your presentation to display incorrectly.

3. Add the selector for the **.TOCEntryNormal** class as shown below. The **.TOCEntryNormal** selector determines the font, font size, and font color for entries in the table of contents when the entry is not playing in the presentation.

```
.TOCEntryNormal
{COLOR: #7D7C6C;
CURSOR: hand;
FONT-SIZE: 12pt;
FONT-FAMILY: Verdana;
FONT-WEIGHT: bold;
LIST-STYLE: none;
LINE-HEIGHT: 18pt;
}
```

A table of contents entry that is not currently playing in the presentation will display using 12-point, bold, Verdana font with a color that is a dark gray. The specified font is part of the standard Windows installation and should be installed on your audience's computers, so this font can be displayed successfully.

When a viewer moves his or her mouse over a table of contents entry that is not playing, the cursor appears as small hand that indicates an entry is a clickable link. The height of each line in the table of contents is set to 18 points so that some space appears between entries in the table of contents.

The value for the font color is specified as a hexadecimal value. Many graphics editing programs provide tools for determining color values and their hexadecimal equivalents. In addition, many books and Web sites also provide tools for determining and specifying color values.

4. Add the selector for the **.TOCEntryNowPlaying** class as shown below. The **.TOCEntryNowPlaying** selector determines the font, font size, and color for entries in the table of contents for the entry that is currently playing in the presentation.

```
.TOCEntryNowPlaying
{COLOR: #000033;
CURSOR: hand;
FONT-SIZE: 12pt;
FONT-FAMILY: Verdana;
FONT-WEIGHT: bold;
LIST-STYLE: none;
LINE-HEIGHT: 18pt;
}
```

The table of contents entry for an item that is currently playing displays as black text, whereas entries that are not playing display as dark gray. This helps your audience see which part of the presentation is currently playing.

Make sure the text color you choose contrasts with the background color (or image) that is displayed in the presentation. If the colors do not sufficiently contrast, the entries will be difficult to read.

6. Save the changes to the presentation template file.

6. Start Microsoft Producer. On the **File** menu, click **Open**, and open the project you saved in the earlier exercise.

   If you did not do the earlier exercise, you can, open the project archive named \StepByStep\Chapter12\ContosoSample.MSProducerZ from the companion CD, and then unpack and work with the resulting project.

7. Click the **Presentation Templates** folder for the current project. Choose the customized template named **Custom Standard Video (320x240) - Resizable Slides and HTML** and add it to the timeline.

8. On the **View** menu, click **Preview Presentation Tab**, and then play your presentation.

CHAPTER 13

Customizing Your Presentations

Up to this point, much of what has been discussed deals with working in Producer to create a presentation. However, you can perform many tasks before and after publishing that can enhance your final presentation. The tips and tricks in this chapter discuss how you can work inside and outside of Producer to create content for a future presentation, and how to edit your published presentation outside of Microsoft Producer.

Opening Web Content in a New Window

As mentioned earlier in this book, you can add static HTML files to your presentation, as well as live Web links. Having the ability to incorporate static and dynamic Web pages into your presentation opens up many design possibilities.

In Producer, static HTML pages or live Web sites are displayed in the area defined by the values for the **#HTML1Div** CSS selector in the template. Because the area is only a portion of the presentation, when a full Web page is displayed in that area, parts of the page are cut off. If viewers want to see other parts of the page, they can use the scroll bars to move around in it. However, this can be distracting if the Web page is large and complex.

To avoid this problem, you can offer viewers a link instead of embedding the whole page. When they click the link, the Web page opens in a separate browser window. Viewers can then choose to look at the whole Web page in one window or the presentation in the other window.

Another thing to consider with embedded HTML content is the use of links within the embedded Web page. The page you are embedding might be sized correctly, but what about the pages that your viewers will access from the links? Normally, linked content opens in the HTML area on the presentation page, replacing the original embedded page. If the linked page is long and complex, you can run into design issues. Also, you may not want the original embedded page to be replaced. To solve these problems, you can add parameters to the links on the embedded page that open the linked page in a separate browser window. The embedded page displays as you intended in the presentation, and when a viewer clicks the link, the new page opens in its own window.

The following procedure shows you how to add the parameter to the link.

Step-by-Step: Editing a Web Content Link

The following describes the step-by-step process for creating a link in an HTML file that will open the linked page in a new Web browser window.

1. Open the HTML file you want to embed in your presentation in an HTML or text editor (such as Notepad). It doesn't matter whether the HTML file has been imported into Producer already.

   For this exercise, Notepad is used to edit the HTML file.

2. Use the following HTML code for all links on the page.

   ```
   <A HREF="TargetSite" TARGET="_blank">LinkedText</a>
   ```

   TargetSite is the Web page you want to link to, and *LinkedText* is the text that viewers can click to access the link. Target="_blank" opens the link in a new browser window.

   For example, if you have an HTML file in your presentation that you want to link to the Microsoft Web site and open the site in a new browser window, the link would contain the following script.

   ```
   <A HREF="http://www.microsoft.com" TARGET="_blank">Microsoft Web site</a>
   ```

3. Save your changes. You can then import this HTML file and add it to your presentation.

   If you have already imported and added the HTML file to the timeline for your current project in Producer, the HTML file is updated automatically in your presentation. The new window will not open in the Producer **Preview Presentation** tab, but it will open in your finished presentation.

Customizing CD AutoPlay

The **Select a Presentation** page contains a listing of the Producer presentations that are located on a particular piece of storage media, such as a recordable or rewriteable CD. The window is a result of the scan.hta file, which is a Microsoft HTML Application file that is created automatically by Producer when a presentation is published.

If you distribute the CD, the **Select a Presentation** page automatically opens after the CD is inserted (as long as the AutoPlay capabilities of the CD drive have not been disabled). If your CD contains multiple presentations, your audience can then choose which presentation they want to watch, and then click the link for that presentation.

You may decide that you want to enhance the **Select a Presentation** page either by editing the existing scan.hta file or by creating an entirely new scan.hta file. Both of these methods let you customize the **Select a Presentation** page for your own organization.

The following sections describe how to edit an existing scan.hta file or how to create an entirely new page that lets your viewer select the presentation they want to watch.

Make sure you edit the scan.hta file before you write the file and the associated presentation files to the recordable or rewriteable CD.

Creating a New Scan.hta File

You can create your own **Select a Presentation** page to replace the one that displays when your presentation CD is inserted into a CD drive. This allows you to customize the look of the page by adding new art, adding your company's logo, or arranging the layout to suit your preference. In fact, you can do virtually anything in your custom **Select a Presentation** page that you do in an Internet Explorer-compatible Web page.

To customize the **Select a Presentation** page, first create your presentations and publish them to a folder on your local computer using the **My Computer** option in the **Publish Wizard**. Think of this folder as a temporary version of the CD you will create later.

Next, create a custom Web page to replace the **Select a Presentation** page. You can use an HTML editor, such as Microsoft FrontPage, or just a plain text editor like Notepad. The key is to include a link to each presentation that will appear on the CD. When the presentations were published, Producer created an HTML document for each presentation that has the same name as the presentation. This small Web page acts as a shortcut to the presentation introduction page. Since your custom Web page will be located in the CD root directory with the shortcuts, you don't need to include a path in each link tag; simply link to the shortcut using its name and file name extension. For example:

```
<A HREF = "CEO_Pricing.htm">Our new fall pricing policies</a>
```

Now make the Web page into an HTML application file named scan.hta. When you publish your presentation, Producer creates a file called scan.hta. This file is an HTML application that runs using the Microsoft HTML Application host.

If you are familiar with HTML, creating an HTML application is easy. To make a simple HTML document into an HTML application:

1. Add the following code in the <HEAD> section of the HTML:

    ```
    <HTA: APPLICATION>
    ```

2. Save the HTML document with a .hta file name extension.

The version of scan.hta that Producer creates adds two parameters to the application tag. You should specify these parameters as well, because they'll make your custom page look and behave more like a Windows-based application than a Web page. The first parameter specifies an icon to display in the title bar when the HTML displays; the second hides any toolbars and the menu bar in the Internet Explorer window. The full code for the application tag that you add to the <HEAD> section takes the form:

```
<HTA: APPLICATION ICON="page.ico"/>
```

In your publishing folder on your local hard drive, replace the Producer file named scan.hta with the custom HTML application file you created. Finally, write all the presentation files to a blank CD using Windows XP or whatever CD writing software you prefer. When you distribute your CD, be certain to advise your audience about the minimum system requirements for viewing your Producer presentations. You can find these in the Microsoft Producer Help.

Editing an Existing Scan.hta File

Editing the existing scan.hta file lets you change how the **Select a Presentation** page appears. Some of the changes you can make include changing the title of the page, the icon displayed, and the colors and font used in the page.

Do not edit the script that appears in this page. Editing this script can cause this page to not display or to display incorrectly.

You should edit the scan.hta file after you have published all the presentations you plan to include on the CD or other media. If you edit the scan.hta file and then publish another presentation to the same folder, the scan.hta you edited will be overwritten with a new file and your changes will not appear.

Before editing scan.hta, save a copy of the file in case you make a mistake and want to go back to the original.

Step-by-Step: Editing the Select a Presentation Page

The following procedure describes the step-by-step process for editing an existing scan.hta file to customize the appearance for the page.

For this exercise, you can open and edit a scan.hta file you have, or you can open and edit the scan.hta file in the folder \StepByStep\Chapter13\EditScanHTA on the companion CD. A sample, edited scan.hta file appears in the same location on the CD and is named SampleScan.hta.

A sample scan.hta page is shown in Figure 13.1.

If you plan on editing the sample scan.hta file, copy the file and the entire EditScanHTA folder to your computer first. This lets you edit scan.hta file and save your changes. The scan.hta and SampleScan.hta pages link to empty presentations.

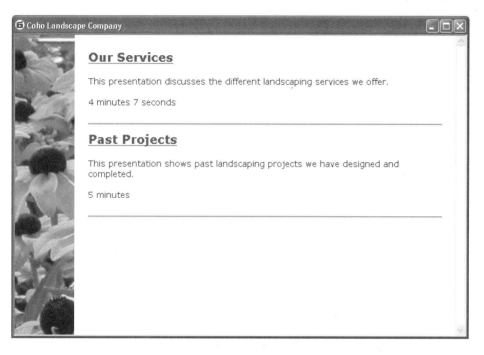

Figure 13.1 — A sample scan.hta page.

When you move the scan.hta without copying the presentation files, the links will not work properly. For this exercise, if you are using the sample scan.hta file, this is OK. The goal is for you to be able to see how your edits affect the appearance of the **Select a Presentation** page. If you are editing your own scan.hta, make sure you click the presentation links to ensure that they remain and link properly after editing the scan.hta file.

1. Open the scan.hta file in an HTML editor or a text editor such as Notepad.

2. The first change you might want to make is for the title of the page. To change the title, select the text between the <TITLE> and </TITLE> tags and then type a new title. To help locate the tags in Notepad, use **Find**.

3. If you have an icon file (that has a .ico file name extension) that you want to use in place of the existing one, do the following:

   • Copy of the icon file you want to use in Windows Explorer or My Computer.

   • Rename the icon file, giving it the new name page.ico.

   • Copy page.ico to the folder that contains the scan.hta file you are editing. When asked if you want to replace the current file with the new file, click **Yes**.

4. You can edit the different styles that appear in the scan.hta file. Figure 13.2 shows an example of the scan.hta page containing elements that you can edit.

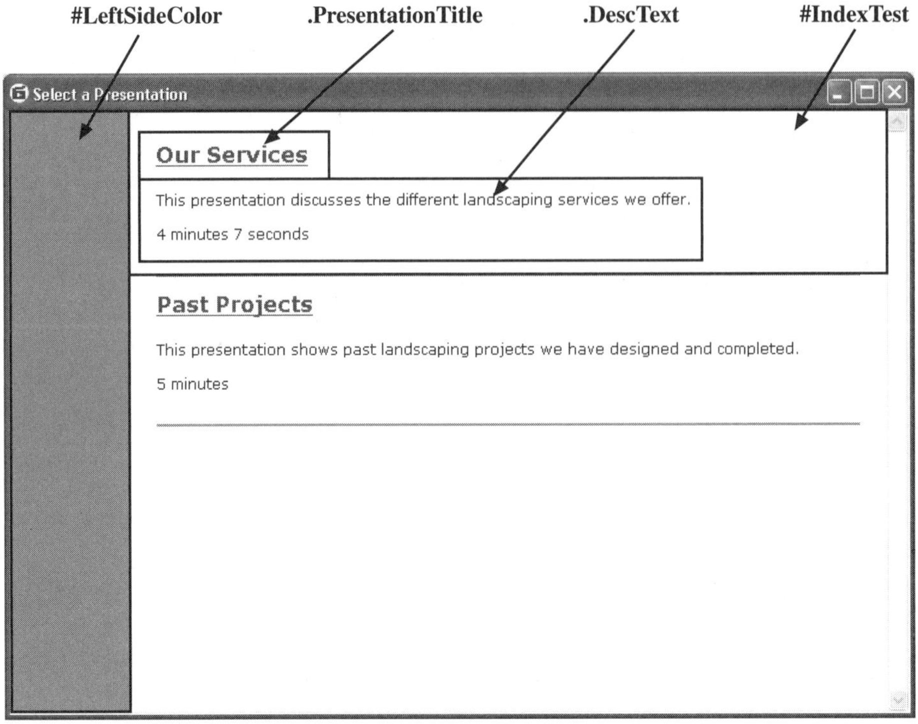

#LeftSideColor   .PresentationTitle   .DescText   #IndexTest

Our Services

This presentation discusses the different landscaping services we offer.

4 minutes 7 seconds

Past Projects

This presentation shows past landscaping projects we have designed and completed.

5 minutes

Figure 13.2 — The styles in scan.hta that can be safely edited.

5. In Notepad, you can edit the style for the **#LeftSideColor** selector in the scan.hta file. The style for the **#LeftSideColor** determines the size and color of the left side background.

For example, in the SampleScan.hta file, the values and properties appear as follows:

```
#LeftSideColor {
POSITION: absolute;
BACKGROUND-COLOR: transparent;
TOP: 0px;
LEFT: 0px;
WIDTH: 100px;
FLOAT: left;
BACKGROUND-IMAGE: URL(leftback.jpg);
}
```

The value for the **BACKGROUND-COLOR** property is set to transparent, so a background color does not appear. A background image named leftback.jpg was also added, so it appears on the left side of the page where the solid background color formerly appeared. This image file appears in the same folder as the scan.hta page.

If you want to use a color for the background, you must enter the color using hexadecimal numbers. The default page uses a shade of blue, which is entered like this:

```
BACKGROUND-COLOR: #0099FF;
```

Values for some other basic colors include red (#FF0000), green (#00FF00), and basic blue (#0000FF).

When editing the style for the **#LeftSideColor** selector, you should avoid editing the values for the **POSITION**, **TOP**, **LEFT**, **WIDTH**, and **FLOAT** properties. Editing the values for these properties may cause your presentation to display incorrectly.

6. Edit the style for the **#IndexText** selector in the scan.hta file. The **#Indextext** determines the size and background color of the right side of the page that displays the individual presentation entries.

   For example, in the SampleScan.hta file, the style for the **#IndexText** selector appears as follows:

```
#IndexText {
POSITION: absolute;
BACKGROUND-COLOR: #FFFFFF;
TOP: 0px;
LEFT: 100px;
PADDING: 20px;
}
```

   The value for the **BACKGROUND-COLOR** property is set to white. Just as shown in the sample for the style for the **#LeftSideColor** selector, you could insert a background image if you like.

   When editing the style for the **#IndexText** selector, you should avoid editing the values for the **POSITION**, **TOP**, **LEFT**, and **PADDING** properties. Editing the values for these properties may cause your presentation to display incorrectly.

7. Edit the style for the **.PresentationTitle** class. The **.PresentationTitle** class determines the font, font size, and color for the individual presentation entries.

   For example, in the SampleScan.hta file, the style for the **.PresentationTitle** class appears like this:

```
.PresentationTitle {
FONT-FAMILY: Verdana, sans-serif;
FONT-SIZE: 20px;
FONT-WEIGHT: bold;
COLOR: #000000;
CURSOR: hand;
}
```

The font for the title of the presentation displays with 20-pixel, bold Verdana font. The font color for the title is black (#000000); however, the font appears as the default color for linked text because the title serves as the link to the actual presentation. You could change the font that is used for the title, as well as the font size and weight. If you do change the font, make sure you choose a font that is likely to be installed on your audience's computers.

8. Edit the style for the **.DescText** class. The **.Desctext** class determines how the text for the description of each presentation is displayed.

   For example, in the SampleScan.hta file, the style for the **.DescText** class appears:

   ```
   .DescText {
   FONT-FAMILY: Verdana, sans-serif;
   FONT-SIZE: 14px;
   COLOR: #000000;
   CURSOR: hand;
   }
   ```

   The font for the title of the presentation displays with 14-pixel Verdana font. The font color for the description text is black (#000000). You could change the font that is used for the description, as well as the font size and color.

   If you add a background image for the **#IndexText**, make sure there is enough contrast in color for the description text. If you add a background image and the font color does not contrast with the image, the text could be difficult to see.

9. After you have edited the scan.hta file in Notepad, on the **File** menu, click **Save**.

10. Double-click the file. The HTML Application should open and your edited listing of available presentations should appear.

Getting a Jump Start on a Presentation

When creating presentations in Microsoft Producer, one presentation might be part of a series of presentations you create and publish to a Web site, intranet site, or to a CD. For example, you may be creating a series of online training classes where each presentation discusses a specific topic or feature in a software application. You might have a standard video, audio, or image, such as a logo, that you show at the beginning of each presentation. Likewise, you might have a closing video clip for each presentation that contains additional contact or copyright information. To save time, you can save a project that has these files already imported into Producer and added to the timeline.

When you start a new project that includes digital media files that have already been imported and added to the project, you can open that project file, then import, add, and edit the additional content. You can then use the **Save As** command on the **File** menu and save the project with a new name. You will then have a project file that contains the content for the entire presentation, and you'll still have the smaller template project file that contains the standard digital media files you commonly include in your presentations. This can save you a lot of time when you are using standard digital media files in your presentations.

You can help standardize your company's presentations by storing standard and commonly used digital media files and the template project file on a shared network location. This way, if others in your organization or company are creating presentations, they could also use this template project. After they import and add additional content, they could save the project they create on their own computers.

An ideal way to share this "template" project is to use the Producer **Pack and Go** feature to create a project archive. Multiple users can then simply copy the project archive and unpack it on their local computers. The project would contain all of the standard files. From there, users could then import additional content and continue creating their presentations as usual. Chapter 7 discusses packing and unpacking a project archive.

Step-by-Step: Using the Save As Command

The following procedure describes the step-by-step process for using the **Save As** command to create a new presentation from a basic project file. The goal of this procedure is to walk through using the **Save As** command to work more efficiently in Producer.

1. Create and save a template project that contains the digital media files you commonly include in all of your presentations. These files can contain corporate logos, copyright information, contact information, or other content you don't want to have to import every time you start a new project in a series.

2. On the **File** menu, click **Save**. In the **File name** box, type a name for the template project such as StartingProject.MSProducer. Click **Save** to save the template project.

3. Import any additional digital media files that you want to include in a particular presentation. Add the files to the timeline and edit your project as usual.

4. When you are ready to save your project, on the **File** menu, click **Save As**. In the **File name** box, type a new name for the particular project, and then click **Save**. This project contains the standard files, as well as the additional digital media files imported and arranged for this particular presentation.

5. On the **File** menu, click **Pack and Go**. Name and then save the project archive. This would allow you and others to copy the project archive and then unpack it on their own computers to continue editing the project that has been started.

Creating a Microsoft PowerPoint Template

Chapter 12 discussed how you can create and customize your own Microsoft Producer presentation templates. To further customize your presentations, you can also create your own design templates in Microsoft PowerPoint for the slides you use in your Producer presentations. You can match the colors and designs of your PowerPoint templates with the colors and images used in your Producer presentation templates. This can help to improve the continuity of your presentations.

When you create a PowerPoint design template, you can choose to create a new one from the beginning, or you can choose to open an existing design template or PowerPoint presentation, edit it, and then save it as a new PowerPoint design template. In PowerPoint, design templates are saved with a .pot file name extension.

Step-by-Step: Creating a PowerPoint Design Template

The following describes the process for creating and saving a PowerPoint design template.

1. In Microsoft PowerPoint, start with a new, blank presentation.

2. On the **View** menu, point to **Master**, and then click **Slide Master**.

   This lets you create a design for the master slide. The slide design you create can then be applied to other slides in your PowerPoint presentation.

3. In the **Slide Master** view, create a new design template. Some of the changes you can make to your slide design include the following:

   - On the **Format** menu, click **Background**. In the **Background** dialog box, shown in Figure 13.3, there are a number of options for choosing a background for the master slide. Click **Apply to All** or **Apply** to accept the background choice.

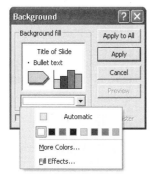

Figure 13.3 — Background choices you can select for your PowerPoint slides.

   You can choose **More colors** to specify a new background color. For example, if you know the RGB code for a color in your Producer template or presentation scheme, you might enter that RGB code (or adjust it slightly) on the **Custom** tab so the colors in your PowerPoint slides and Producer templates are coordinated.

You can choose **Fill Effects** if you want to add a pattern, texture, or picture. Again, the background you choose can coordinate with images or colors used in your Producer template.

- Click **Click to edit Master title slide**. On the **Format** menu, click **Font**, and then choose a font, font size, font style, effects, and the color for the title of your slide. Click **OK**.

  When choosing the font properties, you may choose to match the font with the font used in the table of contents for your Producer presentation. Furthermore, when you choose the font color, choose a color that contrasts with the background color or image you chose for your design template.

- Click **Click to edit Master text styles**. On the **Format** menu, click **Font**, and then choose the font, font size, font style, effects, and the color for the selected bulleted list level. Click **OK**.

- If you would like to change the bulleted list style for the selected bulleted list level, on the **Format** menu, click **Bullets and Numbering**. You can then choose a new bulleted list style. Click **OK**.

These are only a few of the choices you can make for your design template.

4. On the **Slide Master View** toolbar, click **Close Master View**.

5. On the **File** menu, click **Save**. In the **Save as type** box, choose **Design Template (*.pot)**. In the **File name** box, type a name for your design template, and then click **Save** to save the design template.

After you have saved your design template, you can then apply the design template to new PowerPoint presentations you create or to an existing PowerPoint presentation. You can then import the PowerPoint presentation into Producer and incorporate the slides in your Producer presentations.

Annotating Slides for Your Presentation

During your presentations, you might want to annotate or add a pointer to the slides as you narrate them. You would add marks to your slides as you explain the item or concept related to the slide, like drawing on a whiteboard.

You can use the **Video screen capture with audio** capture option in Microsoft Producer to create the illusion of annotating a PowerPoint slide during your presentation. Although it looks as though the annotation is made on a PowerPoint slide, you actually are displaying a video screen capture of the slide and annotation.

Step-by-Step: Annotating Slides

The following procedure shows you how to simulate the appearance of annotations on slides in your presentation.

1. Close any other open applications on your computer, so only Microsoft PowerPoint and Microsoft Producer are open.

   When using the video screen capture option in Microsoft Producer, you can improve the quality of your screen capture by closing unnecessary applications, which consume resources on your computer.

2. In Microsoft PowerPoint, open the PowerPoint presentation that contains the slide you want to annotate. On the **View** menu, click **Slide Show**.

   You can save time by opening the PowerPoint presentation and going to the slide you want to annotate. It also reduces the amount of editing you have to do for the video screen capture because these preliminary tasks, which are not pertinent to the presentation, are not captured.

3. In the **Slide Show** view in PowerPoint, right-click the slide you want to annotate, point to **Pointer Options**, and then choose **Pen**.

   This displays a pen, which you can then use to "write on" or annotate your slides. This also works well if you have images inserted in a slide that you want to annotate.

4. Right-click the slide you want to annotate, point to **Pointer Options**, point to **Pen Color**, and then click the color you want to use for the pen. This is the color that is used for your annotation.

   When you choose a pen color, choose a color that contrasts with the colors in the slide so the pen marks can be seen clearly in the video screen capture.

5. Hold down the Alt key and press the Tab key until Microsoft Producer is selected, and then release the Alt key.

6. In Microsoft Producer, on the **Tools** menu, click **Capture**. Choose the **Video screen capture with audio** option, and then click **Next**.

7. Choose the audio device you want to use for any audio you want to capture, such as a narration, and then click **Next**.

8. In the **Capture Wizard**, select the **Minimize while capturing** check box. Choose the capture setting display size that lets you capture the area of the slide that you want to annotate. Click **Capture** to begin your video screen capture.

9. In the **Slide Show** view of PowerPoint, slowly draw on the slide that you want to annotate with the appropriate marks. If you have an audio capture device configureed, you can describe the slide and the narration will be recorded along with the video screen capture.

10. After you have completed the annotation and narration, hold down the Alt key and press the Tab key until Microsoft Producer is selected, and then release the Alt key. This stops capturing.

11. In the **File name** box, type a name for the screen capture video, and then click **Save**. Click **Finish** to close the **Capture Wizard**.

12. Choose the video screen capture, and then add it to the timeline. You can then continue editing your project as usual.

13. On the **File** menu, click **Save** to save the current project.

Make sure that the video display size is the same as that of your video screen capture by using an appropriate presentation template while the screen capture plays. This prevents the video from appearing distorted.

Your video screen capture will contain the task pane that displayed when you stopped capturing. You can remove this part by trimming the video on the timeline. Chapter 9 discusses trimming video and audio.

Switching Published Video Files

It is possible to manually replace the Windows Media Video (WMV) files that Microsoft Producer creates during the publishing process. You might want to do this if the published video loses a significant amount of quality compared to the original, perhaps due to undesirable re-encoding of the digital media. To do this, you need to be aware of certain restrictions:

- The original source video must be in Windows Media Format.

- The video in the published presentation must have the same content as the original source video. If you have added video files, created clips and re-edited the video, or trimmed the original, for example, the published video will be different from the original. Therefore, when you replace the final video with the original, the presentation will not play as expected.

- The entire presentation must use a single template.

To prepare your original video file for use in the published presentation, you also need to copy the script data that was added to the published file by Producer. To do that, you can use Microsoft Windows Media Advanced Script Indexer. (Advanced Script Indexer can be installed from the CD included with this book.) The script data in the published file contains information that Producer added to play back your presentation.

Once you copy the script data to the original file, you can simply replace the file that Producer created with the modified file. To locate the published file, use Windows Explorer to browse to the folder containing your presentation files. Producer names the file in the form of 0MM0.wmv.

In order to prevent loss of data, it's important that you create backup copies of any files you plan to manipulate.

Step-by-Step: Changing the Video in a Published Presentation

The following steps illustrate how you can replace the WMV file in a presentation that has already been published.

1. Import the original WMV file, create your presentation, and then publish it.

2. Make a backup copy of your original WMV file. It's also wise to make a backup copy of the WMV file that Producer created during publishing.

3. Run Advanced Script Indexer.

4. In Advanced Script Indexer, from the **File** menu, click **Open**. Browse to the WMV file in your presentation that you want to replace and click **Open**.

5. From the **File** menu, click **Export script file**. In the **File name** box, type a name for the script file, and click **Save**. Click **OK** when prompted.

6. From the **File** menu, click **Open**. Browse to the original WMV file and click **Open**.

7. From the **File** menu, click **Import from script file**. Browse to the script file you saved in step 5 and click **Open**. Click **OK** when prompted.

8. From the **File** menu, click **Save As**. Browse to the location where Producer published the presentation. Click the WMV file that you want to replace (for example, 0MM0.wmv) to highlight it. Click **Save**. Click **Yes** when prompted to replace the original published WMV file.

9. Exit Advanced Script Indexer.

Be sure to watch your entire presentation to ensure that the process worked correctly.

Copying a Published Presentation

There may be times when you want to copy a published presentation to a new destination. This can save a significant amount of time compared to republishing the presentation, especially if the presentation is long or you require several publishing profiles. You can simply copy all the files from one location to another if the transfer involves the following locations:

- Between folders on your local computer.

- From your local computer to a CD. Note that you'll need to create the necessary Autorun files if you want the CD to start automatically.

- From a CD to your local computer.

- From your local computer to a Web server.

- From a Web server to your local computer.

- From one Web server to another Web server.

The process is a bit more complex when you want to copy a presentation to a system that uses Windows Media Services to stream content. In this case, the WMV files in your presentation must be copied to the publishing point on the Windows Media server, and the Windows Media metafile playlist file must be edited to reflect the new publishing point.

Step-by-Step: Copying Presentation Files

The following procedure describes how to copy a presentation published using the **My Computer** option in the **Publish Wizard** to a system using a Web server and a Windows Media server:

1. Using the **Publish Wizard**, publish your presentation to your local computer with the **My Computer** option.

2. Using **Windows Explorer,** locate the folder to which you published the presentation.

3. Copy all the published files, including the WMV files, to the Web server folder that will deliver your presentation to your audience.

   Optionally, delete the WMV files from the Web server. If you leave the WMV files on the Web server, your audience can copy your entire presentation to their local computers. If this is a security issue for you, delete the digital video files. There is an advantage to having them duplicated on the Web server—if the streaming server is unavailable for some reason, the presentation will still be able to play the video from the Web server.

4. Copy only the WMV files to a publishing point on the Windows Media server.

6. Edit the playlist metafiles on the Web server to point to the publishing point on the Windows Media server.

There is one playlist file generated by Producer for each publishing profile you choose. You can view and edit playlist metafiles using any text editor, such as Notepad. The playlist metafile acts as a shortcut that redirects requests for playback to the correct path where the digital media content is located. When you published to **My Computer**, Producer placed the digital media files and the metafiles into the same folder, so a path in the playlist metafile contains only the name of a WMV file, not the entire path. For example, the playlist metafile for the file named 0MM0.wmv is 0Media.asx. When you open the metafile in a text editor, it might look like this:

```
<ASX version = "3.0">
<!--Producer-generated file-->
   <ENTRY>
     <REF  HREF = "0MM0.wmv"/>
   </ENTRY>
</ASX>
```

When you move a WMV file to a Windows Media server, you must edit the playlist script and add the complete protocol and path for the WMV file. Additionally, you can enter the publishing point URL just before the existing file name reference as a backup. The presentation will attempt to play back the file from the Windows Media server first, then if that fails play the file from the Web server, if one exists. Be sure to specify the MMS protocol for the streaming server.

The following example playlist changes the preceding example to point to a Windows Media server named MyMediaServer using a publishing point named MyPublishingPoint:

```
<ASX version = "3.0">
<!--Producer-generated  file">
    <ENTRY>
     <REF HREF = "mms://MyMediaServer/MyPublishingPoint/0MM0.wmv"/>
     <REF HREF = "0MM0.wmv"/>
    </ENTRY>
</ASX>
```

If you used multiple profiles, you'll need to repeat this process for each playlist metafile in your Web server folder.

CHAPTER 14

Creating Custom Publishing Solutions

In chapter 11, you learned about the publishing process. You used the **Publish Wizard** to make your presentations available for viewing in a variety of different ways. You saw that the wizard made publishing easy because you simply provided the necessary information and Producer handled the details for you. You also learned a bit about e-services.

The **Publish Wizard** is an exciting and useful tool, and Microsoft has provided ways that you can customize the publishing process. Some of these are fairly simple; others require some programming skills. Here are some of the things you can do:

- Easily distribute a small file that users can run to add a Web server to the **Publish Wizard** on their computers.

- Author a complete custom e-service that replaces the default **Publish Wizard** user interface.

- Create a small file that users can run to change the page that displays when they click the **Learn More** button.

- Write a Web page that replaces the default **Learn More** page in the **Publish Wizard**. This page can contain links that users click to add new Web servers or to add complete e-services.

This chapter will explain how to do each of these things, while providing you with plenty of background information to help you to understand how and why these things work. You'll find the information here easier to grasp if you have some understanding of HTML and the Microsoft JScript programming language. Some familiarity with the Windows registry is also helpful. Even if you don't have any background in these areas, you should still read the chapter. You may find that these concepts aren't hard at all; perhaps you'll even be inspired to learn more about programming. Every effort has been made to keep things as simple as possible.

A detailed reference, programming guide, and complete sample code are provided in the Microsoft Producer for PowerPoint 2002 Software Development Kit (SDK). The SDK documentation is installed by default with Microsoft Producer. You can locate the SDK Help file, named ProdSDK.chm, in the folder named Shared, which can be found within the folder where you installed Producer.

There are several reasons why customizing the publishing process in Producer is useful:

- You can simplify the process for the user.

- You can restrict the choices you offer to the user. For instance, you might only allow publishing using a specific profile.

- You can make the publishing process uniform across an entire organization. For instance, everyone in the marketing department can publish to the same server.

- You can make it easy to update or change the behavior of the **Publish Wizard** on many computers across your organization. For example, if the marketing department changes to a new Web server, employees can be directed to update their computers with new server information and settings simply by clicking a link.

Customizing Registry Keys

When you used the **Publish Wizard** to add a new item to the **Web server** list in chapter 11, Producer stored the data associated with the new Web server in the *registry*. The registry is a database that is an integral part of Microsoft Windows. Windows uses the registry to store data about all kinds of things important to the operating system. Programmers who write Windows-based applications can access the registry to store and retrieve system data, as well as manipulate custom data that they require for their programs.

You can work with the registry by using an editing program provided with Windows, called Registry Editor. To use Registry Editor, run the file regedit.exe.

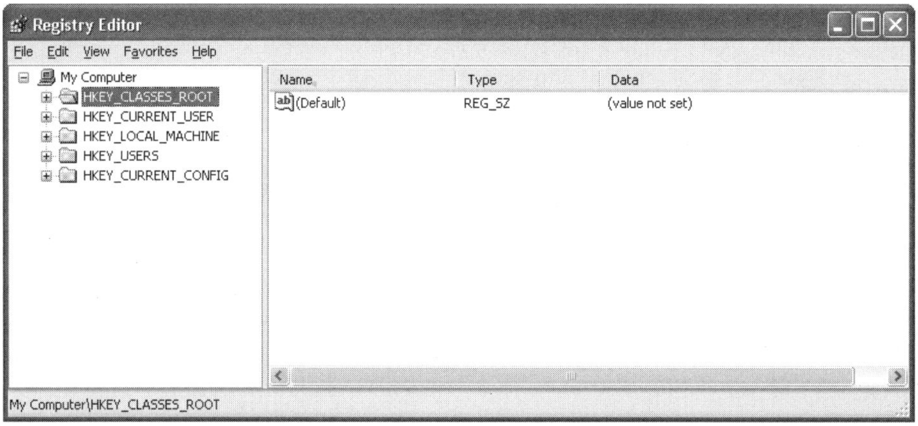

Figure 14.1 — The Registry Editor program

Figure 14.1 shows a screen shot of the Registry Editor program. You can see that the layout of the program is similar to Windows Explorer. The left pane of the window shows an arrangement of folders, the right pane shows details associated with the currently selected folder, and there is a menu bar at the top of the window. If you were to click on a + symbol next to one of the folders, you'll see that there are many subfolders.

This hierarchical tree structure should be familiar to you by now from using Windows—the organization of the registry database in Registry Editor looks just like the file system in Windows Explorer. However, the items stored in the registry are not files; they are data. The folder system is a convenient way to organize the data, but each data item is identified by a unique name.

The terminology you'll use when referring to items in the registry may be new to you, because it is closely tied to database terms. Each level in the hierarchy represented by the folders in Registry Editor is called a *key*. A level that exists below a particular key in the tree is referred to as a *subkey* of that key. For instance, in Registry Editor you can see a key named **HKEY_CURRENT_USER**. All the data relative to a particular user of the computer would logically be organized beneath that key. There is a subkey of **HKEY_CURRENT_USER** named **Identities**.

The data stored in a subkey is called a *value*. Each value occupies one line in the right pane of the Registry Editor window, and consists of a name, a type (which you can ignore for now), and the data for that value. There is a value in the **Identities** subkey named **Last Username**, which stores the name of the most recent user (not the last name of the user). You can see in Figure 14.2 that the name of the most recent user is Jim.

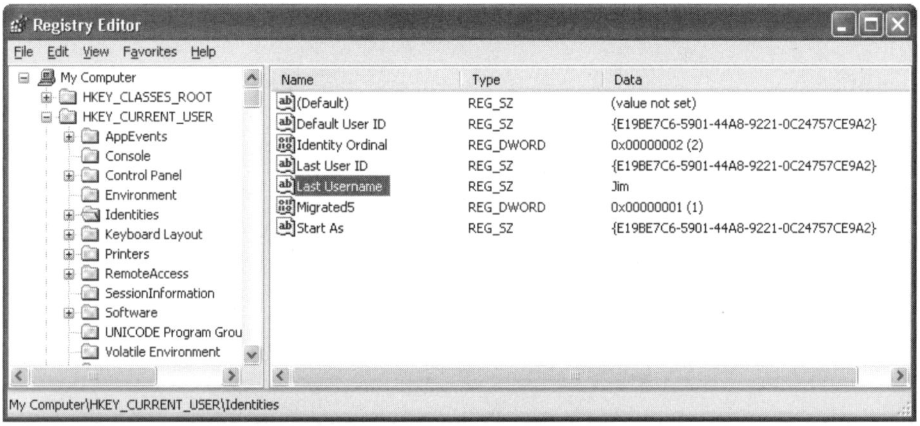

Figure 14.2 — Registry Editor showing **Identities** key values

When you want to describe a set of keys and subkeys to show their relationships, you separate each key from the highest in position to the lowest using a backslash character. For example, the complete name for the **Identities** subkey would be **HKEY_CURRENT_USER\Identities**.

How Producer Uses the Registry for Publishing

Producer, like most software, uses the registry to fill a variety of data storage needs. The focus in this chapter is on how Producer stores the data related to the publishing process and the **Publish Wizard**.

The root key for Producer Web servers and e-services is **HKEY_CURRENT_USER\Software\Microsoft\Producer\WebHosts**. Each time you add a new Web server in the **Publish Wizard**, Producer creates a new subkey below **WebHosts** and gives the subkey the name you provided in the **Friendly host name** box. Producer then creates values in the new subkey, and stores any data you provided when you created the new Web server. This new subkey (and all the data it contains) is called a Web host.

Producer also creates a new Globally Unique Identifier (GUID) for the new Web host, which it stores using the name **ID**. GUIDs are long, complicated strings of numbers and letters. Each combination is considered unique across space and time. You don't need to be concerned with the details of GUIDs; just understand that a GUID is a way to be certain that you can uniquely identify something. GUIDs are used throughout the programming world, and Producer uses them most notably to identify Web hosts and profiles.

Finally, Producer creates a subkey for each new Web host key, and gives it the name **Profiles**. Later, you'll see that you can use this subkey to store a list of default profiles that your Web host can use when publishing.

Table 14.1 describes the minimum set of values placed in the registry by Producer when you add a new Web server in the **Publish Wizard**:

Table 14.1 — Default registry values created by Producer.

Name	Description
(Default)	Not used. It is common for a new key to be created with an empty default value.
DiscussionServerAddress	Stores the address you provided in the **Discussion server** box.
ID	Stores the GUID for the Web host generated by Producer.
PlaybackAddress	Stores the address you provide in the **Playback presentation address (optional)** box.
PublishDestination	Stores the path or address you provided in the **Publish Web files to** box.
WindowsMediaPlaybackAddress	Stores the address you provided in the **Playback address for Windows Media files** box.
WindowsMediaPublishDestination	Stores the path or address you provided in the **Publish Windows Media files to** box.

There are other possible values for a Web host key that you'll learn about later. For now, just use Registry Editor to see what a Web host key looks like in the registry on your computer. Follow these steps:

1. Start Microsoft Producer. If you haven't already added your own Web server, use the **Publish Wizard** to add one now. The **WebHosts** subkey is not created by Producer until you add a Web host key. Refer to chapter 11 for instructions.

2. Click **Start**, and then click **Run**. In the **Open** box, type **regedit**.

3. Click **OK**. The **Registry Editor** window appears.

4. Click the + symbol to expand the key folder **HKEY_CURRENT_USER**.

5. Click the + symbol to expand the subkey folder **Software**.

6. Click the + symbol to expand the subkey folder **Microsoft**.

7. Click the + symbol to expand the subkey folder **Producer**.

8. Click the + symbol to expand the subkey folder **WebHosts**.

9. Click the folder that has the name of the Web host you want to inspect. The values for that Web host appear in the right pane of the window.

Figure 14.3 shows a Web host key as viewed in the regedit.exe program:

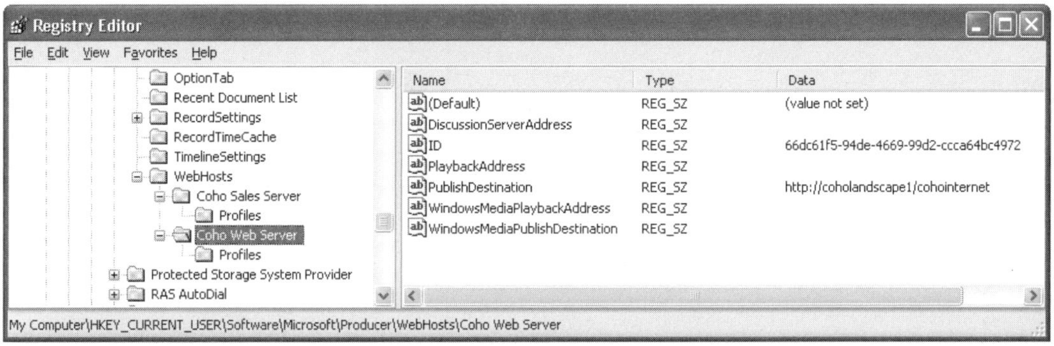

Figure 14.3 — A Producer Web host key.

Next, you'll learn some techniques for working with the registry directly.

Using Data in the Registry

Now that you have a basic understanding about how Producer stores Web host data in the registry, you can start putting that information to good use. First, though, here is a word of caution. As stated previously, Windows and Windows-based programs make extensive use of the registry to store important data and keep track of the system configuration.

Incorrectly editing the registry may severely damage your system. Before making any changes to the registry, you should make a backup of the part of the registry you plan to edit so you can restore the original condition of the system, if need be.

Step-by-Step: Backing up Registry Data

Follow these steps to create a backup copy of the Producer **WebHosts** key on your computer:

1. Run Registry Editor.

2. Navigate to the key **HKEY_CURRENT_USER\Software\Microsoft\Producer\WebHosts**. Click on the **WebHosts** folder to select it.

3. On the **File** menu, click **Export**. The **Export Registry File** dialog box appears as shown in Figure 14.4.

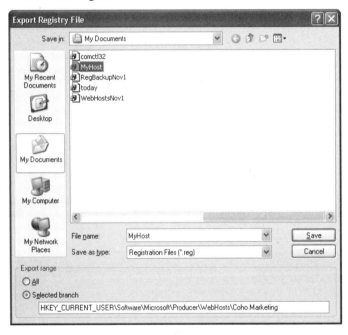

Figure 14.4 — Exporting a registry file.

4. In the **Export range** area of the dialog box, click **Selected branch**.

5. In the **Save in** list box, choose a location to which to save your backup registry file. Typically, the **My Documents** folder is the default, and that works fine.

6. In the **File name** box, type a name you'll remember. It's a good idea to include a date in the name, such as "WebHostsNov18". That will make it easy to find the file when you need to.

7. Click **Save**. You might have to wait a moment while the system creates the registry file.

You can use the **Export** command to create a copy of your entire registry for reference purposes. To do this, click **All** instead of **Selected branch** in step 4 in the previous procedure. The registry file you export will contain all the data in the registry. This is not a good way to create a backup of the registry, however, because attempting to import the entire registry using Registry Editor will usually fail. The failure is the result of the operating system locking parts of the registry that are in use at any given time.

You can create an entire backup copy of your registry by using the Microsoft Backup utility included with Windows. The wizard included with this utility allows you to create a backup file that contains only system state data, which includes the registry. For more information, see Microsoft Backup Help.

Step-by-Step: Restoring Registry Data

If you need to restore the **WebHosts** key and its subkeys, you can follow these steps:

1. Start Registry Editor.

2. From the **File** menu, choose **Import**. The **Import Registry File** dialog box appears.

3. Locate the registry file you saved previously, and click the file to select it.

4. Click **Open**.

5. Click **OK** when prompted.

Changing the Values of Registry Keys

Once you're confident that you have a backup of the area of the registry you plan to edit, you can use Registry Editor to make specific changes to the values in the registry. For instance, you might want to change the address of the server to which a particular Web host copies the published presentation. The preferred (and safest) method for doing this would be to use the **Edit** button in the **Publish Wizard** to make the appropriate change, letting Producer update the registry for you. If you're the adventurous type, you could manually change the value using Registry Editor.

Step-by-Step: Editing Registry Values

This is the procedure you can use to edit any registry value. As an example, try editing a **PublishDestination** key:

1. Start Registry Editor.

2. Navigate to the Web host key that contains the address you want to change. Click the folder for that key to select it and the values appear in the right pane.

3. Right-click the name **PublishDestination**.

4. Choose **Modify** from the shortcut menu. The **Edit String** dialog box appears.

5. In the **Value data** box, type the new address for the publishing destination.

6. Click **OK** to close the dialog box.

7. Start Producer. Try publishing to the new destination using the **Publish Wizard** by choosing the Web host you edited from the **Web server** drop down list.

You may never want to edit your Web host keys in this manner, but it's good to become familiar with the **Registry Editor** program and the functionality it offers. Be warned—you can just as easily delete keys and values from the registry using Registry Editor, so think twice and be sure of what you are doing before you click the **OK** button.

Copying and Distributing a Registry Key

Now you can do something really useful. Suppose you have set up a Web host to publish in a particular configuration, and you want your colleagues to be able to publish exactly the same way you do. Using Registry Editor, there's an easy way for you to distribute your Web host to as many people as you like.

When you created a backup of your **WebHosts** key in a previous procedure, the export function in Registry Editor saved the information in a *registry file*. A registry file is a plain text file with a .reg file name extension. You can open registry files in Microsoft Notepad to view and edit the contents, if you like. But the great thing about registry files is that they are executable. This means you can double-click a registry file and Windows will ask you for permission to add the information in the file to the registry. If the file contains keys that already exist on the system, Windows overwrites the existing data to update it.

The first thing you want to do in order to distribute your Web host configuration is to create a registry file that contains only the particular Web host key you want to share, along with its subkeys. The process is similar to what you did to create a backup.

Step-by-Step: Copying a Registry Key

Follow these steps to make a copy of a registry key that you can share with other users:

1. Start Registry Editor.

2. Navigate to the key you want to export and click on the folder to select it. The folder will have the name that appears in the **Web server** list in the **Publish Wizard**.

3. From the **File** menu, choose **Export**.

4. In the **Export range** area of the dialog box, click **Selected branch**. You should see the entire name of the key you selected to export.

5. In the **Save in** list box, choose a location in which to save your registry file. The **My Documents** folder is the default, and that works fine. Remember that you'll need to retrieve the file soon.

6. In the **File name** box, type a meaningful name for the registry file. Remember that you'll be distributing the file, so you might want to keep it unique somehow.

7. Click **Save** to create the registry file.

Here is what the finished registry file might look like if you opened it using Notepad:

```
Windows Registry Editor Version 5.00

[HKEY_CURRENT_USER\Software\Microsoft\Producer\WebHosts\MyNewWebHost]
"DiscussionServerURL" = ""
"ID" = "13003B9C-83ED-4c95-B950-D163C33B0C15"
"Password" = ""
"PlaybackLocation" = ""
"PublishDestination" = "\\coholandscape1\cohointernet"
"WindowsMediaPlaybackAddress" = ""
"WindowsMediaPublishDestination" = ""
```

Sharing the Registry File

Now that you've created the registry file, you can distribute it in any number of ways:

- Copy the file to a shared network folder and point people to the location.

- Send the file in e-mail as an attachment.

- Link to the file from a Web page.

- Place the file on a floppy disk and physically move it from one computer to another.

When your colleagues run the registry file, they will be prompted for permission to make changes to the registry. Since they might not be as well-versed in the registry as you are by now, you should probably let them know in advance about what the file does and that it is safe for them to accept the registry changes. You should also tell them that any changes made to the registry require that Producer be restarted to take effect.

Custom Publishing with E-services

You've now learned quite a bit about how Producer uses the registry to store publishing data, including a technique that exports a Web host key from the registry on your computer so you can distribute your publishing settings. This provides you with some "under the hood" understanding of how Producer stores its publishing parameters. By itself, though, it isn't quite enough. What you really need is a mechanism to allow you to customize the entire publishing process from beginning to end. This would allow you to control the entire user experience and determine how and where publishing takes place. You need to create an e-service.

In Producer, an e-service is a service that provides a Web server location and hosting for Producer presentations. That sounds pretty basic, and in reality both of those things are required any time you publish a presentation for viewing on a corporate network or the Internet. The key difference is found in the word *service*. A service implies that the Web server and hosting are being provided by someone other than the creator of the presentation, perhaps for a fee.

In fact, this is exactly the intent of the **Learn More** button in the **Publish Wizard**. When the user clicks **Learn More**, by default a Web page appears that offers commercial publishing e-services. The user can take advantage of an e-service by following the directions on the Web page, which includes programming code to add the proper publishing details to the registry on the user's computer. Once the e-service has been added to the user's computer, the user can publish a presentation using the e-service by simply selecting it from the **Web server** list in the **Publish Wizard**.

However, e-services are not limited to commercial ventures. Anyone can be an e-service provider if they have a Web server—such as Microsoft Internet Information Server (IIS)—that is connected to a corporate network or the Internet. This means you can offer custom publishing solutions for your department, your entire corporation, or the world.

The remainder of this chapter will show you how to do the following:

- Create a registry file that adds your e-service to the **Web server** list on the user's computer.

- Create a custom user interface for the **Publish Wizard**.

- Use the Producer object model to control the entire publishing process.

- Create a registry file that changes the Web page that displays by default when the user clicks **Learn More**.

- Create a custom **Learn More** Web page you can use to offer your publishing services and add your e-service to the **Web server** list on the user's computer.

Getting Started

Before you can offer your e-service to anyone, you'll need to set up the Web server (and possibly the Windows Media server) to which you want to let people publish presentations. It is beyond the scope of this book to provide details about configuring IIS or a Windows Media server. Refer to chapter 11 for an overview of the types of servers required for publishing and the differences between Web servers and Windows Media servers.

In addition to the space you allocate for hosting Producer presentations, you'll need to set up a Web site to host your e-service. A good deal of the work you'll be doing will involve authoring Web pages, and those pages must be hosted somewhere so users can see them. The Web pages can be hosted on an intranet or the Internet; in either case, you'll use the HTTP protocol to deliver the content.

The primary Web page you will create performs two functions. First, it replaces the default user interface in the **Publish Wizard**, allowing you to customize what the user sees in the wizard. Because the **Publish Wizard** window contains a hosted version of Microsoft Internet Explorer, the wizard can display Web page content just like the standalone Web browser. Second, the Web page contains the JScript code that allows you to take control of the publishing process. This code can access the Microsoft Producer object model, which exposes the functionality you'll need to perform the functions that the **Publish Wizard** does by default.

About the Microsoft Producer Object Model

Using JScript, you can take advantage of the Producer *object model*, which was mentioned earlier. The object model exposes a set of programming interfaces that make it easy to write code that tells Producer (specifically, the **Publish Wizard**) how to behave. The functionality you require is logically distributed among a variety of *objects*, each of which has a particular name. Of course, these objects don't exist in the physical world; they exist in your computer's memory.

Each object in the Producer object model exposes one or more *properties* or *methods*. You can think of a property as representing a state of being for the object. A property must have a name and a value. For instance, you could have a property named color with a value of red. You can think of a method as an imperative, a definite instruction that tells the object to do something. An important method in the Producer object model is named **PublishPresentation**. As its name implies, a call to this method starts the publishing process, which then proceeds to completion on its own.

Programming objects typically exist in a hierarchy, and those in the Producer object model are no exception. The highest-level Producer object, or *root* object, is called the **Application** object. All the other objects in the Producer object hierarchy derive from this object. It is common to refer to this relationship as a parent/child relationship, where the **Application** object is the parent and the lower-level objects are the child objects. You will access each child object through an **Application** object property that has the same name as the child object you want to access.

In JScript, properties and methods are accessed by using a *dot operator* to separate the object from the property or method. For example, to create a JScript variable that stores a **ProfileManager** object, you would use the following code:

```
var MyProfileMgrObject = Application.ProfileManager;
```

Sometimes you'll use multiple dot operators to access a property or method through a series of objects in the hierarchy.

Table 14.2 lists the objects in the Producer object model hierarchy of objects.

Table 14.2 — Producer objects.

Object	Description
Application	Represents the root of the Producer object model.
Error	Represents the errors that Producer can generate.
Options	Provides properties that let you retrieve local security settings and add or remove Web hosts.
ProfileManager	Represents the collection of all available **Profile** objects.
Project	Represents a Producer project.
Properties	Represents the metadata of a project.
Publisher	Provides methods to support the publishing process.
Windows	Represents a collection of **Window** objects.

There are additional objects that you may use when creating e-services. You can use the objects in Table 14.3 as return values from methods or as parameter values that can be passed to a method as an argument.

Table 14.3 — Additional useful objects.

Object	Description
Profile	Represents a publishing profile.
Profiles	Represents a collection of **Profile** objects.
StreamConfig	Represents a video or audio stream.
WebHost	Represents the e-service.
Window	Represents a Producer window.

You can refer to the Producer SDK for detailed information about the individual objects and the properties and the methods associated with each.

Displaying a Custom Publish Wizard

In order for your e-service to be useful, you must create a Web page that functions as a custom user interface in the **Publish Wizard**. While you are in the process of developing the Web page, it is helpful for you to be able to see the results of your programming each step of the way. Therefore, you need a way to tell Producer where to look for your Web page. You do this by registering your e-service with Producer before you author it.

You learned earlier that you can create a Web host key using a registry file. Now, you'll add a Web host key to the registry by creating a simple registry file from scratch. The new Web host key will contain only two values: a GUID for the **ID**, and a new value you haven't seen before called **HTMLBasedUIURL**. The data you store with this value is a Web address that instructs Producer to look for a Web page to use as a custom user interface in the **Publish Wizard**. It isn't necessary to store other values in this Web host because the e-service will be responsible for providing the details needed for publishing.

Step-by-Step: Creating the Registry File for a New E-service

Here's how to create the new registry file for the e-service you will build:

1. Open a new text document in Microsoft Notepad. Type the following code exactly as it appears here:

```
Windows Registry Editor Version 5.00

[HKEY_CURRENT_USER\Software\Microsoft\Producer\WebHosts\My New E-
service]
"HTMLBasedUIURL" = "http://yourserver/yourpath/MyNewEservice.htm"
"ID" = "C1C8024B-3667-4245-BB8C-0556D61D6166"
```

    The name of the e-service is the text between the last backslash and the closing square bracket on the line that begins with **[HKEY CURRENT USER** (in this case, My New E-service). This is the name that appears in the **Web server** list in the **Publish Wizard** user interface, and also the name of the Web host key in the registry.

    Normally, you won't be creating GUIDs manually. You can use the GUID provided to follow these steps, but you should never use it for a finished product. Later, you'll learn to use the Producer object model to register your e-service, and that is the preferred method. If you have a GUID generating utility, such as guidgen.exe, you can manually register e-services as often as you like.

2. Change the path specified following **HTMLBasedUIURL** in the preceding text to match a valid URL on your Web server. Be sure to retain the file name MyNewEservice.htm.

3. Save the text file as MyNewEservice.reg. Do not add a .txt file name extension. You should select **All Files** in the **Save as type** list to prevent Notepad from adding the .txt file name extension automatically.

4. If necessary, copy the file MyNewEservice.reg to the computer on which you will be running Producer.

5. Use Windows Explorer to browse to the folder where you saved or copied the MyNewEservice.reg file.

6. Double-click the MyNewEservice.reg file. Click **Yes** and **OK** when prompted. You've now registered the MyNewEservice Web host key. This is the registry key that makes the e-service accessible from the **Web server** list in the Publish Wizard.

At this point, if you start Producer and open the **Publish Wizard**, you'll see **My New E-service** as an option in the **Web server** drop-down list. Of course, you haven't created the Web page that displays in the user interface yet. You'll do that next.

Step-by-Step: Creating a Simple Web Page

Now that you've registered your first e-service, you can write a Web page to display some text in the **Publish Wizard**. The goal here isn't to do anything fancy, just to demonstrate that you can indeed create a custom user interface for publishing. Once you understand how to do that, you can then move on to learning the details of how to control the publishing process.

The Web page you'll create will be as simple. It will merely display a single line of text that says, "Behold my new e-service!" To create the Web page, follow these steps:

1. Using Notepad, create a new text file. Type the code exactly as it appears here:

```
<HTML>
<BODY>
Behold my new e-service!
</BODY>
</HTML>
```

2. Save the text file as MyNewEservice.htm. Do not add a .txt file name extension.

3. Copy the file MyNewEservice.htm to the Web server URL location you specified for the value of **HTMLBasedUIURL** in the registry file you created in the previous procedure.

Now, when you select **My New E-service** from the **Web server** list in the **Publish Wizard**, the associated value in the **WebHosts** key in the registry will point the **Publish Wizard** to the simple Web page you created, and it will display in the **Publish Wizard** window when you click **Next**. Give it a try. The result should look like Figure 14.5.

Figure 14.5 — The custom **Publish Wizard** Web page.

Building a Simple E-service

Now that you've seen the mechanism by which an e-service displays itself in the **Publish Wizard**, you can move on to writing an e-service that actually publishes a presentation. The e-service you create will still be fairly simple, but will meet the minimum requirements for a complete e-service. The following restrictions will apply:

- The e-service can only publish presentations that have at least one video clip on the timeline.

- It displays a single, static user interface page.

- It publishes using a single, medium-quality audio/video profile.

- The publishing destination is supplied by the e-service.

- The only data provided by the user is the presentation name.

- The e-service will only publish using a new presentation name. No code is provided to overwrite an existing presentation.

This e-service is based upon the sample called *A Complete Simple E-service* and the programming guide topic *A Simple E-service*, which you can find in the Producer SDK.

Since you've already created a simple Web page, you can use that as the starting point for this e-service. Open the MyNewEservice.htm Web page using Notepad or your favorite HTML editor. You can delete the line that says, "Behold my new e-service!" leaving only the HTML and BODY sections.

First, you need to include some instructions for users to tell them what they need to know about your e-service. You should place this text between the <BODY> and </BODY> tags, as shown in the following example:

```
<BODY>
Thanks for using my new e-service.<BR>
Please supply a name for your presentation.<BR>
The presentation must contain content on the video timeline<BR>
or an error will result.<BR>
<BR>
Publish Destination: http://MyServer/MyPath<BR>
Profile: MediumQualityAudioVideo<BR>
<BR>
Click<B> Next </B>to publish the presentation.
<BR>
</BODY>
```

Next, add code to create a text input element. This is the box where users will type the presentation name. You can add this code just after the text that prompts the user to supply a name for the presentation:

```
<!--This is the text box that retrieves the name
  of the presentation from the user.-->
<BR>
Presentation name:
<INPUT TYPE = "TEXT" ID = "presName" NAME = "presName">
<BR>
<BR>
```

This would be a good time to start Producer and take a look at your work in the **Publish Wizard**. Of course, the Web page doesn't publish anything yet, but you can check the layout of the text and the input control on the page. You don't have to restart Producer each time you make changes to the Web page. Just exit the **Publish Wizard** and start the wizard again to see the changes.

So far, you've been using basic HTML. Now it's time to start using some JScript and the Producer object model. You'll need a JScript function block that executes by default when the page initially loads, which you'll name **OnLoad**(). You'll use this function block to contain some setup code. Change the <BODY> tag to match the following:

```
<BODY onload = "OnLoad()">
```

Now you can type some JScript code. Start by establishing some variables you will use to store Producer objects and publishing data, and also to include the code for the **OnLoad**() function.

```
<SCRIPT language = "JScript">

// These are global variables.
var Application; //   Stores an Application object.
var WebHost; //  Stores a WebHost object.
var ProfileMgr;  //Stores a Profile Manager object

// Stores the path to the Web server.
var PublishDestination = "http://MyServer/MyPath";

// This function executes automatically when Producer loads the page.
function OnLoad(){
    // You must set the value of the Application object to window.external
    // to gain access to the Producer object model.
    Application = window.external;

     // Retrieve a WebHost object that represents the current e service.
    WebHost = Application.Project.Properties.PublishWebHost;

    // Create a Profile Manager object for working with profiles.
    ProfileMgr = Application.ProfileManager;
}
</SCRIPT>
```

Be certain to change the path assigned to the **PublishDestination** variable to your server's address and path.

Notice the values assigned to the variables **WebHost** and **ProfileMgr**—the code to the right of the = symbol. These are great examples of using properties of the root **Application** object to retrieve child objects. It is convenient to store these objects in this manner because it saves you the trouble of typing the entire object hierarchy each time you need to use a particular object. In the rest of the code, you can simply refer to these objects by the shorter variable names to the left of the equals signs.

Next, add some code to the **OnLoad()** function to specify two events. These are the events that will execute when the user clicks **Next** or **Back** in the **Publish Wizard**. This code simply tells Producer the names of the functions to use. You can add this code at the beginning of the function, just after the first curly bracket.

```
// Specify the functions to handle the Next and Back
// button events in the Publish Wizard.
window.document.OnWizardNext = MyOnWizardNext;
window.document.OnWizardBack = MyOnWizardBack;
```

Now, add some code to check the Producer version. The following code verifies that the user has Producer version 1.0, which is the requirement for this e-service. You can add this code to the **OnLoad()** function just after the line that sets the value of the **Application** object.

```
// Test whether the user's Producer version is compatible
// with the WebHost.
var AppVersion = Application.Version;
if (AppVersion.substring(0,3) != "1.0")
    alert ("Warning: Producer version doesn't match.");
```

Version is a property of the **Application** object that returns a string representing the Producer version. The preceding example code assigns that value to a variable named **AppVersion**. The code then tests the first three characters of the string and compares that to the value "1.0". If there is not an exact match, a message box alerts the user that there is a potential problem.

That's it for the **OnLoad()** function. Now, write a simple function to handle the **OnWizardBack** event, which occurs when the user clicks **Back**. Not much needs to happen here; the **Publish Wizard** simply must return to the first page. You can add this code just after the closing curly brace of the **OnLoad()** function block.

```
// This function executes when the user clicks Back
// in the Publish Wizard UI.
function MyOnWizardBack(){
    // Return to the first page of the Publish Wizard.
    return false;
}
```

Returning the value false from the function tells Producer to display the first page of the **Publish Wizard**.

Add the function that handles the **OnWizardNext** event, which occurs when the user clicks **Next**. This is the function that will set up the objects for publishing. You'll write a separate function, called **PublishMe()**, that will contain the code to validate and publish the presentation. The following code includes a call to **PublishMe()**, which you'll write shortly. You can add the following code just after the closing curly bracket of the **OnLoad()** function block.

```
// This function executes when the user clicks Next.
function MyOnWizardNext(){

    // Test whether the user has entered a name for the presentation.
    if (presName.value.length <= 0){
        alert("Please enter a presentation name.");
        return true;
}


    // Set the profile to one of the Producer built-in profiles.
    var myProfile = ProfileMgr.MediumQualityAudioVideo;
    WebHost.AddProfile(myProfile);

    //Set the presentation name.
    Application.Project.Properties.PublishName = presName.value;

    // Set the presentation publish destination.
    WebHost.PublishDestination = PublishDestination;

    // Call the function that begins the publishing process.
    PublishMe();
    return;
}
```

The first part of the function tests whether the user has typed a name for the presentation. If the **presName** text box is empty, the code warns the user and stops further execution.

If the user has done his or her duty and provided a name for the presentation, the function retrieves the built-in profile named **MediumQualityAudioVideo** from the **ProfileMgr** object and then stores the retrieved **Profile** object in a variable named **myProfile**. The code then calls the **WebHost.AddProfile()** method, passing along the **myProfile** object. Producer will use each profile that exists in the **WebHost** object to publish the presentation, and the resulting Windows Media files will be created and numbered in the order in which the profile objects were added to the Web host. This e-service, of course, uses only one profile.

Finally, the function sets the **PublishName** property using the text the user typed into the **presName** box, then sets the **PublishDestination** property using the Web server path you provided in the code, and then calls the **PublishMe()** function to start the publishing process.

There are two functions left to write for this e-service: the **PublishMe()** function, which you'll write next, and the **ClosePubWiz()** function that closes the **Publish Wizard** window, which you will call from the **PublishMe()** function.

To add the **PublishMe()** function, type the following code after the closing curly bracket of the **MyOnWizardBack()** function.

```
// This function starts the publishing process.
function PublishMe(){
    // Use try/catch error handling to verify publish validation.
    try{

        // Verify that a presentation doesn't exist with the same name.
        var bDoesNotExist =Application.Publisher.ValidatePublishPresentation();

        // Test whether ValidatePublishPresentation was successful.
        if (bDoesNotExist == true){
            // Publish the presentation.
            Application.Publisher.PublishPresentation()

            // Tell the user it is done.
            alert("Publish complete.");

            // Close the wizard.
            ClosePubWiz();
        }

        else{
            // Tell the user the there is a problem.
            alert ("Cannot publish because the name exists.")
        }
    }
    catch(e){

    // Show an error message.
    alert ("There were errors. Publish failed.");
    }
}
```

Starting the publishing process is easy. It only requires one method: **Publisher.PublishPresentation()**. There is, however, a test you should perform before calling this method. You should call the method named **Publisher.ValidatePublishPresentation()**, which will determine for you whether the presentation can be published using the current settings. This method must be called within a JScript try/catch block so you can handle any errors returned should the method determine that it isn't possible to publish the presentation. The method also tests whether a presentation exists with the same name as the one the user provided, and returns true if the presentation does not exist, or false if the presentation exists already. This e-service will only publish the presentation if **ValidatePublishPresentation** returns true, but you can refer to the Producer SDK Samples section to see examples of how to permit overwriting an existing presentation.

The final function you must add to this e-service is called **ClosePubWiz()**. This is the function that **PublishMe()** calls to close the **Publish Wizard** window when publishing is completed. You can add this code immediately following the **PublishMe()** function.

```
// This function closes the Publish Wizard.
function ClosePubWiz(){
    // Get a window object that represents the Publish Wizard.
    var WizardWin = Application.Windows.FindByName("PublishWizard");

    // Close the Publish Wizard.
    Application.Windows(WizardWin).Close();
}
```

This function retrieves the **Window** object that has the name "PublishWizard" and then stores that object in a variable named **WizardWin**. The code then calls the **Windows.Close()** method passing the stored **Window** object as an argument. The **Close** method simply closes the window that corresponds to the object it receives as a parameter, in this case the **Publish Wizard**.

You've now completed the code necessary for this simple e-service. Be sure to save the file as MyNewEservice.htm and copy the file to the Web server location pointed to by the **HTMLBasedUIURL** value in the **My New E-service** Web host key.

Start Producer and open a project that has video on the timeline. Click **Publish** to open the **Publish Wizard** and select your e-service from the **Web server** list. Then, go ahead and use your new e-service to publish your presentation. The finished Web page should look like Figure 14.6.

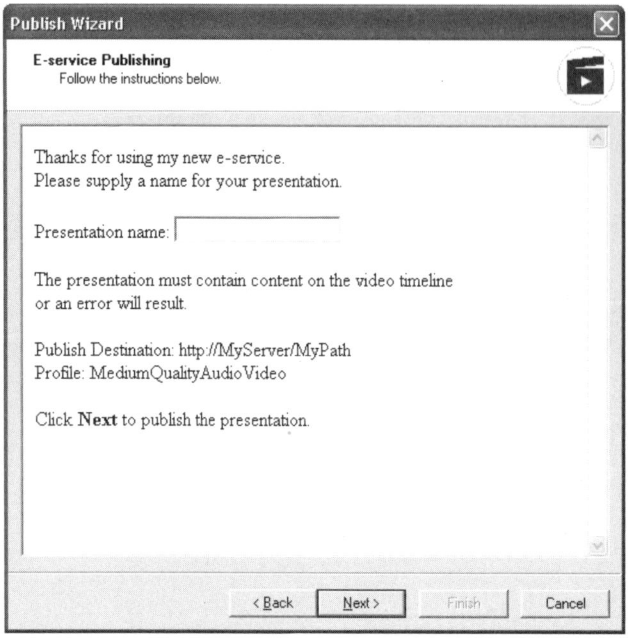

Figure 14.6 — The sample e-service in action.

Making Your E-service Public

There are basically two ways that you can enable users to add your e-service to their computers. You've already learned how to create a registry file to do this—both by exporting one from the registry and writing one from scratch in Notepad. This method works fine, but there is a second method that you can use that is more efficient, especially if you make your e-services available to a large organization.

This method takes advantage of the **Learn More** button in the **Publish Wizard**. The **Learn More** button displays a Web page in a separate browser window that, by default, offers information about commercial e-services. You can, however, create a registry file that, when executed on the user's computer, directs the **Learn More** Web page to any Web site you choose. This means that you can create a Web page that contains links to your corporate e-services, and members of your organization can update or add to the list of e-services that they can use for publishing at any time. This is far more convenient for you as the e-service provider because it means you don't have to constantly distribute new registry keys. You simply distribute a single registry file one time to everyone in your organization, and then maintain the **Learn More** page.

Changing the Default Learn More Web Page

Since you are already familiar with the Windows registry, creating the registry file that changes the default **Learn More** page is easy. The file simply needs to change a single value—a URL value named **PublishEServiceLearnMoreURL**. This value is located in the subkey named **HKEY_CURENT_USER\Software\Microsoft\Producer\Producer Options**. You can use the following example registry file to create your own:

```
Windows Registry Editor Version 5.00

[HKEY_CURRENT_USER\Software\Microsoft\Producer\Producer Options]
"PublishEServiceLearnMoreURL" = "www.microsoft.com";
```

The preceding code example creates a registry file that directs the **Learn More** page to the Microsoft home page. You can simply replace the URL for the Microsoft site with your own. Once you've tested the file to ensure that it works as expected, you can distribute it among members of your organization through whatever method is most convenient.

Authoring a Learn More Web Page

Creating the Web page that allows users to add your e-services to their computers is quite a bit easier than writing the e-service. The **Learn More** page has three basic goals:

- Explain to users what each e-service is used for so they can make an informed choice as to which e-services to install.

- Provide users with a mechanism to choose and install e-services.

- Use the Producer object model to add the e-service details to the registry on users' computers.

For now, you'll learn to create a Web page that adds a single e-service. First, create an HTML document that explains to the user about the e-service. The following example is intended to offer the e-service you created in the previous sections:

```
<HTML>
<BODY>
<!--Create the Web page that displays in Producer.-->
My New E-service<BR>
<BR>
This e-service publishes video presentations<BR>
to my Web server using the default<BR>
MediumQualityAudioVideo profile.<BR>
<BR>
```

```
Please click the button below to add this service <BR>
to the <B>Microsoft Producer Publish Wizard</B> as a <BR>
new <B>Web server</B>. <BR>
<BR>
</BODY>
</HTML>
```

Next, add some code to create a command button. You can add this code just after the last <BR> tag.

```
<INPUT TYPE = "BUTTON" ID ="addEservice" NAME = "addEservice" VALUE =
"Click Me" onClick ="addEservice();">
```

The button displays the text "Click Me" and runs the function named **addEservice** when clicked. You'll write that function shortly.

Now, you must add some JScript code. You can add the following code just after the input button code:

```
<SCRIPT language = "JScript">
// Retrieve an Application object to gain access
// to the  Producer object model.
var Application = window.external;
</SCRIPT>
```

Next, add the function that executes when the user clicks the button. This is the function that adds the new Web host key to the registry on the user's computer. This works exactly like the registry files you've created in the past, except now the Producer object model does the work. You can add this code immediately following the line that retrieves the **Application** object:

```
function addEservice(){
// Use the Producer object model to add the Web host key to the
// registry on the user's computer.
Application.Options.AddWebHost("My New E-service","http://MyServer/
MyNewEservice.htm", true);
}
```

The first argument of the **AddWebHost** method specifies the name of the Web host key. The second is the URL of the e-service, and becomes the **HTMLBasedUIURL** value in the registry. Be sure to change the URL to match the path to your server. The value true for the third parameter tells Producer to allow an overwrite of any existing Web host key with the same name.

It's only polite to let the user know that the e-service was added successfully. You can add the following code just before the closing bracket in the **addEservice()** function:

```
alert("Thank you. You can now use this e-service.");
```

Finally, you should close the browscr window so the user can return to the **Publish Wizard**. This process is identical to the one you performed previously to close the **Publish Wizard**, except the name of the window is different. You can add the following code just after the line that alerts the user:

```
// Use the Windows.FindByName method to get the index
// of the browser window hosted by Producer.
var nWin = Application.Windows.FindByName("EServiceWindow");

// Retrieve the hosted window object.
var pWin = Application.Windows.Item(nWin);

// Test whether the hosted window was successfully retrieved.
if (pWin){
    // Close the window.
    pWin.Close();
}
```

Figure 14.7 shows the completed **Learn More** Web page as displayed by Producer.

Remember, you're not limited to offering only one e-service in your **Learn More** page. Also, you can use any HTML that you would normally use with Internet Explorer to make the page look more interesting. Try authoring your Web page using Microsoft FrontPage instead of Notepad.

For a complete sample **Learn More** page, see the topic *Adding an E-service Using a Learn More Page* in the Samples section of the Producer SDK.

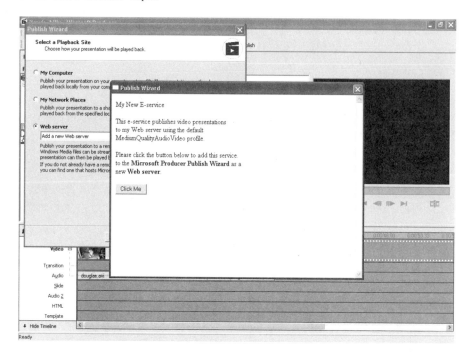

Figure 14.7 — The customized **Learn More** Web page.

Taking the Next Step

There's plenty more that you can do with e-services. Now that you have the fundamentals, you can refer to the Producer SDK for details about how to do the following:

- Work with profiles and the Profile Manager. See the topic *Working with Profiles* and the sample *Allowing the User to Select Profiles*.

- Check the timeline content to verify that the content is compatible with the selected publishing profile. See the topic *Checking the Timeline* and the sample *Allowing the User to Select Profiles*.

- Write code that uses HTML div elements to simulate multiple pages in the **Publish Wizard**. See the topic *A Simple E-service* and the sample *Using Properties and Multiple Pages*.

- Write code that allows the user to preview the published presentation. See the topic *Previewing the Presentation* and the sample *A Complete E-service*.

- Write code that displays the list of published files. See the sample *A Complete Simple E-service*.

- Check the user's security settings to prevent publishing errors. See the topic *Working with Security Settings*.

- Display details about the available profiles. See the sample *Displaying Profile Information*.

Glossary

A

announcement

A Windows Media metafile with an .asx extension that gives a player the information needed to connect to a Windows Media server and receive content.

B

bandwidth

The data transfer capacity of a digital communications system, such as the Internet or a local area network (LAN). Bandwidth is usually expressed in the number of bits that a system is capable of transferring in a second: bits per second (bps) or kilobits per second (Kbps).

bit rate

The speed at which digital audio and video content must be streamed to be rendered properly by a player; or the speed at which digital content in general is streamed on a network. Bit rate is usually measured in kilobits per second (Kbps), for example, 28.8 Kbps.

C

capture

To record audio, video, or still images as digital data in a computer file.

clip

Small segments of a larger video file that are created when the video has been clip detected.

compression

The coding of data to reduce file size or the bit rate of a stream. Content that has been compressed is decompressed for playback.

content

Audio, video, images, text, or any other information that is contained in a digital media file or stream.

D

digital video (DV)

Video images and sound stored in a digital format.

download

To deliver or receive content over a network by copying the content to a computer on which it can be played locally. In contrast, when content is streamed, the data is not copied to the receiving computer.

DV

See definition for: digital video (DV)

F

frame

One of many sequential static images that make up video.

frame rate

The number of frames displayed per second in video. High frame rates generally produce better quality video because there are more frames, which makes movement in the video appear smoother.

I

IEEE 1394

See definition for: Institute of Electrical and Electronics Engineers (IEEE) 1394

import

The process of adding existing digital audio, video, HTML, Microsoft PowerPoint slides, or still image files to a project.

Institute of Electrical and Electronics Engineers (IEEE) 1394

The standard for a high-speed serial bus that provides enhanced computer connectivity for a wide range of devices, including consumer electronics audio/video (A/V) appliances, storage peripherals, other computers, and portable devices.

M

moire pattern

Video artifacts that occur when recording an object that has many thin, parallel lines.

monitor

The area of the user interface in which video clips and still images are displayed.

P

presentation

The final version of a project that is published. The presentation contains any slides, video, audio, HTML code, still images, or other digital media files that have been added to the timeline in Microsoft Producer.

project file

The file that contains information about the files that have been imported into the current project and how files or clips have been arranged on the timeline. This file is saved with an .MSProducer extension.

R

record

See definition for: capture

S

source

Content that you can capture. Source audio and video content can be captured and encoded from devices installed on your computer or from a file.

still image

A graphic file, such as file with a .bmp, .gif, .jpg, or .png file name extension.

T

timeline

The area of the user interface that shows the timing and arrangement of files that comprise a presentation.

transition

The method of smoothly moving from one video clip or still image to another.

trim points

The points where playback of a file or clip begins and ends. There are two trim points: start trim point and end trim point.

trimming

The process of hiding parts of a file or clip without deleting them from the original source material. Files and clips can be trimmed by adjusting the start or end trim points.

W

Windows Media file

A file containing audio, video, or script data that is stored in Windows Media Format. Depending on their content and purpose, Windows Media files use a variety of file name extensions, such as: .asx, .wma, .wmd, .wme, .wms, .wmv, .wmx, .wmz, or .wvx.

Index

Symbols

.asf 164
.jpg. *See* JPEG
.png. *See* Portable Network Graphic (PNG)

A

ActiveX controls 51
animation 95
archiving projects 19, 124
audio 48
  adding to presentations 163
  capture devices 66, 72, 154
  capturing 7, 66, 72, 114, 131, 141
  editing 45, 169, 175
  effects 175
  file formats 89
  importing 120, 123, 131
  in slides 207
  in templates 106, 250, 261, 264
  narrations 52, 135, 137
  options 139, 143, 150
  playback level 175, 176
  recording 77, 78, 82, 89, 101, 130
  synchronizing with slides 116, 117, 199
AutoPlay 276
AVI 9, 10. *See also* audio

B

background colors 109
bandwidth 91
bit rates 90, 151, 214, 241
broadcasting standards 59

C

cameras 55
capture devices 4, 7, 60, 130, 154

capture profiles 90, 138, 143, 151
Capture Wizard 6, 49, 114, 129
  starting 131
capturing digital media 4, 7, 90, 114, 129, 131, 141
  audio 66, 72
  options 138, 143, 151
  screen captures 146, 148
  still images 145
  time limit 144
  video 57
  video screen captures 51
Cascading Style Sheets (CSS) 247, 275
CD AutoPlay 276
clips 144, 169, 187
  combining 171
  creating 23, 123, 163, 170
  splitting 183
codecs 89, 90, 214, 216
command reference 17
component video 62
composite video 61, 68, 71
compressing files 89, 90
configuring hardware 155
connection speeds 91, 154, 215
copying files 5, 174, 288
creating files 18
  clips 23, 163
  presentations 48, 105
  projects 119
CSS. *See* Cascading Style Sheets (CSS)

D

decompressing files 89, 90
deleting files 168, 188
device drivers 155
Digital 8 56

discussion servers 51
display duration
   slides 166
   video 169, 187
distributing presentations. *See* publishing
   presentations
downloading files 212

E

e-services 216, 217, 299
editing files 5, 20, 161, 169, 182
   audio 175
   templates 247, 252, 254
effects 188

F

fade in 173, 175
fade out 173, 175
file formats 4, 7, 55, 89, 113, 114, 120
FireWire 63
fonts 109
frames 90, 149

G

GIF 190, 251
grayscale 173

H

hardware 154
   video capture 55
   video interfaces 60
   Web cameras 58, 71
Hi-8 56
HTML applications 276

I

IEEE 1394 connection 8, 55, 63, 67, 71
IIS. *See* Internet Information Server (IIS)
iLink 63
images 95, 113, 163
   capturing from video 145
   importing 120, 131

   in slides 195
   in templates 255, 256, 259
   screen captures 146
importing files 4, 5, 7, 19, 21, 131
   audio 114, 123
   slides 11, 113, 121, 135
   still images 113
   video 114, 123
input level 140, 144
installing hardware 55
Internet 50, 210
   retrieving digital media 9
   Web discussions 51
Internet Information Server (IIS) 211
introduction pages 111, 178, 189

J

JPEG 145, 190, 251

L

LAN. *See* local area network (LAN)
lavaliere microphones 78, 83
lighting 80
local area network (LAN) 91

M

media player 261, 264
Media tab 21, 162
microphones 66, 78, 83, 101
Microsoft PowerPoint 11, 75, 113, 116,
   117, 121, 193, 196, 283, 285
MiniDV 55
moving files 5, 124, 174, 184
Moving Picture Experts Group (MPEG) 10
MP3 10
MPEG. *See* Moving Picture Experts Group
   (MPEG)

N

narrations 135, 137
National Television System Committee
   (NTSC) 59
networks 91, 131, 154, 210

New Presentation Wizard 18, 105, 121, 131
normalizing audio 175
NTSC. *See* National Television System Committee (NTSC)

O

opening files 18
options 9
  audio 150
  capture 4, 138, 143, 151
  display duration 166
  e-services 217
  hardware 155
  playing files 240, 242
  preview 179
  publishing 214, 216
  slides 121
  video 123, 149, 150, 151
organizing presentations 41

P

Pack and Go 19, 124, 282
PAL. *See* Phase Alternate Lines (PAL)
Phase Alternate Lines (PAL) 59
playing files 26, 240, 241
  options 242
Portable Network Graphic (PNG) 146, 190
presentations 11, 44
  copying 288
  creating 18, 23, 29, 48, 105, 119, 282
  editing 20, 23, 25, 29, 45, 161, 174, 182, 287
  introduction pages 111
  narrating 52, 135, 137
  opening 19
  options 179, 240
  organizing 41, 73, 85
  previewing 6, 32, 33, 179, 204, 206
  profiles 241
  publishing 7, 19, 91, 209, 218, 276
  table of contents 21, 109

templates 106, 110, 153, 168, 185, 215, 247
Preview Presentation tab 22
previewing files 6, 179, 204, 206
profiles 151, 214, 216, 241
projects
  archiving 19, 124
  creating 18, 119, 282
  editing 20, 161, 182
  properties 20
  saving 124, 131
Publish Wizard 209, 218, 289
  customizing 216, 291
publishing presentations 7, 19, 91, 209, 218, 276, 291
  e-services 216, 299
  profiles 214, 216
  servers 210

R

recording 89, 130
  audio 77, 78, 82, 101
  video 77, 92, 96, 97, 100
Registry Editor 292
registry keys 292, 293, 295, 297, 299

S

S-VHS 57
S-Video 62, 69
saving files 19, 124, 131
scan.hta 277
screen captures 51, 146, 148, 285
SECAM 60
security 201
servers 210, 233
sharing presentations. *See* publishing presentations
slides 47, 48, 75, 113, 193
  adding to presentations 163
  annotating 285
  audio and video 207
  creating 11
  editing 20, 194, 196

effects 203, 204, 206
images 195
importing 120, 121, 135
in templates 106
narrating 135, 137
synchronizing 6, 49, 116, 117, 121
templates 250, 266, 283
timings 166, 199, 200, 204
sound cards 66
splitting clips 170, 183
Standard 8 56
still images. *See* images
streaming media 9, 10, 212
synchronizing slides 5, 6, 23, 49, 116, 117, 121, 199, 204

T

table of contents 5, 21, 23, 32, 49, 109, 176, 189, 190
customizing 271
television 58, 65, 69
templates 38, 48, 50, 106, 110, 153, 185, 215
adding to presentations 168
customizing 247, 252, 254
image files 255, 256, 259
media players 261, 264
slides 266
Web pages 269
time-lapse video 95
timeline 5, 22, 23, 25, 26, 34, 37, 161, 163, 182
deleting files 188
editing commands 20
removing files 168
tracks 164
toolbar 22
transitions 95, 171, 188
trim points 169, 187
TV tuner 58, 65, 69

U

Universal Serial Bus (USB) 63, 65, 70, 71

USB. *See* Universal Serial Bus (USB)

V

VCRs 55, 58
VHS 57
video 48, 90
adding to presentations 163, 182
broadcasting standards 59
cameras 55, 92
capture devices 60, 154
capturing 7, 114, 131, 141, 145
clips 123, 144, 163, 170, 171, 183
editing 45, 169
formats 55, 89
importing 120, 123, 131
in slides 207
in templates 106, 261, 264
narrations 135, 137
options 139, 143, 149, 150, 151, 185
recording 57, 75, 77, 80, 89, 92, 96, 97, 100, 130
replacing files 287
screen captures 51, 148, 285
synchronizing with slides 116, 117, 199
transitions and effects 5, 23, 25, 30, 37, 95, 96, 171, 173, 188
TV tuner 58, 65, 69
video cameras 55, 89, 92
accessories 77
features 93
MiniDV 55
Web cameras 58, 71
video capture devices 55, 66
Video for Windows (VFW) 155
video interfaces 60

W

WAV 9
Web cameras 58, 71
Web pages 19, 21, 50, 167, 275, 285
adding to presentations 167, 188, 276

HTML applications 276

importing 120

in templates 269

links to presentations 240

templates 250

Windows Driver Model (WDM) 155

Windows Media Advanced Script Indexer
    287

Windows Media Audio (WMA) 89, 135

Windows Media Encoder 10

Windows Media Format 9

Windows Media Player 7, 10, 212

Windows Media Services 10, 212

Windows Media Video (WMV) 89, 135,
    148, 164, 287

Windows registry 292, 293, 295, 297,
    299

WMA. *See* Windows Media Audio (WMA)

WMV. *See* Windows Media Video (WMV)

About the Authors

Matt Lichtenberg worked as a technical trainer before turning his interests to written and online computer instruction. During and after his undergraduate work, Matt worked as a computer training instructor at two universities in the Washington D.C. area, as well as a non-profit agency. He also taught at and received a Master of Technical and Scientific Communication degree from Miami University (Ohio). At Microsoft, he is the lead writer for the Windows Movie Maker and Microsoft Producer for PowerPoint 2002 Help.

Jim Travis is employed by Microsoft Corporation as lead programmer/writer for the Microsoft Producer for PowerPoint 2002 Software Development Kit (SDK). Jim is also a contributing programmer/writer for the Windows Media Player SDK and various other SDK projects. Prior to working at Microsoft, Jim owned his own multimedia software company, which supplied automation software to the entertainment industry. Jim has also been a live sound engineer and video technician, and once owned and operated a multi-track recording studio.

Get a **Free**
*e-mail newsletter, updates,
special offers, links to related books,
and more when you*
register on line!

Register your Microsoft Press® title on our Web site and you'll get a FREE subscription to our e-mail newsletter, *Microsoft Press Book Connections.* You'll find out about newly released and upcoming books and learning tools, online events, software downloads, special offers and coupons for Microsoft Press customers, and information about major Microsoft® product releases. You can also read useful additional information about all the titles we publish, such as detailed book descriptions, tables of contents and indexes, sample chapters, links to related books and book series, author biographies, and reviews by other customers.

Registration is easy. Just visit this Web page and fill in your information:

http://www.microsoft.com/mspress/register

Microsoft®

- -

Proof of Purchase

Use this page as proof of purchase if participating in a promotion or rebate offer on this title. Proof of purchase must be used in conjunction with other proof(s) of payment such as your dated sales receipt—see offer details.

Creating Dynamic Presentations with Streaming Media
0-7356-1436-9

CUSTOMER NAME

Microsoft Press, PO Box 97017, Redmond, WA 98073-9830

MICROSOFT LICENSE AGREEMENT
Book Companion CD

IMPORTANT—READ CAREFULLY: This Microsoft End-User License Agreement ("EULA") is a legal agreement between you (either an individual or an entity) and Microsoft Corporation for the Microsoft product identified above, which includes computer software and may include associated media, printed materials, and "online" or electronic documentation ("SOFTWARE PRODUCT"). Any component included within the SOFTWARE PRODUCT that is accompanied by a separate End-User License Agreement shall be governed by such agreement and not the terms set forth below. By installing, copying, or otherwise using the SOFTWARE PRODUCT, you agree to be bound by the terms of this EULA. If you do not agree to the terms of this EULA, you are not authorized to install, copy, or otherwise use the SOFTWARE PRODUCT; you may, however, return the SOFTWARE PRODUCT, along with all printed materials and other items that form a part of the Microsoft product that includes the SOFTWARE PRODUCT, to the place you obtained them for a full refund.

SOFTWARE PRODUCT LICENSE

The SOFTWARE PRODUCT is protected by United States copyright laws and international copyright treaties, as well as other intellectual property laws and treaties. The SOFTWARE PRODUCT is licensed, not sold.

1. **GRANT OF LICENSE.** This EULA grants you the following rights:

   a. **Software Product.** You may install and use one copy of the SOFTWARE PRODUCT on a single computer. The primary user of the computer on which the SOFTWARE PRODUCT is installed may make a second copy for his or her exclusive use on a portable computer.

   b. **Storage/Network Use.** You may also store or install a copy of the SOFTWARE PRODUCT on a storage device, such as a network server, used only to install or run the SOFTWARE PRODUCT on your other computers over an internal network; however, you must acquire and dedicate a license for each separate computer on which the SOFTWARE PRODUCT is installed or run from the storage device. A license for the SOFTWARE PRODUCT may not be shared or used concurrently on different computers.

   c. **License Pak.** If you have acquired this EULA in a Microsoft License Pak, you may make the number of additional copies of the computer software portion of the SOFTWARE PRODUCT authorized on the printed copy of this EULA, and you may use each copy in the manner specified above. You are also entitled to make a corresponding number of secondary copies for portable computer use as specified above.

   d. **Sample Code.** Solely with respect to portions, if any, of the SOFTWARE PRODUCT that are identified within the SOFTWARE PRODUCT as sample code (the "SAMPLE CODE"):

      i. **Use and Modification.** Microsoft grants you the right to use and modify the source code version of the SAMPLE CODE, *provided* you comply with subsection (d)(iii) below. You may not distribute the SAMPLE CODE, or any modified version of the SAMPLE CODE, in source code form.

      ii. **Redistributable Files.** Provided you comply with subsection (d)(iii) below, Microsoft grants you a nonexclusive, royalty-free right to reproduce and distribute the object code version of the SAMPLE CODE and of any modified SAMPLE CODE, other than SAMPLE CODE, or any modified version thereof, designated as not redistributable in the Readme file that forms a part of the SOFTWARE PRODUCT (the "Non-Redistributable Sample Code"). All SAMPLE CODE other than the Non-Redistributable Sample Code is collectively referred to as the "REDISTRIBUTABLES."

      iii. **Redistribution Requirements.** If you redistribute the REDISTRIBUTABLES, you agree to: (i) distribute the REDISTRIBUTABLES in object code form only in conjunction with and as a part of your software application product; (ii) not use Microsoft's name, logo, or trademarks to market your software application product; (iii) include a valid copyright notice on your software application product; (iv) indemnify, hold harmless, and defend Microsoft from and against any claims or lawsuits, including attorney's fees, that arise or result from the use or distribution of your software application product; and (v) not permit further distribution of the REDISTRIBUTABLES by your end user. Contact Microsoft for the applicable royalties due and other licensing terms for all other uses and/or distribution of the REDISTRIBUTABLES.

2. **DESCRIPTION OF OTHER RIGHTS AND LIMITATIONS.**

   - **Limitations on Reverse Engineering, Decompilation, and Disassembly.** You may not reverse engineer, decompile, or disassemble the SOFTWARE PRODUCT, except and only to the extent that such activity is expressly permitted by applicable law notwithstanding this limitation.

   - **Separation of Components.** The SOFTWARE PRODUCT is licensed as a single product. Its component parts may not be separated for use on more than one computer.

   - **Rental.** You may not rent, lease, or lend the SOFTWARE PRODUCT.

   - **Support Services.** Microsoft may, but is not obligated to, provide you with support services related to the SOFTWARE PRODUCT ("Support Services"). Use of Support Services is governed by the Microsoft policies and programs described in the user manual, in "online" documentation, and/or in other Microsoft-provided materials. Any supplemental software code provided to you as part of the Support Services shall be considered part of the SOFTWARE PRODUCT and subject to the terms and conditions of this EULA. With respect to technical information you provide to Microsoft as part of the Support Services, Microsoft may use such information for its business purposes, including for product support and development. Microsoft will not utilize such technical information in a form that personally identifies you.

- **Software Transfer.** You may permanently transfer all of your rights under this EULA, provided you retain no copies, you transfer all of the SOFTWARE PRODUCT (including all component parts, the media and printed materials, any upgrades, this EULA, and, if applicable, the Certificate of Authenticity), **and** the recipient agrees to the terms of this EULA.

- **Termination.** Without prejudice to any other rights, Microsoft may terminate this EULA if you fail to comply with the terms and conditions of this EULA. In such event, you must destroy all copies of the SOFTWARE PRODUCT and all of its component parts.

3. **COPYRIGHT.** All title and copyrights in and to the SOFTWARE PRODUCT (including but not limited to any images, photographs, animations, video, audio, music, text, SAMPLE CODE, REDISTRIBUTABLES, and "applets" incorporated into the SOFTWARE PRODUCT) and any copies of the SOFTWARE PRODUCT are owned by Microsoft or its suppliers. The SOFTWARE PRODUCT is protected by copyright laws and international treaty provisions. Therefore, you must treat the SOFTWARE PRODUCT like any other copyrighted material **except** that you may install the SOFTWARE PRODUCT on a single computer provided you keep the original solely for backup or archival purposes. You may not copy the printed materials accompanying the SOFTWARE PRODUCT.

4. **U.S. GOVERNMENT RESTRICTED RIGHTS.** The SOFTWARE PRODUCT and documentation are provided with RESTRICTED RIGHTS. Use, duplication, or disclosure by the Government is subject to restrictions as set forth in subparagraph (c)(1)(ii) of the Rights in Technical Data and Computer Software clause at DFARS 252.227-7013 or subparagraphs (c)(1) and (2) of the Commercial Computer Software—Restricted Rights at 48 CFR 52.227-19, as applicable. Manufacturer is Microsoft Corporation/One Microsoft Way/Redmond, WA 98052-6399.

5. **EXPORT RESTRICTIONS.** You agree that you will not export or re-export the SOFTWARE PRODUCT, any part thereof, or any process or service that is the direct product of the SOFTWARE PRODUCT (the foregoing collectively referred to as the "Restricted Components"), to any country, person, entity, or end user subject to U.S. export restrictions. You specifically agree not to export or re-export any of the Restricted Components (i) to any country to which the U.S. has embargoed or restricted the export of goods or services, which currently include, but are not necessarily limited to, Cuba, Iran, Iraq, Libya, North Korea, Sudan, and Syria, or to any national of any such country, wherever located, who intends to transmit or transport the Restricted Components back to such country; (ii) to any end user who you know or have reason to know will utilize the Restricted Components in the design, development, or production of nuclear, chemical, or biological weapons; or (iii) to any end user who has been prohibited from participating in U.S. export transactions by any federal agency of the U.S. government. You warrant and represent that neither the BXA nor any other U.S. federal agency has suspended, revoked, or denied your export privileges.

DISCLAIMER OF WARRANTY

NO WARRANTIES OR CONDITIONS. MICROSOFT EXPRESSLY DISCLAIMS ANY WARRANTY OR CONDITION FOR THE SOFTWARE PRODUCT. THE SOFTWARE PRODUCT AND ANY RELATED DOCUMENTATION ARE PROVIDED "AS IS" WITHOUT WARRANTY OR CONDITION OF ANY KIND, EITHER EXPRESS OR IMPLIED, INCLUDING, WITHOUT LIMITATION, THE IMPLIED WARRANTIES OF MERCHANTABILITY, FITNESS FOR A PARTICULAR PURPOSE, OR NONINFRINGEMENT. THE ENTIRE RISK ARISING OUT OF USE OR PERFORMANCE OF THE SOFTWARE PRODUCT REMAINS WITH YOU.

LIMITATION OF LIABILITY. TO THE MAXIMUM EXTENT PERMITTED BY APPLICABLE LAW, IN NO EVENT SHALL MICROSOFT OR ITS SUPPLIERS BE LIABLE FOR ANY SPECIAL, INCIDENTAL, INDIRECT, OR CONSEQUENTIAL DAMAGES WHATSOEVER (INCLUDING, WITHOUT LIMITATION, DAMAGES FOR LOSS OF BUSINESS PROFITS, BUSINESS INTERRUPTION, LOSS OF BUSINESS INFORMATION, OR ANY OTHER PECUNIARY LOSS) ARISING OUT OF THE USE OF OR INABILITY TO USE THE SOFTWARE PRODUCT OR THE PROVISION OF OR FAILURE TO PROVIDE SUPPORT SERVICES, EVEN IF MICROSOFT HAS BEEN ADVISED OF THE POSSIBILITY OF SUCH DAMAGES. IN ANY CASE, MICROSOFT'S ENTIRE LIABILITY UNDER ANY PROVISION OF THIS EULA SHALL BE LIMITED TO THE GREATER OF THE AMOUNT ACTUALLY PAID BY YOU FOR THE SOFTWARE PRODUCT OR US$5.00; PROVIDED, HOWEVER, IF YOU HAVE ENTERED INTO A MICROSOFT SUPPORT SERVICES AGREEMENT, MICROSOFT'S ENTIRE LIABILITY REGARDING SUPPORT SERVICES SHALL BE GOVERNED BY THE TERMS OF THAT AGREEMENT. BECAUSE SOME STATES AND JURISDICTIONS DO NOT ALLOW THE EXCLUSION OR LIMITATION OF LIABILITY, THE ABOVE LIMITATION MAY NOT APPLY TO YOU.

MISCELLANEOUS

This EULA is governed by the laws of the State of Washington USA, except and only to the extent that applicable law mandates governing law of a different jurisdiction.

Should you have any questions concerning this EULA, or if you desire to contact Microsoft for any reason, please contact the Microsoft subsidiary serving your country, or write: Microsoft Sales Information Center/One Microsoft Way/Redmond, WA 98052-6399.

HWLC LEARNING CENTRE

PN 097-0002296